NEGOTIATING THE NEW EUROPE

To Rachel, with love

Negotiating the New Europe

The European Union and Eastern Europe

DIMITRIS PAPADIMITRIOU
University of Bradford

Ashgate

Published by
Ashgate Publishing Limited
Gower House
Croft Road
Aldershot
Hants GU11 3HR
England

Ashgate Publishing Company
131 Main Street
Burlington, VT 05401-5600 USA

Ashgate website: http://www.ashgate.com

British Library Cataloguing in Publication Data
Papadimitriou, Dimitris
  Negotiating the new Europe : the European Union and Eastern
  Europe
  1.European Economic Community 2.European Union 3.Europe,
  Eastern - Economic policy - 1989- 4.Europe, Eastern -
  Foreign relations - 1989- 5.Europe, Eastern - Foreign
  relations - European Union countries 6.European Union
  countries - Foreign relations - Europe, Eastern
  I.Title
  337.1'42'09049

Library of Congress Control Number: 2001099962

ISBN 0 7546 1865 X

Printed and bound by Athenaeum Press, Ltd.,
Gateshead, Tyne & Wear.

Contents

PART I: THE NEGOTIATION OF THE FIRST WAVE
OF EUROPE AGREEMENTS

PART II: THE NEGOTIATION OF THE SECOND WAVE
OF EUROPE AGREEMENTS

PART III: THE EUROPE AGREEMENTS,
EASTWARDS ENLARGEMENT AND THE EU's
STRATEGY IN THE BALKANS

vi

List of Figures

List of Tables

Acknowledgements

The completion of this book would not have been possible without the generous support of the Department of European Studies at the University of Bradford and the assistance of its academic and secretarial staff. I am also grateful to the European Parliament's Directorate General for Research for giving me the opportunity to acquire some first hand knowledge of the working practices of the European Union as well as for facilitating the conduct of my fieldwork. My gratitude is also due to the Bulgarian and Romanian Delegations to the European Union for their co-operation and to all the interviewees who, despite their busy schedules, were always keen to support and enlighten me.

My special thanks go to Kevin Featherstone and George Kazamias for their friendship and for providing me with inspiration and guidance throughout the laborious process that led to the completion of this book. I am also obliged to William Wallace, Claudio Radaelli and Kenneth Dyson for their valuable comments. Moreover, I am hugely indebted to my family for tolerating my long absences and giving me their unconditional love and support. Without them the pressure of finishing this work would have been almost impossible to bear. Last, but by no means least, my greatest debt of gratitude is due to Rachel Viner, for being so beautiful and wonderfully supportive. It is to her that I dedicate this book.

List of Abbreviations

AAA: Association of Association Agreements
ACP: African, Caribbean and Pacific countries
AP: Association Partnership
ARC: Rainbow Group (EP)
BANU: Bulgarian Agrarian National Union
BBC SWB: British Broadcasting Corporation Summary World Broadcast
BSP: Bulgarian Socialist Party
CAP: Common Agricultural Policy
CDU: Christian Democratic Union (Germany)
CECD: Committe Europeen du Commerce de Retail
CEE: Countries of Eastern Europe
CEECs: Central and Eastern European Countries
CEFTA: Central European Free Trade Area
CEJA: European Council of Young Farmers
CEPR: Centre for Economic and Political Research
CFSP: Common Foreign and Security Policy
CFSR: Czechoslovak Socialist Republic
CG: Left Unity (EP)
CMEA: Council of Mutual Economic Assistance
COGECA: General Committee for Agricultural Co-operation in the EC
COM: Communist and Allies Group (EP)
COPA: Committee of Agricultural Organisations in the EC
CPE: European Farmers Co-ordination
CSCE: Conference on Security and Co-operation in Europe
CSU: Christian Social Union (Germany)
PDC: Partido della Democrazia Christiana (Italy)
DG: Directorate General
DR: Technical Group of the European Right (EP)
DTI: Department of Trade and Industry (Britain)
EA: Europe Agreement
EBRD: European Bank of Reconstruction and Development
EC: European Community
ECJ: European Court of Justice
ECLA: European Association for Clothing Industries

ECSC: European Coal and Steel Community
ED: European Democratic Group (EP)
EEA: European Economic Area
EEC: European Economic Community
EFA: European Federation of Agricultural Workers
EFTA: European Free Trade Area
EIB: European Investment Bank
EKEM: Elliniko Kentro Evropaikon Meleteon (Greece)
EMS: European Monetary System
EMU: Economic and Monetary Union
EP: European Parliament
EPC: European Political Co-operation
EPP: European People's Party (EP)
ESC: Economic and Social Committee
ETUC: European Trades Union Congress
ETUI: European Trades Union Institute
EU: European Union
EUROFER: European Confederation of Iron and Steel Industries
FCO: Foreign and Commonwealth Office (Britain)
FDI: Foreign Direct Investment
FDP: Free Democratic Party (Germany)
FEWITA: Federation of European Wholesale and International Trade Association
FN: Front National (France)
FNSEA: Federation Nationale des Syndicats d' Exploitants Agricoles (France)
FRY: Federal Republic of Yugoslavia
FTA: Free Trade Area
FYROM: Former Yugoslav Republic of Macedonia
GATT: General Agreement of Trade and Tariffs
GEDIS: European Group of Integrated Distribution
GDP: Gross Domestic Product
GDR: German Democratic Republic
GSP: Generalised System of Preferences
GUE: Group for the European United Left (EP)
IGC: Inter-Governmental Conference
IMF: International Monetary Fund
JHA: Justice and Home Affairs
LDR: Liberal and Reformist Group (EP)
LP: Liberal Party (Britain)
MAFF: Ministry of Agriculture, Fisheries and Food (Britain)
MEP: Member of the European Parliament

MFA: Multi Fibre Agreement
MRF: Movement for Rights and Freedom (Bulgaria)
MSI: Movimento Sociale Italiano (Italy)
NACC: North Atlantic Co-operation Council
NATO: North Atlantic Treaty Organisation
ND: Nea Dimocratia (Greece)
NFU: National Farmers Union (Britain)
NI: Non-attached (EP)
NSF: National Salvation Front (Romania)
OBNOVA: European programme for the rehabilitation and reconstruction of
Bosnia-Herzegovina, Croatia, the Federal Republic of Yugoslavia and
the FYR Macedonia
OEEC: Organisation for European Economic Cooperation
OPT: Outward Processing Trade
OSCE: Organisation for Security and Co-operation in Europe
PASOK: Panellinio Socialistiko Kinima (Greece)
PHARE: Poland and Hungary. Assistance for Economic Reconstruction
PS: Parti Socialiste (France)
PSE: Group of European Socialists (EP)
RDE: European Democratic Alliance (EP)
RPR: Rassemblement pour la Republique (France)
SAA: Stabilisation and Association Agreement
SAP: Stabilisation and Association Process
SEA: Single European Act
SDP: Social Democratic Party (Britain)
SPD: Social Democratic Party (Germany)
UDF: Union of Democratic Forces (Bulgaria)
UDF: Union pour la Democratie Francaise (France)
UK: United Kingdom
UN: United Nations
UPA: Union Professionel Agricoles (Belgium)
USA: United States of America
USSR: Union of Soviet Socialist Republics
V: Greens (EP)
VER: Voluntary Export Restraints
VRA: Voluntary Restraint Agreement

Introduction

On 25.6.88 the European Community (EC) and the Council for Mutual Economic Assistance (CMEA) signed their Joint Declaration in Luxembourg, ending more than 30 years of political and ideological bickering which had prevented the two largest trading blocks in Europe from recognising each other's existence. The EC/CMEA Joint Declaration marked a significant breakthrough in East-West relations in Europe and was the result of a less confrontational phase of the Cold War which began with Gorbachev's rise to the Soviet leadership in 1985. From a different perspective, the Soviet compromises that made the signature of the Joint Declaration possible were a spectacular sign of how far the USSR and its satellites were prepared to go in order to combat the problems that decades of mismanagement had inflicted on their economies.

Whilst the causes behind the fall of socialism in Eastern Europe were rooted far deeper, the Soviet change of policy vis à vis the EC was the first concrete manifestation of the forthcoming Soviet decline. During the eighteen months that followed the Joint Declaration, the signs of such decline intensified, starting with the Polish government's decision to negotiate with Solidarity in August 1988 and reaching their most dramatic climax in November 1989 with the fall of the Berlin Wall. In parallel to the revolutionary changes in Eastern Europe, the European Community was embarking upon its own odyssey towards deeper economic and political integration. Following almost two decades of Eurosclerosis, the drive towards further integration during the second half of the 1980s constantly gained momentum, leading to the signature of the Single European Act (SEA) in 1986 and, by April 1989, to plans for Economic and Monetary Union (EMU) amongst the 12 EC member states.

As the economic and political crisis in Eastern Europe sprang out of control during the last few months of 1989, the pressure on the EC - already an economic giant and an emerging foreign policy actor in the international scene - to act as a stabilising factor in the region increased dramatically. By that time the EC had already begun the process of negotiating Trade and Co-operation agreements (also referred to as First

Generation agreements) with the former communist countries, while also co-ordinating the G-24's assistance to Eastern Europe (also known as the Phare programme). Nevertheless, the First Generation agreements and the Phare programme soon proved insufficient tools for the containment of the crisis in Eastern Europe.

In December 1989, the Strasbourg European Council concluded that the strengthening of the EC's relations with the Central and Eastern European countries (CEECs) was necessary and instructed the Commission to draft a new form of Association agreement for these countries. Following more than eight months of internal deliberations, the Commission's proposals were published in August 1990 and agreed by the General Affairs Council in September 1990. The new Association agreements with the CEECs were to be given the symbolic name 'Europe' agreements (EAs) and envisaged provisions for the comprehensive regulation of trade relations between the two parties (eventually leading to the creation of a Free Trade Area) as well as procedures and institutions for political consultation. Moreover, the EAs provided for co-operation in a wide range of issues including finance, transport, culture and environmental protection.

While the overall structure of the Europe agreements remained the same for all East European applicants, the precise content of each agreement was negotiated bilaterally and not on a block-to-block basis as, for example, was the case with the Lomé Convention. Moreover, not all East European applicants negotiated their Association with the EC at the same time. Taking into consideration the progress of their economic/political reform process, but also the timing of their applications, the East European applicants were divided into different waves. Poland, Hungary and Czechoslovakia (also referred to as first wave applicants) were the first group of countries to begin Association negotiations with the EC in January 1991. Bulgaria and Romania (also referred to as second wave applicants) formed the second group of countries to negotiate their Association to the EC between May and December 1992. Subsequently, the EC negotiated Association agreements with the successor republics of the former Czechoslovakia in 1993, the Baltic states in 1994 and Slovenia in 1995. More recently the European Union has concluded similar agreements (known as Stabilisation and Association agreements) with the Former Yugoslav Republic of Macedonia (FYROM) in 2000 and Croatia in 2001.

The Europe agreements marked an important turning point in the EC's relations with Eastern Europe in the post-Cold War era. From the outset, they were greeted by EC leaders as an historic development which manifested the EC's determination to assist the reform process in Eastern Europe. For the CEECs too, the EAs assumed great economic and political significance as not only did they offer desperately needed markets, but were also regarded as the first step towards full EC membership; the epitomisation of a passionately desired 'return to Europe'. Despite the optimism of the early days, however, the negotiation of the Association agreements soon evolved into a rather turbulent process, tarnished by delays, quarrels and disillusionment, particularly as the EC often failed to match the expectations that the East European applicants had attached to the Association negotiations.

This book looks, in a theoretically informed manner, at the evolution of the Europe agreements from their conception in early 1990 through to their negotiation with Poland, Hungary and Czechoslovakia in 1991 and Bulgaria and Romania in 1992. Yet this is not a complete narrative of the negotiations which, for most of their duration, concentrated on highly technical issues. Neither is it claimed that all players, features and phases of the Association process as it unfolded during the period 1990-92 have been adequately and equally analysed. Whilst in some chapters the reader may find extensive references to the Association applicants' strategies during the negotiations, this is a book that looks at the Association agreements predominately from an EC perspective. But even within this framework, not every aspect of the EC's policy in relation to the Association agreements has been exhaustively analysed. Instead, the book focuses on five main questions which, it is argued, have not been sufficiently covered by the existing literature. These questions are:

- Why was 'Association' selected as the main tool of the EC's strategy in Eastern Europe?
- Why did the EC fail to adopt a more generous position during the Association negotiations with the first and second wave of East European applicants?
- Why did Bulgaria and Romania fail to be included alongside Poland, Hungary and Czechoslovakia in the first wave of Association applicants?
- What were the implications of the Association agreements becoming an *iterated* game for the strategies of both the EC and the second wave of Association applicants?
- What were the long term consequences of the Association agreements for the EC's strategy in Eastern Europe, both within the setting of its

eastwards enlargement and its attempts to stabilise the volatile Balkan region?

It is argued that providing well-grounded answers to the five questions raised above is important for understanding the outcome of the Association negotiations and for assessing the strategies of their participants. In addition, their importance stretches far beyond the 1991-92 period. In fact, strategies and patterns of behaviour that were developed during this early period continued to shape the EC's relationship with Eastern Europe throughout the 1990s and are, indeed, very much connected to the way in which the processes of the EU's eastwards enlargement and the reconstruction of post-Kosovo Balkans have been thought through and conducted.

For its empirical base, the book depends upon the extensive examination of primary sources such as official EC documents, newspaper articles and newsletters published in the English and foreign language press. Moreover, the author was also granted access to the official correspondence between the EC's institutions and the East European governments as well as to confidential documents relating to the formation of the EC's negotiating position vis à vis the Association applicants. Finally, a number of lengthy interviews were conducted with EC and East European officials who participated in the Association negotiations. Due to the confidential nature of these interviews, the names of the interviewees are not disclosed. The dates and places where these interviews were conducted are listed in the bibliography.

The book is divided into three parts. Part I looks predominantly at the first wave of Association agreements between the EC and the Visegrad three - Poland, Hungary and Czechoslovakia. Chapter 1 provides a theoretical framework for the study of the Association agreements and reviews the main theoretical tools with which the negotiations are later analysed. Chapter 2 examines the EC's initial response to the revolutions in Eastern Europe and explores the main reasons behind the EC's decision to use 'Association' as the main instrument for the management of its relations with Eastern Europe. It then looks at how the main principles of the EC's Association strategy were formulated during 1990 and reviews the more contentious issues of the negotiations with the first wave applicants during 1991.

Chapter 3 addresses one of the most intriguing questions surrounding the EC's strategy in Eastern Europe: why did the EC fail to adopt a more generous position in the Association negotiations despite the insignificant threat posed by the CEECs to the EC's economy? In order to address this paradox, chapter 3 examines a series of internal (e.g. CAP reform) and international (e.g. GATT negotiations) bargains which ran in parallel to the Association negotiations and explores how the EC's need to maximise its gains from those bargains affected its offers to the first wave of Association applicants.

Part II concentrates mainly on the second wave of Association agreements between the EC and Bulgaria and Romania. Chapter 4 looks at the EC member states' response to the Bulgarian and Romanian requests for the opening of Association negotiations with the EC. Attention is given to the evolution of bilateral relations between the key EC member states and the two Balkan applicants as well as to the domestic factors (i.e. position of the main political parties, the reaction of sectoral interests and of public opinion, the levels of economic inter-penetration) that shaped the policy of the EC member states vis à vis Bulgaria and Romania.

In chapter 5 the focus shifts from the EC's member states to the EC's institutions and in particular onto how the Commission and the European Parliament responded to the Bulgarian and Romanian Association requests. The chapter traces the development of relations between the two Balkan applicants with the Commission and the EP since 1988, assesses the way in which the EC's institutions influenced Bulgaria's and Romania's separation from the first wave applicants and examines how, in 1992, they finally consented to the opening of Association negotiations with the Bulgarian and Romanian governments. Chapter 6 looks at the Association negotiations between the EC and the two Balkan applicants in 1992. The chapter examines the changes in the EC's internal and external environment since the negotiation of the first wave of EAs and assesses their effect on the EC's position during the second wave of Association negotiations. Moreover, a substantial part of chapter 7 looks at the negotiating strategies of the second wave applicants with particular emphasis on three themes: firstly, how the precedent of the Visegrad agreements affected the strategies of the Bulgarian and Romanian delegations during the negotiations; secondly, the different way in which each of the two delegations reacted to the EC's offers and thirdly, how the second wave applicants' position changed from the pre-negotiation stage to the more substantive part of the Association bargain.

In Part III (chapter 7), the book concludes with a reflection on how some of the main features of the EC's strategy during the negotiation of the Association agreements continue to dominate its policies vis à vis Eastern Europe to the present day. In this respect, it is argued that the ongoing process of the EU's eastwards enlargement as well as the EU's involvement in the efforts to reconstruct the Balkans cannot be fully understood without reference to its early post-Cold War involvement in the region. With this in mind, it is hoped that this book will not only provide a historical account of the Association negotiations, but will also contribute towards a more productive EU policy in Eastern Europe for the 21st century.

PART I

THE NEGOTIATION OF THE FIRST WAVE OF EUROPE AGREEMENTS

1 Putting the Association Agreements into Theoretical Perspective

The existing literature on the Association agreements

In the decade following the conclusion of the first wave of Association agreements, an extensive literature has been published on the subject. Despite the large number of studies available however, our knowledge in this field remains somewhat fragmented. Employing some degree of simplification, the existing literature on the Association agreements can be divided into four broad categories:

Studies that challenge the economic and political rationale of the EC's Association strategy

As far as economics is concerned, the EC's strategy during the Association negotiations is no stranger to criticism (see, for example, Winters, 1992; Messerlin, 1993). Perhaps the most authoritative study in this field has been conducted by Rollo and Smith (1993). Modelling the effects of complete trade liberalisation between the EC and Eastern Europe in the so-called sensitive sectors, the two authors concluded that the gains of the EC's taxpayers and consumers (as a result of increased competition, lower prices and subsidies) far outweighed the losses of the EC's producers. Consequently, in addition to the gains it would have brought to Central and East European producers, such a trade liberalisation would also have been beneficial for the EC economy, even in the event that the EC had to fully compensate its producers for their losses (Rollo and Smith, 1993:155). A year before, Baldwin *et al.* (1992) reached a similar conclusion and argued for the reciprocal benefits of the CEECs being included in a European Economic Space which would involve free trade, but not labour mobility (1992: 91). Nevertheless, while making a convincing case as to why the EC's trade protectionism in the

9

Association negotiations was unnecessary (since such a practice was damaging for both the EC and the CEEC economies), most of these studies shed little light on the fundamental question of how and why such a policy came about.

A similar criticism can also be directed towards studies that concentrated on the political aspect of the EC's Association strategy. Bonvicini *et al* (1991: 81), for example, argued that the Association agreements should prepare the CEECs for EC membership within a decade. Inotai (1994) also criticised what he regarded as a defensive and counter-productive EC strategy during the Association negotiations. In addition to his criticism against the EC's lack of generosity in relation to trade concessions and financial assistance to the region (1994: 29-32), Inotai vigorously attacked the EC's refusal to offer a clear membership commitment to the newly emerged democracies in Eastern Europe (1994: 35) which he regarded essential for both economic/political and psychological reasons. Like Rollo and Smith, Inotai did, in fact, offer a well-substantiated critique of the EC's early strategy in the region. Nevertheless, the dynamics behind the formation of such a strategy were once again either disregarded or identified in very general terms by reference to the EC's 'self interest' and the EC's 'lack of imagination and strategic planning'.

Studies that look at the legal technicalities of the EAs and studies that concentrate on specific aspects of the EAs

In the first category one can include the works of Maresceau (1993, 1997: introduction) and Muller-Graff (1997) both of which analysed the legal basis of the Association agreements and gave an overview of the provisions of each of their chapters (i.e. Political Dialogue, Trade, Competition, Movement of Workers, Establishment and Supply of Services, Payments and Capital). Notwithstanding the fact that references to EC law such as the legal basis of the EAs and the Court of Justice rulings in previous Association agreements are essential for the understanding of the content and character of the Europe agreements, these studies shed little light on the politics behind the CEECs' Association to the EC. Once again, the motives behind the initiation of the EAs negotiations as well as the factors that shaped the EC's position in them are largely overlooked.

The same can also be argued about the studies that concentrated on sectoral aspects of the Association agreements. Here amongst the plethora of studies available, one should distinguish the works of Tracy

(1992) on the agricultural arrangements of the EAs; Sedelmeier (1995) on the process behind the formation of the EC's Association strategy in relation to steel products; Van den Bossche (1997) on the similarities and differences of competition provisions in the EA's with each of the CEECs; Cremona (1997) on the EAs provisions in relation to free movement of Persons, Establishment and Services; and Van den Hende (1997) on the EAs' safeguard clauses. Despite their usefulness in explaining the implications of the EAs' provisions in specific sectors of the EC's and the CEECs' economies, their scope and explanatory power remain rather limited.

Studies that focused on the Association agreements between the EC and a particular Association applicant or a group of Association applicants belonging to the same wave

Stawarska (1992), in her analysis of the negotiation of the Polish Association agreement with the EC, offered perhaps the most authoritative work in this category. The negotiation as well as the impact of the Hungarian and the Czech Association agreements with the EC have also been examined by Janacek (1992) and Drabek (1993) respectively. As far as the second wave applicants are concerned, Wallden (1993) offered a general account of the Bulgarian and Romanian Association agreements with the EC, while Eskenazi (1993) and Wallden (1993b, 1994b) looked in more detail at the Bulgarian strategy and expectations during (and after) the negotiation of the country's Association with the EC.

Whilst providing useful insights into the interaction of certain CEECs with the EC, these studies normally lack a comparative perspective and do not address the crucial question of the EC's alleged discriminatory treatment against certain (waves of) Association applicants. Most importantly, they fail to capture the evolutionary character of the EC's Association strategy in Eastern Europe and often ignore important internal and international factors that shaped the EC's policy in specific phases of the Association negotiations.

Studies that look at the Association agreements as part of a broader examination of the EC's relations with Eastern Europe

This is the largest category in the existing literature. Within it, one can identify three sub-categories. Firstly, those studies whose chronological scope stretches from the outbreak of the Cold War to the negotiation and conclusion of the Association agreements with Poland, Czechoslovakia and Hungary in 1991. Perhaps the most influential example of such studies can be found in the work of Van Ham (1993) who offered a comprehensive narrative of East-West relations during the Cold war and attempted an interesting conceptualisation (through a neo-Realist and neo-Liberal institutionalist perspective) of the new multi-polar post-Cold war setting and its effects on the EC's relations with Eastern Europe. Distinguished, though more descriptive, examples in this sub-category can also be found in Pinter (1991) and, for the EC's relations with the Balkan region, in Wallden (1994).

A second sub-category includes works whose chronological scope stretches from the 1988 EC-CMEA Joint Declaration but ends before December 1995 when the Madrid European Council set a concrete timetable for the EU's eastwards enlargement for the first time. Here, the works of Reinicke (1992) and Kramer (1993) offered useful insights into the problems surrounding the crystallisation and execution of the EC's strategy vis à vis Eastern Europe, while Sedelmeier (1994) successfully captured the conflict between the EC's political and economic objectives in the region. Baldwin (1994), on the other hand, highlighted the disadvantages of the 'hub and spoke' nature of the EC-CEECs economic relations and argued for the benefits of greater trade liberalisation as well as for the inclusion of all of the CEECs who have signed EAs with the EC into an 'Association of Association Agreements' (AAA).[1] Guggenbuhl (1995) also provided an interesting narrative of the making of the EC's Association strategy. Moreover, at a theoretical level, his conception of the Association agreements as an attempt on behalf of the EC to reduce 'negative externalities' (1995: 214) coming from Eastern Europe carried significant explanatory power. Finally, Sedelmeier and Wallace (1996 and 2000) offered perhaps the most authoritative and systematic attempt to identify the disjointed nature of the EC's strategy in Eastern Europe and analyse the main dynamics behind the EC's policy formation in this area.

The final third sub-category includes more recent publications which are strongly influenced by the opening of the enlargement negotiations. Here, the most important examples include the works of Van den Bempt and Theelen (1996), Maresceau (1997), Mayhew (1998), Van Brabant (1999), Mannin (1999), Gurzon Price *et al* (1999), Baun (2000), Tang (2000) and Lord (2000). In the studies of this sub-category the Association agreements are largely treated as the starting point of a process which will come to an end with the Union's eastwards enlargement (which remains their main research focus). While crucial for understanding the evolution of the EU's strategy in Eastern Europe during the last decade (and before), studies with such broad chronological scope inevitably fail to examine the Association agreements in much depth. As a result, in some cases (e.g. Maresceau, 1997; Van Brabant, 1999; Tang, 2000) the EA negotiations are largely ignored. In others (e.g. Kramer, 1993, Mannin, 1999; Baun, 2000), the treatment of the EA negotiations between the EC and the CEECs as 'identical' misses important aspects of each Association applicant's interaction with the EC.

The problem of theorising the Association agreements

Despite attracting a great deal of empirical research, the EU's relations with Eastern Europe (including the process of the EU's eastwards enlargement) has remained a largely under-theorised field of the EU's activities. With few exceptions (see Van Ham, 1993; Guggenbuhl, 1995; Shaffer, 1995; Friis, 1998), the Association agreements have followed this rule. In addition to the more general problems relating to the theory-building on the EU (see, for example, Keohane and Hoffmann, 1991: chapter 1; Risse-Kappen, 1996; Caporaso, 1996; Wallace and Wallace, 2000: chapters 2, 3 & 19), the application of a theoretical straitjacket to the Association negotiations entails further difficulties:

The treaty base of the Association agreements

The EC's Association strategy in Eastern Europe was formed on the basis of Article 238 of the Treaty of Rome according to which: "The Community may conclude with a third State, a union of States or an international organisation agreement establishing an association involving reciprocal rights and obligations, common action and special procedures". Article 238 stipulated that after receiving an Association application "the Council shall act unanimously after consulting the Commission and after receiving the Assent of the European Parliament...". Moreover, when new institutions are established under an Association agreement (i.e. when an agreement is 'mixed' as was indeed the case with the EAs), then "...this agreement shall be submitted for ratification by all the contacting states in accordance with their respective constitutional requirements".[2]

The treaty base of the Association agreements differs quite substantially from other areas relating to the EC's external relations. Unlike foreign and security policy which formed a separate intergovernmental pillar under Maastricht, Association remains a fully 'communitised' policy where the Commission retained its exclusive role as the EC's policy initiator and international negotiator. Moreover, unlike the EC's common commercial policy (the procedure of which is set in Article 113) where the EC's negotiating position is decided by the Council on the basis of qualified majority voting (QMV), the EC's position in Association negotiations requires a unanimous decision by the Council. The conclusion of Association agreements is also different from trade agreements signed under Article 113. The application of the Assent procedure under Article 238 (as compared with the consultation procedure under the Article 113) strengthens the role of the European Parliament which, in Association agreements, becomes a constitutionally veto-holding player. The number of veto players is further increased by the need for ratification of the Association agreements by 'all contracting parties', meaning in this case the twelve (in 1991-92) national parliaments, the parliaments of the Association applicants as well as the European Parliament.

The treaty base of the Association process points to a complex network of relationships between its main actors which can be captured by a variety of theoretical perspectives. The unanimity required within the Council as well as the need for ratification of the EAs by national parliaments point, for example, to the literature on intergovernmentalism and its main proposition on the supremacy of national governments over the EC's decision making process (Moravcsik, 1991, 1994, 1998). Yet, the fully 'communitised' nature of the Association process, in particular the Commission's role as policy initiator and negotiator with the Association applicants as well as the European Parliament's increased powers under the Assent procedure, can point in the opposite direction. An extensive literature exists on how the EC's supranational institutions (Bulmer, 1994a, 1994b; Peters, 1994; Tsebelis, 1994; Pollack, 1997) and their leaders (Nugent, 1995b; Dyson and Featherstone, 1997) can potentially act as effective policy entrepreneurs and thus have a crucial impact on the agenda setting and the outcome of the EC's internal bargaining.

The need for a three-level analysis

The final shape and content of the Association (Europe) agreements were the products of bargaining at many different levels. At the international level, the Association agreements were negotiated bilaterally between the Commission (on behalf of the EC) and the government of each of the Association applicants. In theoretical terms, the striking power asymmetries between the participants of the Association bargain as well as their very different exit costs from the Association process lends itself to a Realist-inspired explanation (e.g. Wright, 1946; Morgenthau, 1978). However, a full-blown Realist explanation of the Association negotiations fails to account for the identity of the actors involved and the dynamic and complex interaction between them. In this sense, to view the Association negotiations as a 'traditional' inter-state bargaining or, worse, to regard its participants as monolithic 'black box'-like actors would be misleading.

Since the late 1950s a large number of scholars have argued for the interdependence between domestic politics and international behaviour. Waltz's 'second image' (1959), Rosenau's 'linkage politics' (1969), Katzenstein's work on international relations and domestic structures (1976) and Gourevitch's 'second image reversed' (1978), for example, all point to the weakness of the Realist 'black box' thesis. More recently, Putnam (1988) has described the interaction between domestic politics and international behaviour as a 'two level' game whereby negotiators are engaged in simultaneous bargaining with their international counterparts and their domestic constituencies. In the case of the Association negotiations (and the EU's international presence in general), however, another layer of analysis may be required to supplement Putnam's paradigm. This refers to the EU level where national preferences are mediated within the largely consensus-driven Council and subjected to the influence of the EU's supranational institutions and European-level lobbying before an 'EU preference' is finally agreed upon. At this level, theoretical perspectives need to be sensitive to the special features of the EU's decision making process: notably its fragmentation and receptiveness to lobbying as well as the scope it allows for entrepreneurial behaviour on behalf of the EU's supranational institutions.

Within this context, the book will seek to locate the factors that shape the final outcome of the Association negotiations within a framework of a three-level game (domestic, EC, international) as elaborated by Shaffer (1995: 5-10). The first two levels relate to the process of the EC's preference formation and are explored in chapters 2 and 3 for the first wave applicants (Hungary, Poland, Czechoslovakia) and in chapters 4 and 5 for the second wave applicants (Bulgaria and Romania). The third level which relates to the actual negotiations between the EC and the first and second wave of Association applicants are explored in chapters 2 and 6 respectively.

A high or low politics bargain?

The selection of an adequate theoretical framework for the understanding of the Association agreements is further impeded by the difficulty of distinguishing between their economic and political significance. The vast majority of the EAs' articles are dedicated to the regulation of trade and economic relations between the EC and the CEECs, whilst the agreements also included provisions for co-operation in other areas of 'low politics' (Hoffmann, 1966) including transport, tourism, education and culture. The 'low politics' character of the issues covered by the Association agreements lends itself to a theoretical explanation based on more liberal propositions.

Yet, to treat the EAs as an exclusively 'low politics' exchange would be misleading. From the outset the Association agreements were rich in symbolism, regarded by both sides as an important step towards the re-unification of the Continent and a long-term guarantee for the stability of the newly emerged democracies in Eastern Europe. The security ramifications of the EAs were also reinforced by the fact that the opening of the EC markets was considered pivotal for the economic survival of the CEECs which at that time were desperately seeking to re-direct their trade flows away from the former Soviet block and earn badly needed hard currency. Moreover, the agreements substantially increased the level of political interaction between the EC and the Association applicants, notably through the process of Political Dialogue introduced in Title I. Within this process the EAs made references to the convergence of the two parties' positions on foreign and security matters and the exchange of information on issues of mutual interest, whilst they also established the institutional framework (i.e. Association Council, Association Committee and Joint parliamentary Committee) to facilitate regular consultation. Within this context the Association agreements fail to fit neatly into Hoffmann's (1966) low/high politics dichotomy. Whilst much of the substance of the agreements remained within the area of low politics, their negotiation was very much affected by longer term strategic and security considerations. The impact of high politics on the negotiation of the first and second wave of Association agreements is discussed in chapters 2 and 6 respectively.

The theoretical perspective of the book

The theoretical perspective of this book is anchored on the 'wider' or 'soft' rational choice tradition (see below). In recent years a number of scholars have utilised game theoretic propositions and multi-level bargaining models to study a wide range of issues relating to the EU's integration process. Tsebelis (1994), for example, has used game theory to elaborate on the impact of the European Parliament on the EU's decision making process. Schneider and Seybold (1997) also worked within the wider game theoretic tradition to explain the successes and failures of the EPC, while Schneider and Cederman (1994) and Schneider *et. al.* (1995) have worked with game theory propositions to account for the stops and starts of European integration. On a different level, Dyson, Featherstone and Michalopoulos (1994) have successfully shown the applicability of multi-level bargaining models to the negotiation of EMU, while a similar conclusion was also reached by Wennerlund (1994) and Princen (2001) in relation to the EU's EFTA expansion and the negotiation of the international trapping standards respectively .

Nevertheless, similar theoretical tools have only been used sporadically in the study of the EC's relations with Eastern Europe. Shaffer (1995), for instance, attempted an interesting three-level game analysis to the EC-Visegrad Association negotiations, but according to his own words his model was in need of more parsimony and empirical backing. Friis (1998), on the other hand, made reference to the 'Europe Agreement game', but the attention of his research was largely focused on the post-negotiation (that is the ratification) phase, rather than the actual Association negotiations. Whilst not claiming to have the final word in the field, this book seeks to build upon the literature on wider rational choice and extend, in a systematic manner, some of its propositions to the study of the EC's strategy in Eastern Europe. In doing so, the book also aims to contribute to the more general debate on the EC's role as an international negotiator (Zartman, 1971; Galtung, 1973; Shlaim and Yannopoulos, 1978; Stevens, 1992, 1996; Hill, 1993; Devuyst, 1995; Woolock and Hodges, 1996; Smith, 2000; Princen, 2001 and Young, 2001).

Based upon a wider rational choice perspective, the initiation of the Association process is explained with reference to regime theory (Ruggie, 1975; Krasner, 1983; Keohane, 1984; Rood, 1989). The main argument here is that the EC devised the Association agreements as a means of regulating economic/political relations with the CEECs as well as a tool for reducing uncertainty and enhancing the 'predictability' of the newly emerged democracies in Eastern Europe (see chapter 2). A regime-based explanation of the EAs' initiation, however, should be sensitive to the power asymmetries that existed between the regime's constructors/participants. In this respect, it would be misleading to suggest that both parties (the EC on the one hand and the CEECs on the other) dictated the rules of the Association regime on an equal basis. It would be equally misleading to suggest that both parties participated in the Association regime for the same reasons or anticipated the same benefits from it. Realist-inspired propositions can provide useful insights for the understanding of such asymmetries and their implications for the design of the Association regime as well as the final outcome of the Association negotiations with the first and second wave of Association applicants. These will be discussed in more detail in chapters 2 and 6.

Chapter 3 uses Tsebelis' concepts of *games in multiple arenas* with *variable payoffs* (1988, 1990) in order to account for the formation of the EC's strategy during the negotiation of the first wave of Association agreements with Poland, Hungary and Czechoslovakia in 1991. The main argument of the book is that the EC's inability to 'translate' its positive rhetoric into generous trade and political concessions to the East European applicants cannot be fully understood if the Association negotiations with the first and second waves of applicants are studied 'independently' as one-shot games played in a vacuum. Instead, it is argued, the Association negotiations should be conceptualised as a game nested into a wider network of international and domestic games (which is referred to in chapter 3 as the *Grand* game) in which the EC was involved at the time (1990-1992). Within this *Grand* game, negotiating strategies need to take into account that payoffs in a given game can be affected by the situation prevailing in another game (or the moves of a third player in this game).

The interdependence between the different games (and the EC's anticipated payoffs from them) within the *Grand* game is a crucial factor for the understanding of the EC's strategy during the Association negotiations. This book argues that the EC's caution vis à vis the Association applicants was in most cases dictated, not by the direct threat posed by the CEECs to the EC's interests, but instead by the EC's need to pursue a consistent strategy in a number of domestic and international bargains which run in parallel to the Association negotiations. Thus, what within the context of a one-shot Association game may seem a sub-optimal strategy (in the sense that the EC's caution was disproportionate to the threat posed by the Association applicants), it could after all be an optimal strategy when the distribution of payoffs in the entire *Grand* game is taken into consideration.

The concept of *iterated* games (Axelrod, 1990), as a determinant of the EC's negotiating position vis à vis the second wave of Association applicants (Bulgaria and Romania) is explored in chapter 6. Similar to the *multiple arenas*-based analysis offered in chapter 3, chapter 6 argues that the EC's negotiating position vis à vis the second wave applicants should not be studied in isolation, but in relation to the Association game's 'past' and anticipated 'future'. In this respect, the selection of sub-optimal preferences at a particular phase of an *iterated* game, may be necessary for the maximisation of a player's payoffs during the entire period of the game (Tsebelis, 1990: 73) or for the preservation of its *reputation* (whatever this reputation might have been in a given issue) vis à vis previous or future negotiating partners (Axelrod, 1990: 151, Tsebelis, 1990: 156).

References to the iterated nature of the Association game can, therefore, provide additional resources for the understanding of the EC's position during the second wave of Association negotiations. It is argued that the tightening of the EC's offers to the Bulgarian and Romanian delegations (i.e. the 'improved conditionality' clause, the inclusion of a specific safeguard clause for steel products and the reduction of quotas for agricultural products) can not be explained solely by the direct threat posed to the EC's interests by the second wave applicants. Instead, the EC's strategy towards Bulgaria and Romania can be put into a clearer perspective when one considers the EC's need to preserve its *reputation* vis à vis previous and prospective Association partners as well as to maximise its profits during the entire duration of the Association game.

A soft rational choice approach to the study of the EC's policy in Eastern Europe

An explanation of the EC's Association strategy that is anchored on the wider rational choice tradition is inextricably linked with the question of the EC's rationality. 'Full blown' game theorists have traditionally built their models upon assumptions of optimising behaviour based on strict rationality requirements. This, they argued, ensures that their models possess both explanatory and predictive powers - the latter being, of course, their much prized advantage over 'story-telling'. Even what 'full blown' game theorists describe as 'weak' (Tsebelis 1990: 24-27)[3] rationality requirements (impossibility of contradictory beliefs or preferences; impossibility of intransitive preferences and conformity to the axioms of probability calculus) appear to be a tall order for individual actors let alone complex multinational political entities. The inability of the EC to comply with the rationality requirements prescribed by 'narrow' rational choice is profound: multiplicity of preferences and actors co-existing in a non-hierarchical order, a 'constitutionally' fragmented decision making process, and uncertainty (in terms of the availability and reliability of data regarding the economic and political developments in the CEECs during the early stages of transition) can easily substantiate such an assertion.

However, the impossibility of complying with the rationality requirements of 'full blown' game theorists, does not necessarily strip rational choice from its relevance in explaining behaviour in the international system. Scholars of the 'wider' rational choice tradition have argued about the methodological benefits of "...relaxing the notion of optimisation, though still keeping the overall framework of cost benefit analysis" (Fierke and Nicklson 1999: 3-4). What is lost through such a compromise? Arguably the solidity of the predictive powers of game theory. Yet, as Sharpf argues, the benefits may be substantial since a "...game-theoretic representation allows us to describe and compare, at a very high level of abstraction but with great precision, extremely diverse real-world constellations" (1997: 45).

It is against this background that the book uses the game theoretic concepts of *games in multiple arenas with variable payoffs* and *iterated games* as explanatory tools for framing the strategic interaction between the participants in the Association game. Both terms are used outside the theoretical rigidity of game theory. In this respect, the book 'consumes' (rather than 'produces') game theory in its attempt to find a framework in which to analyse the contextual factors which shaped the EC's strategy from the early conception of the Association agreements all the way through to their negotiation with the East European applicants. By doing so the book follows the example of a long list of scholars (Putnam, 1988; Bates *et al.*, 1998; Radaelli, 1998; Opt, 1999; and Fierke and Nicholson, 1999), who have combined game theoretic representations with narrative accounts in order to capture the complexities of games that 'real actors' play (Scharpf, 1997; see also Green and Shapiro, 1994, 1995).

Whilst rejecting the strong rationality requirements prescribed by full-blown game theorists, an analysis of the Association negotiations based on the wider rational choice tradition still relies on the assumption of purposive and goal-oriented behaviour. After all, the conceptualisation of decision making process during the Association negotiations as a 'garbage can' (Cohen, March and Olsen, 1972, Kingdon 1984) would render a game theoretic representation of the Association bargain obsolete. The problem in this case seems to be exacerbated by the high levels of fragmentation and complexity of the EC's decision making process which is known to encourage paralysis and inertia. Yet in the case of the Association process, there is little evidence to suggest that the EC's behaviour resembles that of a non-purposive, jelly-like, actor.

To begin with the very initiation of the Association process as a means of reducing uncertainty in Eastern Europe is in itself indicative of strategic behaviour. The consensus within and between the EC's institutions over the main principles of the EC's strategy in Eastern Europe (see chapter 2) also served as a guiding light for the EC during the negotiations. Chapter 3 provides further evidence that EC's negotiating position vis à vis the Association applicants was affected by a number of internal and external bargains that run in parallel to the Association negotiations. These adjustments are indeed indicative of strategic behaviour as is the EC's ability to respond to the iterated nature of the Association bargain as illustrated in chapter 5. On a more general level the decisions of the Copenhagen (June 1993) and Essen (December 1994) European Councils offer further evidence of an actor able to review its strategy in the face of changing circumstances and embark upon radical policy changes.

Against this background, the EC's involvement in the Association negotiations can best be described as that of an actor possessing 'bounded rationality' (Simon 1976).[4] The 'bounded rationality' assumption is compatible with the limitations imposed upon the EC's Association strategy by its own decision making structures and the high levels of uncertainty that surrounded its elaboration and execution. It is also compatible with the main propositions of the 'wider' rational choice tradition employed in this book. Keohane, for example, acknowledged the compatibility of 'bounded rationality' with perceptions of self-interest (1984: chapter 7) and associated his regime theory with the efforts of international players to cope with the limitations caused by their 'bounded rationality' (1984: 131). Within the context of the Association negotiations, the conceptualisation of the EC as an actor possessing 'bounded rationality' pursuing games in multiple arenas can offer useful insights into the understanding of the factors that shape its international behaviour and thus put more substance to the often blurred notion of the EC's 'self-interest'.

Notes

[1] Building on Baldwin, Sapir (1999) also explored the future shape of trade relations between the EU and non-EU members in Eastern Europe.

---

[2] Article 238 was slightly rephrased in Maastricht. In the TEU the procedure applicable for Association agreements is described in Article 228 paragraph 3. Articles 228 and 238 were subjected to further changes by the Amsterdam treaty. For more details see Phinnemore (1999).

[3] In addition to his 'weak' rationality requirements, Tsebelis presents what he describes as 'strong' rationality requirements: (i) strategies that are mutually optimal in equilibrium; (ii) probabilities approximate objective frequencies in equilibrium and (iii) beliefs approximate reality in equilibrium. Tsebelis (1990: 27-31).

[4] Herber Simon's concept of 'bounded rationality' was based on the observation that 'real behaviour' always falls short of 'perfect rationality'. This is because: "(i) Rationality requires a complete knowledge and anticipation of the consequences that will follow from each choice. In fact, knowledge of consequences is always fragmentary, (ii) since those consequences lie in the future, imagination must supply the lack of experienced feeling in attaching value to them. But values can be only imperfectly anticipated, (iii) rationality requires a choice among all possible alternative behaviours. In actual behaviour, only a very few of all these possible alternatives ever come to mind". (Simon 1976: 80-81).

2 The EC and the First Wave of Association Agreements: Fixing the Rules of the Game

This chapter looks at the evolution of relations between the EC and Eastern Europe leading to the negotiation and conclusion of the first wave of Association agreements with Poland, Hungary and Czechoslovakia in December 1991. Particular attention will be paid to three main themes: (i) the EC's early strategy in the region, beginning with the 1988 EC/CMEA Joint Declaration and ending in late 1989 with the collapse of the Berlin Wall and the overthrow of most of the communist leaders in Eastern Europe; (ii) the reasons leading to the introduction of Association as the main instrument of the EC's policy in Eastern Europe and the main principles on which the new Europe agreements were to be based; and (iii) the most contentious issues during the negotiations between the EC and the first wave of Association applicants and the way in which these issues were finally resolved.

From a theoretical perspective, the initiation of the Association agreements will be regarded as a regime building exercise on behalf of the EC aimed at reducing the uncertainties produced by the revolutions in Eastern Europe during the second half of 1989 and facilitating co-operation with the region's newly emerged governments. The initiation of regimes as a means of reducing uncertainty and the opportunity costs of co-operation lays at the heart of interdependence/regime theory (Ruggie, 1975; Keohane, 1984; Rood, 1989). By 1990, the creation of an Association regime offered substantial benefits for both the CEECs and the EC. For the CEECs, the Association agreements provided an opportunity for full normalisation of their relations with the EC and, most importantly, offered desperately needed export markets. For the EC on the other hand, the Association agreements provided an opportunity for the creation of an information-rich environment which was clearly beneficial for trade and investment opportunities in the region. Moreover, the establishment of commonly accepted standards of behaviour - what

Krasner called *norms* of the regime (1983: 2) - ensured the 'predictability' of the new and largely unknown governments in Eastern Europe.

The anticipated mutual benefits of the Association regime, however, should not alone lead to the conclusion that both parties (the EC and the CEECs) contributed equally to its construction. It will be argued that the design of the Association regime was exclusively performed by the EC, while the East European applicants' ability to shape even the regime's details - what Krasner called *rules* (1983: 2) - remained extremely limited. In this respect, this chapter fully subscribes to Keohane's assertion that regimes "...should be comprehended chiefly as arrangements motivated by self-interest" (1984: 62), not as instruments contributing to the decline of inequality within the international system (a view, for example, advocated by Haas, 1975: 860 and Scott, 1977). From a slightly different perspective, the Association regime can also be seen as a means of 'institutionalising' (Cox, 1991: 450) a new order in Europe at the heart of which lay the EC as the continent's undisputed economic and, rapidly developing, political super-power.

Facing the avalanche: The EC's initial response to the events in Eastern Europe

For most of the Cold War years, ideological conflict and political considerations prevented the establishment of official relations between the EEC and the CMEA or its members. The deadlock in EC-CMEA relations was finally broken in early 1986, following Gorbachev's decision to retreat from the long standing Soviet insistence on 'block to block' negotiations and allow the EC to enter a parallel process of negotiations with both the CMEA and its individual members. Negotiations between the EC and the CMEA ended on 25.6.88 with the signature of the "Joint Declaration on the Establishment of Official Relations Between the European Economic Community and the Council for Mutual Economic Assistance" (OJ L 157/35) and soon after diplomatic relations were established with each of the CMEA members.[1]

The normalisation of relations with Eastern European countries apparently widened the Community's scope for action in the region. A few months after the establishment of diplomatic relations, the Commission and Hungary signed a Trade and Co-operation agreement, while similar agreements were concluded with other East European countries throughout the period 1988-91.[2] The negotiations of the First Generation agreements presented few difficulties for the Community. The agreements were confined to trade-related matters and did not touch upon politically-sensitive matters. The scope and extent of trade liberalisation were also limited. Agriculture and ECSC products were excluded from the scope of the agreements,[3] while there was no provision for the establishment of a Free Trade Area (FTA). Furthermore, the Community promised the removal of all quantitative restrictions by 31.12.95,[4] but still retained the right to impose preferential duties on imports originating from Eastern Europe. Against this background negotiations between the CEECs and the EC advanced rapidly and, in most cases, were concluded within two or three rounds.

Whilst creating a basic framework for the development of trade relations and bilateral consultation (through the establishment of the Joint Committee), it soon became apparent that the First Generation agreements could not, on their own, provide a sufficient response to the complex problems facing the reforming economies in Eastern Europe. The necessity for more and better co-ordinated assistance for the support of the economic reforms underway in Poland and Hungary was recognised by the G-7 Summit held in Paris on 14-16.7.89. To this end, and following the insistence of German Chancellor Helmut Kohl (Reinicke, 1992: 188), the G-7 Summit finally decided to "...ask the Commission to take the necessary initiatives in agreement with the other members states of the Community, and to associate, besides the Summit participants, all interested countries" (Doc/89/2, 16.7.89).

The Summit's decision was a clear manifestation of the EC's increased influence in Eastern Europe and a great victory for the Commission which was now emerging as the 'conductor' of Western assistance in Eastern Europe. Indeed, the EC was quick to respond to this challenge. Following consultations with the rest of the G-24, the Commission in September 1989 proposed its action plan for Poland and Hungary (Commission of the EC, 1989), known as the Phare programme (Assistance for Economic Reconstruction in Poland and Hungary). The assistance, which was made conditional upon "a firm commitment for substantial economic reforms", involved measures for:

- supporting the revival of domestic agricultural production through the supply of production aids such as pesticides and agricultural machinery,
- supporting investment initiatives in the two countries through loans from the ECSC and the EIB,
- promoting vocational training, especially in the financial and banking sectors, protecting the environment, and

- improving access to the Community markets through the accelerated abolition of quantitative restrictions, improved agricultural and tariff concessions and extension of the benefits of the system of generalised preferences to Poland and Hungary from 1990.

By the end of 1989, most of the Commission's proposals concerning assistance to Hungary and Poland had been accepted by the Council. Furthermore, the Strasbourg Summit (8-9.12.89) and the Brussels Ministerial Conference of G-24 (13.12.89) agreed in principle to the Commission's plans to extend the Phare programme to other East European countries which would fulfil the necessary criteria (IP/89/953, 14.12.89 and Doc/89/3, 9.12.89). However, as unrest spread across Eastern Europe during the winter of 1989, the pressure on Brussels to act as a stabilising factor in the region increased dramatically. Now, five more countries (the GDR, Czechoslovakia, Bulgaria, Romania and Yugoslavia) were knocking on the Community's door seeking assistance in order to avoid total economic and social collapse.

The Community's ability to respond quickly and effectively to the generalised crisis in Eastern Europe, however, was severely restrained by its limited exposure in the region. By the end of 1989 Poland and Hungary were the only CEECs to sign Trade and Co-operation agreements with the EC and to be included in the Phare programme. Romania and Yugoslavia did conclude trade agreements with the EC in the early 1980s but both countries eventually saw their relations with the EC either completely frozen (Romania) or been put in the backburner (Yugoslavia). Czechoslovakia and Bulgaria on the other hand enjoyed no contractual relation with the EC. Moreover at the time of the fall of the Berlin Wall, the Commission did not have a delegation in any of the CEECs. The first such delegation opened in Budapest in November 1990 whist the Commission's offices in Bucharest, Prague and Sofia did not open until 1992. Under these circumstances the Commission often lacked reliable information about the rapidly changing economic and political developments in Eastern Europe. It also crucially lacked a bilateral framework for political consultation with these countries in times of crisis. The alternative of sending fact-finding missions in order to acquire first-hand knowledge about the political and economic situation in the region was both ineffective and time consuming.

Moreover, the scarce resources available for the Phare programme (a consequence of the Western reluctance to engage in a new Marshall Plan for Eastern Europe) limited the scope of the EC's action in the region, particularly as the number of CEECs requesting assistance increased. For example, the Community's entire Phare budget for 1991-93 was just under 3 billion ECU (Mayhew (1998: 140), a rather modest figure if one considers that the new German Länders, over the same period, were granted 3 billion ECU from the Cohesion Fund alone (Wallace and Wallace, 1996: 216). The whole process was further slowed by the complex financing of the G-24 assistance which involved resources from the EC budget, direct contributions from the EC member states as well as contributions from the rest of the G-24 member states.

Finally, the Community's ability to respond swiftly to the events in Eastern Europe was impeded by the dramatic increase in the responsibilities of the Commission's Directorate General for External Relations (DG I). In July 1989, relations with Eastern Europe, including the Soviet Union, were the responsibility of a small Unit within Directorate E (also responsible for relations with the EFTA countries) of DG I, consisting of no more than twenty people. In February 1990, following the changes in Eastern Europe, a new Task Force for Poland and Hungary was established with the responsibility of co-ordinating the G-24 assistance, while Directorate E was left to concentrate on Eastern Europe only (relations with the EFTA countries were assigned to a new Directorate). Even after the internal restructuring, however, (see Figure 2.1), the services dealing with Eastern Europe severely lacked personnel.

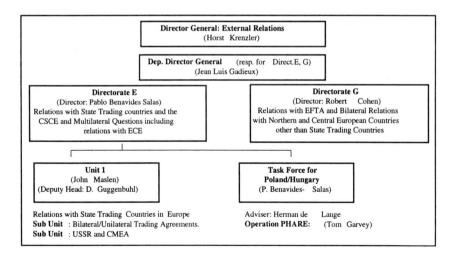

Figure 2.1 Directorate General for External Relations (I), February 1990

For a better understanding of the extensive restructuring of DG I that followed this initial period, one has to observe that the responsibilities of the relatively small Directorate E in 1990 had, by 1996, become the responsibility of three different Directorates (C, B and D) within the new DG IA (see Figure 2.2). Although DG I's internal restructuring was also closely associated with the accommodation of personal rivalries within the Delors III Commission (Edwards and Spence, 1994: chapter 4), the increase in the number of Directorates dealing with Eastern Europe was a clear indication of the burden imposed upon the Commission's services by the collapse of the Iron Curtain.

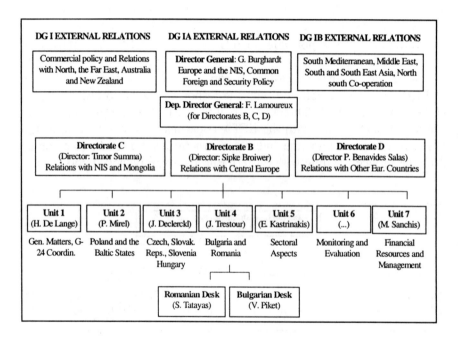

Figure 2.2 Directorates General for External Relations (I, IA and IB), Spring 1996

It is, therefore, arguable that despite some modest progress made in relations with Hungary and Poland, the Community remained largely unprepared to face up to the new challenges posed by the collapse of the Berlin Wall and the end of Europe's division. Inexperienced in dealing with crisis situations, having established channels of communication with very few countries in the region (and for a very short period of time) and lacking adequate financial and human resources, the Community was clearly overtaken by the speed of events in late 1989. It is against this background that, speaking before the Strasbourg European Summit in December 1989, President Delors admitted:

> Things are changing there very quickly. So we have to find the resources, the intelligence and the spirit to go forward and answer the double challenge, the external and the internal challenge. In this new European environment we are facing the shock of necessity. We all have within us a mixture of happiness and anxiety, a mixture of hope and fear (Speech/89/87, 7.12.89).

The construction of the Association regime: the birth of the Europe Agreements

The generalised crisis of late 1989 and the inability of the EC to respond effectively to the developments in Eastern Europe had made it clear that the existing framework of relations between the EC and the CEECs (i.e. First Generation agreements and the Phare programme) could not on its own provide a sufficient basis for future co-operation (Kramer, 1993: 227). Furthermore, as the old communist leaders were disappearing from the political scene, fears began to emerge about the 'predictability' and 'consistency' of the new regimes in Eastern Europe. These fears were fuelled by the lack of any democratic tradition in most CEECs, but also by the highly polarised nature of East European politics in which nationalist and demagogic forces threatened the very existence of the new political systems (White S. *et. al.*, 1993: chapter 1).

Against this background, the idea of granting Association agreements to the CEECs was first put forward by Margaret Thatcher in November 1989 (Van Ham, 1993:138).[5] According to the British idea the new agreements were to include both economic and political elements and their legal basis was to be Article 238 of the Treaty of Rome, according to which the Community "...may conclude with a third State, a Union of States, or an international organisation agreements establishing an association involving reciprocal rights and obligations, common actions and special procedures". In fact, by 1989, Article 238 had served as the legal basis for numerous EC agreements with third parties, including Greece (1961), Turkey (1963), Malta (1969), Cyprus (1971), the ACP countries (1975), the Maghreb (1976) and Mashreg (1977) countries. The vague description provided by Article 238, however, allowed great flexibility on what the specific terms of the Association agreements could be. Consequently, the Community's offers to its associated partners differed substantially. While the Greek and the Turkish agreements, for example, offered a clear prospect for full membership (Articles 72 and 28 respectively), in other cases, similar commitments were either watered down or excluded completely (i.e. Lome convention). Furthermore, the duration of the agreements as well as the timetable of trade liberalisation also varied considerably (Coffey, 1976: 97).

As instability in Eastern Europe continued to increase in December 1989, Thatcher's proposal for concluding Association agreements with the CEECs gained impetus and was eventually endorsed by the Strasbourg Summit (8-9.12.89). The exact form of Association, however, remained unclear. According to the Conclusions of the French Presidency:

> The Community has taken and will take the necessary decisions to strengthen its co-operation with peoples aspiring to freedom, democracy and progress and with States which intend their founding principles to be democracy, pluralism and the rule of law. It will encourage the necessary economic reforms by all means at its disposal, and will continue its examination of the appropriate forms of Association with the countries which are pursuing the path of economic and political reform (Doc 89/3, 9.12.89).

This carefully worded decision of the Strasbourg Summit had a double significance. On the one hand, it provided the vital, in-principle agreement for the beginning of the Association process while on the other, it made it clear that Association would not be granted automatically to all; it would be the Community's 'reward' only to those committed to economic and political reforms. This fundamental principle of conditionality was to be the cornerstone of the EC strategy in Eastern Europe.

In fact, conditionality, as the means of channelling the Community's assistance and encouraging reform in Eastern Europe, was also supported by the Commission. Following his visit to Czechoslovakia, Bulgaria, and Romania, the Commissioner for External Relations Frans Andriessen, reported back to his colleagues on 4.1.90:

> This [Community policy] seeks to associate them [Eastern European countries] with the Community through trade, co-operation and appropriate financial support, the balance between these three elements being determined by the degree of progress made in each country towards open political and economic systems. As democracy and economic liberalisation take root, the agreements can be applied flexibly and further developed to provide for a form of Association corresponding with aspirations in East Europe and the Community's own interest (Commission of the EC, 1990a).

In his Communication to the Council on 17.1.90, Commissioner Andriessen further clarified the Commission's position concerning Association:

> Once the First Generation agreements are complete, the Community should respond positively to aspirations for closer links with the Community by means of a form of Association. Association agreements with the countries of Central and Eastern Europe would have common elements covering trade, co-operation and financial support, modulated according to the needs and the capacities of each country as well as its progress towards open political and economic systems. With respect to trade, such agreements would aim at attaining free trade when conditions for this are right. In this way the countries concerned could eventually be linked to the wider European framework which the Community and EFTA are now in the process of developing (Commission of the EC, 1990b).

On the same day, President Delors in his speech to the European Parliament was more revealing about the Commission's intentions:

> We must therefore look beyond them [Trade and Co-operation agreements] to devise new forms of co-operation and provide a framework for future political co-operation between democratic States. This could be our goal in drawing up new, revised Association agreements. If the six countries [Poland, Hungary, Czechoslovakia, the GDR, Romania and Bulgaria] so wished, these agreements could include an institutional aspect, the creation of a forum for genuine dialogue and economic and political consultation, the extension of co-operation to the technical, scientific, environmental, commercial and financial spheres; but not necessarily involving a common market, since such ill-prepared economies could not cope with one for a number of years (Speech 90/1, 17.1.90).

During this initial stage, the Community chose not to be adventurous. While a 'form of Association' was to be granted to the more advanced CEECs, the new agreements were not to be identical to the advanced Greek and Turkish Association agreements. Instead, a 'revised', less ambitious form of Association would be selected. As far as trade was concerned, liberalisation would be gradual and free trade would be achieved when conditions for the 'ill-prepared' economies were 'right'. Most importantly, the possibility of EC membership for the short and medium term was to be excluded. To this end, President Delors was keen to warn against the danger of "...raising unrealistic expectations" (Speech 90/1, 17.1.90). As a senior EP official put it: "Delors was not very talkative about membership...the whole idea of the EAs and the EEA was to have a string of alternative homes to the European Village" (interview in the EP, 20.3.97).

Having established its main policy priorities, and also having secured the Council's assent in Dublin on 20.1.90 (*Agence Europe*, 22-23.1.90), the Commission was now facing the task of tailoring the precise content of the new Association agreements as well as choosing which CEECs would start Association negotiations first. This process was finalised in three stages, following the Commission's respective Communications on Eastern Europe in February, April and August 1990.

In its Communication on 1.2.90, the Commission suggested that the Association agreements should be based on six principles (IP/90/40, 1.2.90):

- progressive trade liberalisation and eventual establishment of free trade "when the conditions for this are right",
- establishment of political dialogue,
- technical assistance and financial support according to the needs of each beneficiary country,
- joint projects for the support of infrastructure in Eastern Europe,
- strengthening of the co-operation established by the First Generation agreements "embodying new forms and instruments",
- information exchange and cultural co-operation.

Interestingly, the Commission's 'sensitivity' over the issue of membership was again dominant: "Association agreements will be of special value in themselves and should be distinguished from any commitment concerning the question of accession" (IP/90/40, 1.2.90). Furthermore, the Commission was still reluctant to set any solid requirements for granting Association:

> Today it would be premature to fix firm criteria for the passage from co-operation to Association. It is already apparent, however, that these criteria will relate to performance as well as commitments and that before considering this move the Community will expect decisive steps to have been taken towards systems based on political and economic liberties (IP/90/40, 1.2.90).

The Commission's 'wait and see' policy at this stage was hardly surprising. In the period between March and June 1990, elections were scheduled for Hungary, Romania, Czechoslovakia, Bulgaria and the two of the constituent republics of former Yugoslavia, Croatia and Slovenia. Although the end of one-party rule in Eastern Europe seemed, in the eyes of Franz Andriessen, to be 'irreversible' (Commission of the EC, 1990b: 1), the result of the first multi-party elections in Eastern Europe was a crucial component of the Commission's strategy. For this reason, the Commission promised further clarification of its Association policy in a new Communication during the first half of 1990.

The new Communication was presented on 18.4.90 (Commission of the EC, 1990c) and outlined the structure of the agreements which consisted of six sections each of which established:

- political dialogue,
- free trade and freedom of movement,
- economic co-operation,
- cultural co-operation,
- financial co-operation and
- the institutions of Association.

The most important development of this second stage however, was the fact that, for the first time, the Commission put flesh on its conditionality clause:

> The calendar of negotiations for Association agreements and the keeping in enforcement of these agreements will depend on the economic performance of these countries and on the observation of the Law and Human Rights; free multi-party elections; economic liberalisation aimed at a market economy (*Agence Europe*, 21.4.90).

The third and final stage of the process involved the presentation of the remaining details as well as the selection of the countries which would begin Association negotiations first. All of these matters were dealt with in a third Communication presented by the Commission to the Council and European Parliament on 27.8.90 (Commission of the EC, 1990f). As far as the content of the new Europe[6] agreements was concerned the Communication included some important announcements. With regards to Political Dialogue, the Commission proposed the establishment of the Association Council responsible for political consultation at the highest level, while the Association Committee would concentrate on technical issues arising from the agreement. Furthermore, the Parliamentary Association Committee would also promote dialogue between the European Parliament and the national Parliaments of the Associated countries.

With regards to trade in industrial products, the Commission's proposals envisaged total liberalisation in two broad phases whose timetable would be negotiated and during which the Community would "move more rapidly towards free trade than the Associated countries, thus assisting their economic recovery". Agricultural products however, would not receive the same treatment. Despite the fact that the Commission recognised the importance of agriculture for the economies in Eastern Europe, special arrangements would be negotiated in order "to promote trade in agricultural and fisheries products, taking fully into account their particular character and the functioning of the common agricultural and fisheries policies". Furthermore, while the Commission's proposals provided for the Associated countries moving towards the "..full application of Community rules on capital markets" by the end of the transitional period, it remained sceptical towards the establishment of free movement of persons. "Further improvements" in the freedom of movement of persons were to be given consideration "once the social and economic conditions in associated countries have been brought substantially into line with those in the [EC] member states" (Commission of the EC, 1990f).

The second issue addressed by the August Communication was the selection of those countries who would start Association negotiations first. In this field, the elections that took place in most East European countries during the first half of the year had a crucial impact on the Commission's proposals. The two Central European countries in which non-communist governments were formed, Hungary[7] and Czechoslovakia,[8] joined Poland, which already had a Solidarity-led government since August 1989, into the first wave of Association applicants. On the other hand, countries in which communist-dominated governments had prevailed, such as Bulgaria[9] and Romania,[10] were to be left in a second tier. Yugoslavia was also excluded as the result of the elections in Croatia and Slovenia raised doubts about the future of the country, while the case of the Soviet Union was to be examined later due to "...specific questions in the context of internal reform, relations with the Community and integration into the international economic system" (Commission of the EC, 1990f).

The Commission's proposals presented in the August Communication continued to favour a cautious, step-by-step approach to the EC's strategy in Eastern Europe. The refusal to undertake any clear commitment for future membership was once again restated. The objective of the Association agreements was not to provide eventual membership, but rather to:

...strengthen the foundations of the new European architecture and...enable partners in Central and Eastern Europe to participate in the wider process of European Integration, exemplified by the single European market and the new relationship to be negotiated by the Community and EFTA (Commission of the EC, 1990f).

For this reason, the legal basis of the forthcoming negotiations was to be Article 238 (Association); not Article 237 (accession) as many East European governments had hoped.[11] The issue of free movement of persons was also to be treated very carefully in line with the EC member states' sensitivities over the prospect of mass immigration from Eastern Europe. Thus, the EAs were to include moderate provisions only covering those East European workers already legally working within the EC.

As far as trade was concerned, whilst proposing a two-phase transitional period leading to a free trade area, the Commission made no reference to a specific timetable in this direction. The duration of each phase of the transitional period was left to be negotiated at first with the 12 member states, and then with the Eastern European candidates. Moreover, with the exception of agriculture, the August Communication made no reference to other 'sensitive' products such as steel and textiles which later became the centre of the debate during the Association negotiations. Another crucial aspect of the Communication was the Commission's call for a flexible mandate so that, while keeping a common overall structure, "individual agreements would be adapted to the circumstances of the country concerned". The idea of negotiating with each country individually and providing for "differentiation within and between the common elements comprising the agreements" was based on the conclusion that the economic and financial needs in each candidate country varied so substantially that negotiating with Eastern Europe as a group would have been both impractical and ineffective. By opting for differentiation the Commission was thus keeping in line with its long established position of negotiating on a partner-to-partner basis with countries of Eastern Europe.

Finally, the Commission's selection of Poland, Hungary and Czechoslovakia as the first wave of Association candidates, *de facto* recognised the existence of a multi-tier Eastern Europe. Despite the fact that this separation was not to be easily swallowed by those left outside - i.e. Bulgaria and Romania (see chapter 6) - it nevertheless provided a great opportunity for the Commission. A smaller group of candidates as well as partner-to-partner negotiations based on a 'flexible' mandate (which would not commit the Commission to the same concessions for all applicants) as secured by the differentiation principle, was to increase the Commission's negotiating power and provide a more manageable workload for its bureaucratic mechanism.

This section focused on the EC's attempts to shape the *principles, norms* and *decision making procedures* (Krasner, 1983: 2) of the Association regime prior to the opening of the international negotiations with the first wave applicants in early 1991. These international negotiations were to finalise the regime's *rules* as well as to provide the necessary legitimisation of the overall arrangement. The way in which the Association regime was completed as well as the Visegrad group's attempts to alter some of its provisions will be examined in the next section.

Negotiating the first wave of Europe Agreements: the Association regime completed

The Commission's proposals included in the August Communication were discussed and approved in principle by the Council's meeting on 17.9.90 in which the Commission was also authorised to begin exploratory talks with the three selected candidates, Poland, Hungary and Czechoslovakia. Meanwhile, the EC's member states begun an acrimonious internal bargaining in order to tailor the final mandate which would set out the limits of the Commission's position during the negotiations (Sedelmeier, 1994; Guggenbuhl, 1995: 235; Mayhew, 1998: chapter 3). While it was agreed that free trade would be achieved within 10 years (broken down into two 5 years phases), and that, with regards to industrial products, all trade barriers would be eliminated during the first phase of the transitional period, some member states insisted that textiles and ECSC products should be subject to special treatment similar to that envisaged by the Commission for agricultural products and, therefore, full liberalisation should take place by the end of the second (and not the first) phase. Despite efforts by 'liberal' member states such as the UK, the Netherlands, Denmark and the Commission not to widen the list of 'sensitive' products, the 'protectionist' view finally prevailed and as a result textiles, coal and steel were also to be excluded from fast-track liberalisation.

Following the Council's mandate given to the Commission on 18.12.90 (*Agence Europe*, 20.12.90), negotiations with the Visegrad countries began during the second week of February 1991[12] and were concluded after ten rounds on 22.11.91 (Bull-EC, 11-1991: 67). The negotiations were by no means easy and, during these nine months, both the CEE applicants and the Commission struggled on several occasions to save the talks from collapsing. The first major deadlock became clear during the third round of the negotiations (late March 1991) when the Visegrad states refused to accept the Commission's offers over the 'sensitive' products and free movement of persons while they insisted that the objective of accession should be clearly indicated in the agreement (CEPR, 1992). Under heavy pressure from both the Association applicants (Bull-EC, 3-1991: 54 and *Agence Europe*, 4.4.91: 8) and the Western press (*Financial Times*, 26.3.91), the Commission returned to the Council asking for greater "comprehension" (*Agence Europe*, 10.4.91: 11) and a revised mandate to accommodate the Visegrads' demands.

The Commission's proposals called for:

- liberalisation in the steel sector to be concluded within the first phase of the transitional period,
- further concessions in agriculture to be made on a 'product by product' basis,
- the inclusion of a possible reference to accession, without a clear commitment to the automatic passage from Association to membership, and
- further clarification on the issues of labour provisions, cumulating in the rules of origin and year of reference for tariff reductions (*Agence Europe*, 10.4.91: 11).

The Council's decision to accept most of the Commission's proposals and permit "greater flexibility" on the membership question (Bull-EC, 4-1991: 44) was greatly welcomed by the Commission's officials: "We have now the necessary flexibility to go on and complete negotiations with Czechoslovakia, Hungary and Poland, bringing them into the network of European states which have opted for liberalisation and interdependence as the best means to ensure peace and prosperity" argued vice President Andriessen (Speech/91/41, 19.4.91). Commenting on the possibility of further EC concessions in 'sensitive' products, Sir Leon Brittan also agreed "it is an urgent necessity and we should do so" (IP/91/328, 19.4.91).

The initial celebrations over the new concessions, however, did not last long. Whilst the Commission's proposals with regard to steel had been accepted by the Visegrads, the issues of agricultural and textile concessions as well as that of movement of workers still remained unresolved. Thus, by mid-July 1991, despite the wishes of the

Luxembourg Summit for the agreements to be concluded before the end of October, negotiations were once again deadlocked, leaving Polish negotiators demanding "a political decision extending the Commission mandate to be taken before the next round of negotiations" (*Agence Europe*, 13.7.91: 8). Responding to the new crisis, on 29.7.91 the Council authorised the Commission to submit new proposals for breaking the deadlock while it reserved its final decision for its September meeting (*Agence Europe*, 23.7.91: 7). Following a hot summer involving the coup in the Soviet Union and the outbreak of hostilities in Yugoslavia, the Commission's position, presented by vice President Andriessen on 4 9.91, offered some considerable compromises (*Agence Europe*, 7.9.91: 7):

- in relation to textiles, both the EC and the applicant countries would eliminate custom duties within 6 years with the same timetable applying for quantitative restrictions.

- in relation to agriculture, the basic quantities of the applicants' imports from which the tariff quotas were calculated would increase 10% annually over a period of 5 years while tariffs and levies for these products would be reduced 20% annually for 3 years and then frozen for the final 2 years. Furthermore, tariff and levy reductions granted previously under the Generalised System of Preferences (GSP) would be consolidated as such within the agreements which would also include a specific safeguard clause in the event of a serious upset in the Community market.

- in relation to financial co-operation the Community would continue to provide assistance through the Phare programme and EIB loans while it would also consider the possibility of providing assistance for economic stabilisation and currency convertibility. No clear commitment would be made however on the amount of money to be spent on these operations.

- in relation to the free movement of workers, the EC member states which had not concluded bilateral agreements with the applicants would do so while social security provisions regarding workers legally employed in the EC would be co-ordinated with the aim of ending any form of discrimination against them.

- in relation to coal the EC member states would eliminate all existing national restrictions within 5 years.

- in relation to transit provisions the Visegrad countries would grant more concessions while the EC would finance transport infrastructure within these countries.

- in relation to the Visegrads' request to participate in the EPC meetings, the Community would develop a form of political co-operation aiming at "...overcoming the sense of isolation felt in Central Europe against the background of turbulence in the Soviet Union and Yugoslavia, and creating a feeling of belonging" (*Agence Europe*, 7.9.91: 7).

Despite the fact that the Commission's proposals were welcomed by the press, (*Financial Times*, 22.8.91) they nevertheless failed to be 'ratified' by the Council's double session on 6 September, as disagreements between member states continued to be irreconcilable. While initial opposition by the Italian and Portuguese delegations over the new textiles offers was overcome following the efforts of the Dutch presidency (*Agence Europe*, 9/10.9.91: 9), French opposition against agricultural concessions (especially for meat products) deadlocked the meeting, thus leaving the Council unable to agree on a revised mandate to be given to the Commission for the Association negotiations. Following the Council's failure to reach an agreement, the Community's policy vis-à-vis Eastern Europe came under an unprecedented attack involving not only the applicant countries and the press, but also the European Parliament, some of the Commission's own members as well as some of the liberal EC member states (*Financial Times* 9.9.91; *Agence Europe*, 11.9.91: 10 and 9-10.9.91: 9) .

Against this background, the Commission faced the difficult task of preparing a compromise deal before the next Council meeting on 30.9.91. The Commission's proposals included:

- for textiles, the abolition of tariffs within 6 years and the elimination of non-tariff barriers within half the period determined by the ongoing negotiations for the Uruguay round. In exchange, the Commission would include a specific safeguard clause for textiles in the agreements as well as producing a study for the effects of liberalisation accompanied by measures modernising and strengthening the industry's competitiveness.
- for meat imports (especially beef and goatmeat), a liberalisation process similar to the rest of the agricultural products (10% annual increase on the quantities imported over 5 years and 20% annual reduction on custom duties and levies over 3 years). However, only half of the quantities provided by the quota would be sold in the EC market. The rest would be channelled back to Eastern Europe through the so-called 'triangular' operations.[13] Furthermore, a

safeguard clause limiting cattle imports to 425,000 head a year as well as provisions for strict veterinary and health controls on agricultural imports from Eastern Europe would also be included in the agreement.

The Commission's proposals were finally accepted by the Council on 30.9.91 and consequently a new mandate was given for the conclusion of negotiations with the Visegrad countries. Having secured the Council's agreement for all major issues, the Commission was now able to resolve all outstanding problems within less than two months.[14] On 16.12.91, the Council formally signed the agreements on behalf of the EC (Bull-EC, 12-1991: 95) and the trade component of the EAs (Interim agreement), entered into force on 1.3.92.

Conclusion

This chapter sought to explain the introduction of the Association agreements as the main instrument of the EC's strategy in Eastern Europe through the lens of regime theory. It was argued that, by the beginning of 1990, the existing framework of relations between the EC and Eastern Europe (i.e. the First Generation agreements and the Phare programme) proved insufficient to respond to the tremendous pressures released by the revolutions in the region during the second half of 1989. As the crisis in Eastern Europe spread out of control, the European Community faced the urgent task of filling the political and economic vacuum which had emerged in the Continent. The EC's response to this challenge came from the initiation of the Association regime. The new Europe agreements, it was hoped, would not only demonstrate the EC's determination to assist the process of reform in Eastern Europe, but most importantly, would provide a more comprehensive framework for the effective management of relations with the region's newly emerged governments.

At a political level, the EAs' Preamble and Final Provisions defined mutual expectations (Ruggie, 1975) and established commonly accepted norms of behaviour (Krasner, 1983). Additionally, the conditionality principle ensured an almost prohibitive (particularly for the CEECs) cost for defective practices (Moravcsik, 1994: 59), while Political Dialogue provided the necessary channels of communication through which compliance with the agreed norms of behaviour would be constantly scrutinised. Clearly, at the heart of these arrangements lay the determination to put an irreversible end to the suspicion which characterised the EC-CEECs relations during the past decades. Moreover, the EAs were expected to have a significant impact on reducing uncertainty in post-Cold war Europe, by ensuring that the largely unknown and inexperienced forces which brought down the old communist order regimes would be 'reliable' and 'predictable' partners and, above all, would remain committed to the process of political reform.

The reduction of, what Rood (1989: 66) called, 'opportunity costs of co-operation' between the EU and the East European economies was also a key element of the Association regime. The first steps to this direction had already begun prior to 1989 with the signature of the First Generation agreements and the trade concessions offered to Poland and Hungary within the framework of the G-24 assistance. Nevertheless, these concessions were moderate, limited to the two countries and non-applicable to a number of so-called sensitive product categories. Moreover, the collapse of economic, legal and administrative order which followed the 1989 revolutions further increased the already high opportunity costs for economic inter-penetration between Eastern Europe and the EC. The Association regime sought to reduce these costs *firstly* through improved (comparing to the First Generation agreements) trade concessions in all products categories, including the so-called sensitive sectors; and *secondly*, through provisions relating to free movement of capital, competition and approximation of legislation all of which aimed at reducing uncertainty, strengthening economic exchanges between the two parties and promoting investment opportunities in Eastern Europe.

Despite been born out of the need to manage commonly shared problems the construction of the Association regime was far from a 'joint exercise' between 'equals'. The CEECs, for example, were never invited to contribute during the early stages of the regime's elaboration and as a result had little impact on setting the agenda for the negotiations to follow. Later, when the Association negotiations began, the Visegrads' attempts of improving the proposed deal ended in only limited success. This is hardly surprising taking into consideration the bilateral nature of the Association bargain, the power asymmetries between the two partners and the EC's 'take or leave it' stance during the negotiations (Stawarska, 1992). Overall, it can be argued that the EC, as the dominant partner of the Association bargain, was able to dictate five crucial features of the Association regime:

- *The membership question.* Despite the Visegrads' fierce opposition, the Association agreements were finally 'separated' from the issue of EC membership. The only EC concession on this front was the acknowledgement in the EAs' Preamble that full EC membership was the candidates' "ultimate objective". Nevertheless, the EC undertook no commitment for the 'automatic' passage from Association to membership.

- *Trade arrangements for the 'sensitive' sectors.* Textiles, Coal and Steel were excluded from the fast-track liberalisation applicable to most industrial products. Consequently, the accomplishment of a Free Trade Area for these products would not take place until the end of the ten-year transitional period. Most importantly, agriculture was altogether excluded from the envisaged Free Trade Area. Concessions in this sector were agreed in a separate protocol on a 'product by product' basis, while the possibility of further improvements in the future was left open subject to a decision by the Association Council.

- *Movement of workers.* The relaxation of the restrictions facing East Europeans for travelling and working in the EC was from the outset one of the most sensitive issues for the EC's member states. Practically all existing restrictions remained untouched by the Association agreements. The only consolation for the Association applicants was the commitment that those East European workers already legally employed in the EC would not be discriminated against, as well as the promise that further improvements in relation to movement of workers would be examined by the Association Council in the second phase of the transitional period (subject to the economic situation in the Associated partners and the employment situation in the Community).

- *The conditionality principle.* The most significant function of the conditionality principle was to determine what would be tolerated as acceptable norms of behaviour within the Association regime. Nevertheless, these norms of behaviour were not the product of negotiation between the two parties. Instead, they were set by the EC unilaterally and then presented to the East European applicants as a non-negotiable in-built feature of the Association agreements. Moreover, the EC was to assume the role of Eastern Europe's 'ultimate judge'. In other words, it would not only set the acceptable norms of behaviour, but would also decide which of the applicants complied with these norms and consequently 'deserved' to be granted the opportunity to negotiate an Association agreement with the EC.

- *The differentiation principle.* Differentiation was one of the two (the other being conditionality) 'cornerstones' of the EC's Association strategy in Eastern Europe. Differentiating within and between the common elements of the EAs was initially portrayed as a necessary practice for ensuring the EC's flexibility during the negotiations, but also as a means of addressing the individual needs of the Association applicants. Nevertheless, differentiation had several 'side effects' (see chapter 6). Above all, differentiation meant the fragmentation of the Association applicants' opposition and the negotiation of the Association agreements on a 'convenient' (for the EC) partner-to-partner basis.

The final arrangements of the Association regime were, therefore, a reflection (Keohane, 1984:62), rather than an instrument for the reduction (Haas, 1975 and Scott, 1977) of the inequality between the two negotiating partners of the Association bargain. The strongest actor, in this case the EC, was in a position to dictate both the terms of the regime as well as the selection of its participants. In this respect, the Association regime can be better understood as an instrument facilitating the pursuit of self-interest, or, using Cox's (1991: 450) terminology, as an instrument for the 'institutionalisation' and perpetuation of a particular order. So, if the Association regime was constructed so as to fit the interests of the stronger player (i.e. the EC), why did the CEECs voluntarily decide to participate in it? The answer to this question rests on the fact that the Association negotiations were not a zero sum game. In other words, no matter how cautious, the EC's proposed deal still remained better than any other alternative available to the CEECs. In this respect, taking the very high *cost of exclusion* (Moravcsik, 1994: 59) into consideration, the CEECs' participation in an 'imperfect' regime can still be perceived as an act motivated by self-interest.

A final feature of these early stages of the Association process has been the quite remarkable consensus between and within the EC's institutions over the main principles of the EC's Association strategy in Eastern Europe. This is, of course, not to say that all aspects of the Association agreements remained uncontroversial. The extent and timetable of trade liberalisation envisaged by the agreements, for example, became the subject of bitter disagreements within the Council. In the Commission, the support of Competition Commissioner Leon Brittan for fast-track trade liberalisation with the CEECs (*Agence Europe*, 11.9.91: 10) was in sharp contrast with the rather protectionist outlook of Martin Bangemann (who headed the DG for Industry - III) as well as with the more cautious approach followed on this matter by the DG I. The disagreements between DGI and DG VIII (Development) over the extent and administration of the Phare programme (*Financial Times*, 13.3.90) point to further bureaucratic infighting within the Commission, whilst the inclusion (or not) of a financial protocol in each Association agreement became a point of significant friction between the EP and the Commission. Yet none of these disagreements undermined the overall consensus on the 'cornerstones' of the EC's strategy such as the principles of differentiation and conditionality, the caution over the membership and free movement of people issues, and the need for special protection of the EC's 'sensitive' sectors. (see Figure 2.3).

	Commission's Position 27.8.90	Commission's Position 15.4.91	EP's Position (A3-0055/91) 18.4.91	Commission's Position 4.9.91	Negotiating Directives given by the Council
Differe-ntiation	Differentiation... within and between the EAs' common elements		Measures to help CEECs on the basis of individual needs[7]		Differentiation incorporated into the EAs
Conditio-nality	Observation of the Law and human rights, free multi party elections and economic liberalisation[6]		Commitment to political and economic reforms & respect for human rights[7]		Conditionality incorporated into the EAs' Preamble
Member-ship Clause	The agreements separate from the possibility of accession	Possible ref. to accession, but no automatic element	stress possibility for entry, but enlargement not to be prejudiced[5]		Membership as the candidates' ultimate objective[2]
Non-sensitive Industrial Products	Liberalisation in two broad phases whose timetable would be negotiated		Immediate and complete opening of the EC market		Elimination of duties by 1993 (Annex IIA); 1996 (Annex IIB); & by 1997 (Annex III)[1]
Agricultu-ral Products	* Special protocol * Liberalisation to take fully into account the particular character of the CAP and Fisheries policy	* Special protocol * Concessions on a "product by product" basis		* Special protocol * 50% quota increase * 60% reduction on tariffs & levies * GSP Consol/tion * Specific safeguard clause	* Special protocol * 50% quota incr. * 60% reduction on tariffs & levies * GSP Consol/tion * Safeguard clause * Triangular oper. * Vet controls[4]
Textiles	Liberalisation in two phases (length to be negotiated)		Step by step approach may be possible	Quantitative and duty restrictions to be eliminated within 6 years	* Elimination of duties by 1998 (protocol 1) * Safeguard clause[4]
Steel	Liberalisation in two phases (length to be negotiated)	Liberalisation within 5 years	Step by step approach may be possible		Elimination of duties by 1997 (Protocol 2)[2]
Coal	Liberalisation in two phases (length to be negotiated)		Step by step approach may be possible	Liberalisation within 5 years	Elimination of custom duties by 1996 (Protocol 2)[3]
Move-Ment of Persons	Equal treatment for legal workers only	Equal treatment for legal workers only	Improvements for legal workers only	Equal treatment for legal workers only	Equal treatment for legal workers only[3]
Financial Co-operation	No commitment on the amount		Guaranteed level of financial commitment	No commitment on the amount	No commitment on the amount [3]

1. Agreed on 18.12.90   3. Agreed on 6.9.91   5. B3-1834/90 (11.10.90)   7. OJ C 38/97 (18.1.90)
2. Agreed on 15.4.91   4. Agreed on 30.9.91   6. SEC (90) 717 final (18.4.90)
Sources: Agence Europe (various), COM(90)398 final, A3-0055/91, B3-1834/90, OJ C 38/97, SEC (90) 717 final, personal interviews.

Figure 2. 3 Position of the EC's Institutions on the Visegrad EAs

At the heart of such a consensus lay the recognition that any further strengthening of EC's relations with the CEECs (and, in fact, any further development towards Scandinavian enlargement) should come after the successful conclusion of the 'deepening' process already underway within the context of the IGC on EMU. In the Council, for example, the attempts of the Eurosceptic delegations led by Britain to use widening as a means of diluting the integrationist agenda failed to gain meaningful support. Margaret Thatcher's passionate pleas for a fast-track integration of the CEECs into a Europe-wide free trade area met with strong opposition by those member states committed to 'deepening'. The position of the 'wideners' was further undermined by the events leading to German unification. The opening of the new IGC on Political Union (June 1990) as a means of tightening a unified Germany to the process of European integration was difficult to resist, particularly since some of the most ardent 'wideners' (i.e. Britain) had also been amongst the most fearful to accept Chancellor Kohl's demands for a fast track German unification.

The prioritisation of 'deepening' was even stronger within the Commission. President Delors, who had since the late 1980s invested much of his energy and credibility to the EMU project, warned the Strasbourg European Council in December 1989 that "since events are accelerating in the rest of Europe we must accelerate construction of the European Community" (*Speech/89/87*, 7.12.89). Delors' enthusiasm over the successful conclusion of the new Treaty prior to any move towards widening was also shared by the majority of his Commissioners, who themselves had a vested interest in supporting the 'deepening' of the Community. The consensus within the Commission became apparent in April 1991 when Commissioner for External Relations Frans Andriessen floated his idea of 'affiliated membership' in an attempt to offer an alternative to the Scandinavian demands for full membership, but also to bridge the ongoing row between the EC member states and the Association applicants over the inclusion (or not) of a membership clause in the Preamble of the agreements. According to the plan:

Affiliated membership would provide membership rights and obligations in some areas, while excluding others, at least for a transitional period. It would give the affiliate member a seat at the Council table on a par with full members in specified areas, together with appropriate representation in other institutions, such as Parliament (Speech 91/41, 19.4.91).

Whilst the suggested 'affiliation' would not bring voting rights in the Council meetings, it would nevertheless, provide a chance of consultation in areas such as energy, transport, the environment, research and development, together with participation in the European Political Co-operation (EPC) meetings and linkage with the European Monetary System (EMS). Andriessen's proposal, however, got a cool reception by his colleagues in the Commission, most of whom saw it as an unnecessary deflection from the deepening agenda which the Commission was pursuing at that time. Against this background Andriessen was forced into a hasty retreat by arguing that the concept of affiliated membership was simply a personal idea and did not represent the Commission's official position (*Agence Europe*, 29-30.4.91: 11).[15]

The European Parliament for its part also aligned itself with the Council and the Commission over the main principles of the Association strategy. The EP was fully supportive of both the differentiation and conditionality principles and was perhaps the most ardent supporter of the 'deepening prior to widening' strategy for the development of the EC (see Figure 2.3). The consensus between the key EC institutions described above can also be extended to other less 'official' (but, probably, equally important) participants in the Association process, including trade unions, employers' organisations as well as other representatives of sectoral interests affected by the EAs. Even those who expressed the greatest opposition against trade concessions to the CEECs during the negotiations of the Association agreements (see chapter 3), never actually challenged the historic significance of the EAs or the EC's decision to include in them some sort of trade liberalisation for textiles, agricultural and ECSC products (interview in the ETUI, 18.3.97).

Notes

[1] GDR, Bulgaria, Hungary and Czechoslovakia established diplomatic relations with the EC on 10.8.88, followed by Poland on 16.9.88. Other East European countries with more 'independent' foreign policy like Romania and Yugoslavia had already established diplomatic relations with the EC.

[2] Hungary was the first CEEC to sign such an agreement on 26.9.88 (which came into force on 1.12.88), followed by Poland on 19.9.89 (which came into force on 1.12.89), the ex USSR in December 89 and the former Czechoslovakia on7.5.90 (entered into force on 1.11.90). Bulgaria and Romania concluded their agreements on 24.9.90 and 5.3.91 respectively (which came into force on 1.11.90 and 1.5.91 respectively).

[3] For the ECSC products, separate protocols were later signed and attached to each First Generation agreement. For agricultural products, the agreement left the Joint Committee to examine "...the possibility of granting eachother reciprocal concessions on a product-by-product basis..."

[4] See, for example, Art. 6 of the Bulgarian Trade and Co-operation agreement, OJ L 291, 23.10.90.

[5] Anecdotal evidence also suggest that the granting of an Association agreement with the EC was promised by German Chancellor Kohl to the Hungarian government in exchange of opening its border with Austria in August 1989.

[6] The symbolic term 'Europe' agreement was used according to the Commission in order to mark "the importance of the political initiative which they represent". See Commission of the EC (1990f).

[7] Following the election of March-April 1990, a coalition government under Jozsef Antall was formed consisting of the Hungarian Democratic Forum, the Smallholders' and the Christian Democrats.

[8] Following the election of 8-9.6.90 a coalition government was formed consisting of the Civic Forum and Public Against Violence. On 5.7.90, Vaclav Havel was re-elected President.

[9] Following the election on 10-17.6.90, the Bulgarian Socialist Party won the majority of the vote, and a new government was formed under Andrei Lukanov.

[10] Following the election on 20.5.90, the National Salvation Front won the majority of the vote and Ion Ilescu was elected President.

[11] Before Maastricht, the legal basis for Association was Art. 238 (EC), while Art. 237 (EC) provided the legal basis for enlargement. Under Maastricht, Art. 238 has been slightly amended, while Art. 237 has been replace by Art. O. The treaty of Amsterdam brought further changes on these Articles.

[12] The negotiations formally opened on 20-22.12.90. The first round of substantive talks however, took place on 8-14.2.91. See *Agence Europe*, 8.2.91.

[13] According to the 'triangular operations', the EC would finance the purchases by the Soviet Union of agricultural products originating from the Visegrad countries. Using this technique, the Community could provide aid needed in the poorer East European countries while reducing the pressure in the EC agricultural markets.

[14] The agreements were initialled on 22.11.91. Until the last moment however, some member states insisted that the agreements should include either a specific safeguard clause in relation to steel products or a commitment by the Visegrads that they themselves will restraint their steel exports to the EC. Their request however, was rejected by the Commission ton he basis that the general safeguard clause included in the agreements was a sufficient guarantee. The Commission's refusal angered Spain in particular, which two days before the initiation of the agreements expressed its disappointment about the Commission's practices in resolving this issue. See *Agence Europe*, 21.9.91: 9.

[15] Andriessen's attempt to insert the concept of 'affiliated membership' into the IGC's agenda (since such reference would require the revision of the treaty of Rome which was already under discussion in the IGC on Political Union) met with severe opposition by the smaller member states of the EC fearful about a future EC design based on multiple speeds or variable geometry. The plan was also rejected by the Scandinavians and the East European applicants who saw it as a device for postponing the EC's enlargement for the foreseeable future (*Financial Times*, 20.4.91; 4.9.91; 6.9.91 and *Agence Europe*, 10-11.6.91: 5-7).

3 Explaining the Outcome of the First Wave of Association Agreements: Games in Multiple Arenas with Variable Payoffs

Chapter 2 discussed the evolution of relations between the EC and Eastern Europe, leading to the negotiation and conclusion of the first wave of Association agreements with Poland, Hungary and Czechoslovakia in late 1991. It was argued that the initiation of the Association regime was born out of the EC's determination to reduce the uncertainties caused by the 1989 revolutions and fill the political and economic vacuum which was created in Eastern Europe following the end of the Cold War. Nevertheless, Eastern Europe's stabilisation was not to be pursued at any cost. The long and difficult negotiations with the first wave of Association applicants, for example, revealed the EC's unwillingness to give in to the East European demands for the speedy accomplishment of a Free Trade Area and a commitment to future EC membership. As a result the agreed Association deal was to be a rather cautious one. Certain products (i.e. agriculture, textiles, coal and steel) were excluded from fast-track liberalisation, concessions in relation to free movement of people were moderate and membership would be the candidates' "ultimate goal", not the EAs' natural progression.

The EC's tough position during the Association negotiations with the Visegrad applicants is, at first glance, puzzling. Taking into consideration that the three countries' combined share of the EC's total external trade in 1990 was just 2.37%, (Commission of the EC, 1994: 545) why did the EC fail to meet their demands for greater trade concessions? Moreover, taking into consideration that agriculture, textiles and coal/steel products accounted for the majority of the applicants' exports to the EC, why did the latter choose to 'penalise' them by insisting on 'special' (that is, more unfavourable) arrangements for these product categories? To put the question in more general terms, what are the factors determining when and which issues will emerge as 'sensitive' and, therefore, will be perceived as vital for the EC's interests during an international bargain?

In order to address these questions, this chapter borrows heavily from Tsebelis' concept of *nested games* (Tsebelis, 1990). In his initial application of *nested games* to French electoral coalitions Tsebelis argued:

Political parties are considered as pursuing strategies in two different but connected arenas. Their choices affect the balance of forces within each coalition, and the balance of forces between coalitions. The game between partners is, therefore, nested inside the game between coalitions (Tsebelis, 1988: 145-146).

Tsebelis also assumed that the game has *variable* (rather than fixed) *payoffs*. Political parties, therefore:

...find themselves in a situation where their payoffs vary according to the specific balance of forces between coalitions, and have to chose strategies that will have implications for the balance of forces both within each coalition and between coalitions (Tsebelis, 1988: 145-146).

Tsebelis' concept of *nested games* was further refined in 1990 to include games which were played in more than two *arenas* and involved a larger number of players than those described in the case of French politics. In what was now called games in *multiple arenas* the player could simultaneously be involved in numerous games, all being connected and interdependent with each other. Therefore:

The payoffs of the players in the principal arena vary according to the situation prevailing in other arenas or the moves made by players in these arenas. The use of games in multiple arenas is in studying situations in which political context is important and the situation is so complicated that reference to exogenous factors is required (Tsebelis, 1988: 60).

According to Tsebelis, the study of games in *multiple arenas* could hold the answer to the fundamental paradox of why players sometimes opt for profoundly sub-optimal choices.

An optimal alternative in one arena (or game) will not necessarily be optimal in respect to the entire network of arenas in which the actor is involved (Tsebelis, 1988: 9).

Viewed outside the rigidity of its parenting Game theory, Tsebelis' concept of *nested games* can serve as an excellent metaphor for the understanding of the EC's strategy during the Association negotiations. If one conceives the negotiation of the Europe agreements as a game, it is clear that such an Association game was not played in a vacuum, but it was instead *nested* within the entire network of games in which the EC was involved during the early 1990s.[1] This entire network of games (the most important of which are illustrated in Figure 3.1) will be referred to as the *Grand* game. A crucial feature of the *Grand* game is that the distribution of payoffs within it are not fixed. In other words, the EC's strategy in a particular game and the payoffs it manages to secure from it, are inextricably linked with the EC's performance (and payoffs) in other games, and vice versa.

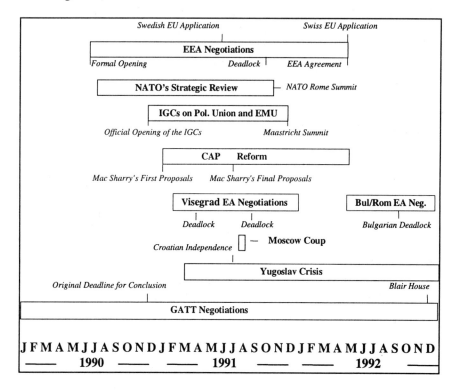

Figure 3.1 Timetable of the EC's Multiple Games, 1990-1992

The interdependence between individual games as well as the variable distribution of payoffs within the *Grand* game are crucial factors for the understanding of the EC's strategy in the Association negotiations. This chapter will argue that the EC's insistence on a cautious Association deal had, in most cases, little to do with the actual 'threat' posed by the Visegrad applicants. The EC's protectionism against the Visegrads, nevertheless, was by no means a sub-optimal choice. On the contrary, a tough line in the Association negotiations was often deemed necessary in order to supplement (or not to undermine) the EC strategy in other games which, for one reason or another, were considered to be more important. For this reason, the first two sections of this chapter look at a number of peripheral games[2] (played both at the domestic and international levels) of the *Grand* game and assess how the preservation of the EC's interests in these games led to the restriction of the EC's Association offers to the Visegrads in the fields of agriculture, textile, coal/steel and free movement of workers. The next section examines a number of *high politics* games and assesses how broader security considerations as well as the process of the EC's EFTA enlargement contributed to the CEECs' efforts to secure more generous payoffs from the Association game. Finally, the last section looks at how the *equilibrium* within the *Grand* game was reached and assess how such an *equilibrium* affected the CEECs' payoffs from the Association bargain.

The impact of the GATT negotiations

As far as trade-related matters are concerned, the most influential event on the international scene since the mid 1980s was, undoubtedly, the GATT negotiations. The Uruguay Round had been proposed by the US in the early 1980s and was finally launched in September 1986 following the Punta del Este Declaration. Together with a large number of issues ranging from the relaxation of trade barriers in industrial goods and services to the strengthening of multilateral trade rules, the participants of the Uruguay round also agreed to include in the negotiations' agenda the partial liberalisation in agricultural and textile markets.

Negotiating in GATT proved to be a painful experience for the EC which in many cases found it impossible to reconcile the differences between those member states committed to maximum liberalisation (i.e. the UK and the Netherlands) and those who adopted a more sceptical stance (i.e. France and the EC's south). Not surprisingly, agriculture and textiles emerged as two of the most controversial issues for the EC, whose inability to accept the proposed GATT deal twice led to the blockage of the conclusion of the Mid Term Review; firstly by France, Germany and Spain in November 1988 over agriculture (*Agence Europe*, 19.11.88) and secondly by Portugal and Italy in April 1989 over textiles (Woolock and Hodges, 1996: 311).

By early 1990, the Uruguay Round entered its final and more crucial phase, aiming to conclude the negotiations in Brussels by December of the same year. All big issues however, including those of agriculture and textiles, still remained open, thus leaving space for intense bargaining both at an international and a domestic EC level.

The 'agriculture' game

From the outset of the Uruguay Round, the EC's Common Agricultural Policy (CAP) emerged as the most controversial issue of the GATT negotiations. The heavy export subsidies provided to EC farmers through CAP, angered the Americans who, during the 1980s, saw a severe deterioration of the US agricultural trade performance (GATT, 1988). In an attempt to reverse this trend, the US put forward proposals which sought to eliminate all trade-distorting subsidies and import barriers within a transitional period of 10 years. The American proposals, however, met strong opposition from the EC. The inability of both sides to bridge their differences led to the stagnation of the Uruguay Round which eventually failed to meet the completion target of December 1990 as initially envisaged by the Punta del Este declaration (Woolcock and Hodges, 1996: 314).

At the international level, the EC took most of the blame for the failure of the GATT negotiations. Domestically, the CAP was also criticised for its escalating costs and the burden it placed on the EC budget. The need for reducing the cost of the CAP had always been a popular theme amongst the 'liberal' EC member states. The pressure for reform however, eased by the late 1980s when the CAP's expenditure was brought under control. In 1990 however, this positive trend was reversed and massive new increases were reported for 1991, while EC's agricultural surpluses soared (Rieger, 1996: 115). Responding to this double crisis, the Commissioner responsible for agriculture, Ray MacSharry, finally revealed his plans for the CAP reform in July 1991 aiming at tackling some long-term imbalances of European agriculture (especially the heavy price subsidies and the huge surpluses in cereals, beef and milk), but also facilitating the EC's negotiating position in the GATT negotiations (*Agence Europe*, 12.7.91: 15).

The new proposals, which included big cuts in the intervention prices for beef (15%) and cereals (30%), but also a whole new thinking in the way the EC supported its farmers, were welcomed by consumer associations (Rieger, 1996: 115 and *Agence Europe*, 12.7.91: 15). On the other hand, producer organisations, both at national and European level, offered a very hostile reception to the MacSharry Plan. At a national level, the greatest criticism came from farmers' organisations in the EC's North which accused the Commission of giving in to the demands of their Southern counterparts (*Agence Europe*, 12.7.91: 15; 19.7.91: 12 and 24.10.91: 15). At a European level the rejection of the plan was universal, with all major pan-European agricultural groups (i.e. COPA, CPE, CEJA) producing damning reports and press releases (*Agence Europe*, 19.7.91: 12).

What is also worth noticing at this point is the fact that producers' opposition to the MacSharry plan was successfully 'transmitted' to their respective governments. "Disappointing", "discriminatory" and "too brutal" are only some of the descriptions used by several delegations (i.e. Belgian, British and Italian) during the first Agricultural Council following the announcement of the proposals (*Agence Europe*, 15-16.7.91: 6). The opposition within the Council continued to be strong, until a compromise on the CAP reform was finally reached by the twelve agriculture ministers in May 1992 (*Agence Europe*, 18-21.5.91: 13).

The EA negotiations between the Commission and the Visegrads over agricultural concessions, therefore, coincided with a turbulent period for European agriculture characterised by domestic quarrels over the CAP reform and the Community's strategy in the Uruguay Round. The prospect of increased competition from the CEECs (resulting from the trade liberalisation envisaged by the EAs) could be anything but appealing to everybody related to European agriculture. Having realised the potential threat that the CEECs could present to their interests, European farmers' organisations were fast to oppose a fast-track liberalisation in agriculture. COPA and COGECA, for example, lobbied the President of the Commission in June 1991, asking for a series of protective measures ranging from the imposition of strict veterinary controls to the introduction of quantitative restrictions and safeguard clauses, while insisting that any EU concession should be based on the principle of reciprocity (*Agence Europe*, 21.6.91: 14). Once again, European farmers seemed to have been successful in 'transmitting' their concerns to their governments, as less than a month following the COPA-COGECA intervention, several agriculture ministers urged the Commission to be "vigilant" regarding imports from Eastern Europe (*Agence Europe*, 18.7.91:9).

In retrospect, the concerns expressed by national governments and farming organisations were only partially justified. During the early stages of transition to a market economy, the agricultural sector in all CEECs remained in deep crisis with rapidly shrinking outputs. Moreover, whilst prices of agricultural products in Eastern Europe were much lower than in the EC, agricultural exports from the CEEC-5 to the EC during the period 1989-1991 rose by just 5% (European Commission, 1995).

So, if the 'threat' from East European agriculture was relatively small, why did the EC appear so cautious during the EA negotiations? Viewed in isolation, the EC's 'reluctance' constituted a profoundly sub-optimal strategy. However, taking into consideration the wider picture and, in particular, the interdependence between the Association game and the other peripheral games (i.e. GATT and CAP reform), such a 'reluctance' makes much more sense. In other words, having proposed big price cuts aiming to reduce its huge agricultural surpluses (i.e. in beef, milk and cereals), how could the EC defend a policy which would encourage more East European agricultural imports to enter the EC markets? Similarly, having upset the farming lobby twice over the reform of the CAP and the GATT negotiations, what were the chances that farmers would 'ratify' a more generous package for Eastern Europe? Finally, how could the Commission appear generous in the Visegrad EA negotiations without undermining its 'tough' negotiating strategy vis à vis the Americans within the GATT process? As a senior official of the Greek Permanent Representation to the EU put it:

> It is very important to remember the background of these Association agreements. The EAs were before the conclusion of GATT and even before the Blair House agreement. Before you close this huge economic and political issue you must be very careful. For France which is the biggest agricultural power in the EU, it was impossible to be generous to the CEECs and then defend its position against the Americans. And do not forget that France was desperate to keep this policy vis à vis the Americans. And that applied to everybody, not just France (Interview in the Greek Permanent Representation to the EU, 21.3.1997).

The 'textiles' game

The decision to negotiate the incorporation of the textile and clothing products into the GATT process and thus gradually phase out the Multifibre Agreement (MFA)[3] which had regulated international trade in these sectors since 1974, was one of the greatest innovations of the Uruguay Round. The new regime under negotiation, however, would result in major changes, including the removal of all quantitative restrictions following a transitional period of 10 years, during which time all textile and clothing products would be integrated into the overall discipline of the GATT. The proposals for limiting international protection came at a time of severe crisis for the EC's textile and clothing industries. According to the Commission's (1993c) estimates, between 1988 and 1992 production had fallen by 4.7% in the textile sector and by 6.4% in clothing. Over the same period, investment in the two sectors was down almost 30%, while employment had fallen by 14%, resulting in the loss of more than 300,000 jobs (European Commission, 1994).

Since the late 1980s, the basic problem of the European textile and clothing industry was its increasing inability to compete successfully with its international rivals, especially those coming from low labour cost regions such as Asia (e.g. China and India) and Latin America (e.g. Mexico). The lack of competitiveness facing European firms (deriving mainly from their very high labour costs) led to the loss of a considerable market share, especially in the US (from 12.4% in 1988 to 8.8% in 1992) and Japan (from 24% in 1988 to 16.2% in 1992), which, in turn, reinforced the problems of low investment and unemployment at home. The Commission's response to this crisis was to encourage European firms to de-localise production for textile and clothing products. The development of Outward Processing Trade (OPT) with developing countries was seen by the Commission as the safest way of proceeding with the restructuring of the two industries since it would allow labour-intensive activities to be performed outside the EC where costs were lower (while the EC's Structural Funds would compensate the regions mostly hit by the loss of their textile and clothing industries).

The restructuring plan, especially as far as the development of OPT was concerned, was nevertheless very much dependent on the relaxation of international protection measures, in particular those affecting trade with the developing (i.e. low labour cost) countries. That partly explains why, within the GATT negotiations, the EC (in contrast to its actions in the case of agriculture) consistently advocated a more liberal approach with regard to trade liberalisation in textiles and clothing (Woolcock and Hodges, 1996: 312). The Commission's aggressive strategy within GATT received a mixed reaction from different interest groups within the textile and clothing industries. While sectoral groups representing commerce (e.g. FTA, CECD and FEWITA and GEDIS) advocated greater liberalisation within the Uruguay round and higher quotas for Eastern Europe as a means of strengthening bilateral trade, those interest groups representing producers and employees (e.g. ECLA, ETUC) appeared to be more reluctant (*Agence Europe*, 20.6.91: 14; 13.9.91: 16, 13.7.91: 10; 29.1.92: 15).

Against this background of dissatisfaction on both sides of the textile and clothing industry, Bruce Millan, the Commissioner responsible for regional policy, promised further aid to the regions hit by high unemployment as a result of the decline of the textile industries and insisted that the Commission "...had no intention of abandoning the textile industry" (IP/91/309, 15.4.91). Similarly, the Commission's vice-President Andriessen (responsible for both the GATT and the Association negotiations) had tried from an early stage to highlight the benefits of the rapid conclusion of the Uruguay Round and the opportunities emerging from the liberalisation of textile trade with Eastern Europe (Speech/90/20, 16.3.90).

By 1991, it had become apparent that Andriessen's early optimism about textile and clothing trade with Eastern Europe was only partially justified. As predicted, Outward Processing Trade (OPT) with the region developed rapidly and consequently, clothing imports from the CEECs between 1989 and 1991 almost doubled (see European Commission, 1994). While this development was highly beneficial for the EC's big industries which could re-locate their production basis into a low labour-cost region, it nevertheless seriously undermined the competitiveness of smaller EC businesses, which lacked the resources needed for investment in Eastern Europe. Furthermore, relocation of the production base to Eastern Europe meant even greater job losses in two sectors which had already lost a considerably high percentage of their workforce, as well as further devastation for those EC regions still dependent on the textile and clothing industries.

The EC's Association strategy with regard to textile and clothing products had therefore to compromise two conflicting interests (Interview in DG IA, 20.2.1997). On one hand, the need to restructure the textile/clothing industries (a need which was better served by a greater liberalisation of the EC-CEEC trade) and on the other, the need to protect the EC's workforce and the EC's regions which were still dependent on the two industries (a need which would be better served by maintaining the existing trade barriers between the EC and CEECs). Indeed, the Commission's position during the EA negotiations clearly reflected this compromise: concessions in textiles and clothing products were to be greater than those granted for agricultural products, but still considerably smaller than those granted for industrial products (see chapter 2).

An assessment of the interdependence between the Association and the 'GATT' games

In relation to both agriculture and textiles/clothing, the GATT negotiations had a decisive, double-faceted, impact upon the EC's strategy in the Association game. Firstly, the EC's simultaneous involvement in the 'GATT' and the Association games meant that its strategy in both games needed to be consistent. This need, in turn, faced the EC with a dilemma: either adopt a liberal stance in the Association negotiations and consequently undermine its position within GATT (which was based on a protectionist agenda), or 'sacrifice' a liberal deal with the Visegrads so as to serve its position within GATT. In fact, the choice between the two options was not difficult to make. Taking into consideration the fact that the EC's economic stakes in GATT were so much higher than its stakes in the EAs, it was clear that the EC's negotiating tactics in the former would dictate the EC's strategy in the latter and not the other way around. Such a choice made sense for yet one more reason. Quite simply, for the EC it was much easier to 'bully' the CEECs into a 'convenient' (for the EC) Association deal than, for example, 'bully' the Americans or the Japanese into a 'convenient' GATT agreement. Such a prioritisation of the 'GATT' game over the Association game was manifested in the most clear manner with the EC's poor agricultural offers to the first wave of Association applicants.

The second facet of the GATT's impact on the EC's strategy in the Association game relates to what Gourevitch (1977) called the 'second image reversed'. Clearly, the significance of the GATT negotiations went far beyond that of 'conventional' international trade agreements. While the GATT deal was not finalised until the end of 1993, by 1991 it was already becoming apparent that the liberalisation timetables negotiated in the Uruguay round would have a major impact on certain sections of the EC economy (i.e. agriculture, textiles) and would most certainly lead to the radical rethink of some of the EC's internal policies (i.e. CAP). In this respect, the formation of the EC's strategy in the Association game would have to take into account not only the EC's negotiating position within the 'GATT' game, but also the opposition from certain sections of its domestic audience which were expected to be hardest hit by the arrangements of the new GATT deal. The domestic dissatisfaction caused by the GATT negotiations was, therefore, crucial to the EC's ability to 'ratify' a more liberal package within the Association game. When such domestic opposition was aggressive and universal (i.e. in the case of agriculture), the Association offers for the CEECs were kept to a minimum (i.e. exclusion of agriculture from the FTA envisaged by the EAs). When, on the other hand, domestic opposition was fragmented (i.e. in the case of textiles/clothing), the Association offers to the CEECs improved noticeably (i.e. accomplishment of a FTA at the end of the second phase of the transitional period).

The evolution of other sensitive issues

The 'coal/steel' game

Since the beginning of the European integration process in the early 1950s, the coal and steel industries had enjoyed a special status within the European Communities. The management of coal and steel by a different Community (the ECSC), and the exclusion of these markets from the competition rules of the European Economic Community (EEC), was a clear manifestation of the importance of these industries for the stability and economic development of post-war Europe. While European coal and steel industries developed rapidly during the '50s, the first structural problems in the sector became apparent in the mid 1960s. Coal was no longer the Community's major energy source and steel lost its pre-eminent position among manufacturing industries. The crisis in the steel sector further deepened in the mid-1970s, following the energy crisis of 1974-78. The Commission's rescue package (the 'Davignon Plan', 1977) for the steel sector included strict regulation and an official "market cartelisation" (Sinn, 1993: 173) in which production quotas and mandatory minimum prices were set by the Commission. Furthermore, the plan provided for strong external protection through a series of bilateral Voluntary Restraint Agreements (VRAs) which the EC negotiated with its main trading partners, including the CMEA countries (Sedelmeier, 1995).

By 1988, despite the fact that the restructuring programme was still incomplete, the situation in the steel sector had improved considerably as, after a long period of continuous decline, domestic demand for steel had increased considerably. The positive circumstances in the late 1980s, however, did not last for long. By 1990, economic recession in Europe had depressed domestic demand for steel and exports were severely hit by the decision of the US to impose anti-dumping measures against EC companies (Sedelmeier, 1995: 5). By the early 1990s, the European Coal and Steel industries were, therefore, facing a double-edged crisis. On a domestic level, a painful process of structural adjustment began aimed at reducing large over-capacities in order to respond to reduced demand, and on an international level the 'closure' of the US steel markets was coupled with increased competition from south-east Asia (i.e. Korea) and south America (i.e. Brazil) (Tsoukalis (1993: 292).

Against this background of generalised crisis, the timing of East European demands for complete liberalisation in the steel market was unfortunate. The prospect of eliminating all trade barriers for the CEECs received a hostile reception by both national (e.g. German Steel Association) and pan-European (e.g. ECSC Advisory Committee, EUROFER) interest groups relating to steel which argued strongly for the better policing of the EC-CEECs trade rules as well as for the continuation of quantitative restrictions for imports originating from Eastern Europe (*Agence Europe*, 8.3.91: 13; 10/11.6.91: 13; 20.9.91: 11 and interview in DG IA on 20.2.97). The concerns of EC steel producers concentrated on three issues: *firstly*, that a dramatic increase in East European imports would upset the EC's domestic steel market and thus jeopardise the restructuring of the industry; *secondly*, that competition rules were not respected since cheap imports from Eastern Europe were heavily subsidised by the respective governments; and *thirdly* that more funds should be available in those regions which would be affected by job losses as a result of the full exposure of the steel industry to the international competition.

In retrospect, the fears of the EC's steel industry were only partially justified. While the EC's trade balance with CEECs in the categories relating to coal and steel products deteriorated severely (see European Commission, 1994), the total volume of the CEECs steel exports to the EU in 1992 was relatively small (4 million tonnes), representing only 3% of the total EC steel imports (Arts and Lee, 1994: 304). It can also be argued that the East European threat with regard to steel was dramatically overestimated, especially if one considers that during the first three years of transition, steel output in the region halved as a result of the collapse of military spending and the impact of macro-economic 'shock therapy' (*Financial Times*, 19.2.93).

So, given this grim situation in the CEECs' steel sector and the relatively limited danger they presented for the EU market, why did the EC refuse to accept a fast-track liberalisation (see chapter 2) for coal and steel products? As in the cases of agriculture and textiles, the EC's reluctance during the EAs negotiations can be better understood in relation to the EC's involvement in other peripheral games. On a domestic level, such peripheral games included the process of restructuring the EC's coal and steel industries, while on an international level this involved the damage inflicted to the EC steel industry by the 'closure' of the American markets and increased pressure by the EC's international competitors. Under these circumstances, how could the Commission persuade the all-powerful steel organisations about the virtues of total liberalisation with the CEECs at a time when EC producers were already suffering from large over-capacities and the loss of considerable international markets? Furthermore, if the Commission opted for a fast-track liberalisation of the coal and steel markets, how could it then justify the large amount of money spent in many EC regions (in the form of Regional Funds and national aid programmes) in order to minimise the social consequences[4] of restructuring the coal and steel industries? Finally, how could the Commission be more lenient towards heavily subsidised imports from the CEECs at a time when subsidies for the EC's domestic producers had almost been eliminated through the Aid Code which authorised public aid for only the financing of social programmes, research development and investments for environmental protection?

The 'free movement of people' game

As discussed in chapter 2, the Community's position in relation to free movement of people was amongst the most controversial issues during the EA negotiations. From the outset, the Commission's proposals dismissed the idea of complete freedom of movement for people at the end of the transitional period. Moreover, with the EC's refusal to give in to the Polish demands for legalisation of all those who had been illegally working within the EC (Pinter, 1991: 67-18), the bargain soon shifted towards the clause of non-discrimination, in other words, whether those CEE nationals (and their families) already legally employed within the EC's territory would enjoy the same working rights as the EC nationals. Nevertheless, the Visegrads' demand for the application of the non-discrimination clause to both contributory and non-contributory benefits was once again rejected by the EC. As a result, the Association agreements were to limit the application of the non-discrimination clause only to contributory benefits.

The EC's tough position during the EA negotiations in relation to the free movement of people was driven by both dor international considerations. Domestically, the Association demands for the relaxation of travelling and working restricti nationals coincided with an unfavourable economic climate w Following a period of spectacular growth during the secon 1980s, by the beginning of the 1990s the EC economy towards recession. GDP growth for 1991 was a moderate 1.6%, while further deterioration was predicted for 1992-93 (by 1993, GDP growth reached -0.5%). As growth stalled, unemployment began to rise reaching, in 1991, an EU average of 8.7% (Eurostat, 1993). In turn, as unemployment rose so did the expenditure for social protection which by 1991 amounted on average to 27.1% of the EC's GDP, rising from a level of 25.1% in 1989 (Eurostat, 1994a).

In addition to the deteriorating economic situation, the EC member states' scepticism over the Visegrads' demands was further aggravated in early 1991 as a result of the Court of Justice's ruling on Bahia Kziber's case against the Belgium government (ECJ, 1991: 129). The Court ruled that Ms. Kziber, daughter of a Moroccan national who worked in Belgium, was entitled to unemployment benefit on the basis of the non-discrimination clause in the EC's Association agreements with the Maghreb countries. The financial implications of the Court's ruling came as a shock to most EC member states and inevitably raised concerns over the application of a similar clause to the Association agreements with the CEECs. Evidently, such concerns were reflected in the EC's determination during the EAs negotiations that the Europe agreements should include a clear reference that the non-discrimination clause would not be applicable to non-contributory benefits.

Arguably, the greatest pressure for a cautious EA arrangement in relation to the free movement of workers came from international rather than domestic considerations. To this end, the fall of the Berlin Wall and the end of the Cold War had a decisive impact. For more than 40 years, Western Europe's main security preoccupation was connected to the military threat posed by the Soviet Union and its allies. By the early 1990s however, the European scene was radically different. As the disintegration process of both the Warsaw Pact and the Soviet Union accelerated, the European security agenda was substantially broadened to include issues such as environmental protection, nuclear safety and, of course, immigration (Collinson *et al.*, 1993: 43).

The fear of 'mass migration' from Eastern Europe, together with the increasing pressure for westward migration from Africa and Asia, 'elevated' the containment of immigration from a mainly economic problem to an issue of national security for almost every member state, especially now that the EC was negotiating the abolition of its internal borders (*Financial Times*, 23.1.91; *Agence Europe*, 13.9.91). Indeed, the figures were alarming. According to UN data, Western Europe received more than 2 million immigrants over the period 1991-92 (*Financial ˙es*, 23.3.93). In Germany alone the number of successful asylum applications by CEE nationals grew from 193,000 in 1990 to 256,112 in 1991, while in 1992 it reached 438,000, a new record for the Federal Republic (Reinicke, 1992: 192). The problem was further aggravated by the unknown number of East Europeans illegally working in the EC as well as by the dramatic increase in the number of people who were forced to migrate as a result of the Yugoslav crisis.

Under such an unfavourable combination of developments on both its internal and external fronts, the EC's ability/willingness to tolerate a more generous package for the CEECs was, therefore, severely restricted. In other words, at a time of political and economic turmoil on their borders how could the EC's member states accept measures which would facilitate the entrance of large numbers of desperate East Europeans to the EC 'heaven'? Furthermore, with rising unemployment across the EC, what would the consequences be for the EC's least skilled labour force, if cheap labour was to become available from Eastern Europe as a result of the Association agreements? At the international level, how would the EC justify the relaxation of restrictions to free movement for East European workers to other Associated partners (i.e. Turkey) whose requests for similar treatment had been repeatedly refused by the EC? Finally, how could the EC member states 'be persuaded' to pay non-contributory benefits to all CEE nationals (and their families) legally working in the EC in a period when social security bills were soaring as a result of high unemployment?

An assessment of the interdependence between the Association game and the 'coal/steel' and 'free movement of people' games

In fact, the interdependence between the 'coal/steel' game and the EAs presents many similarities to the one already described for the cases of agriculture and textiles. All three cases involved a double bargain: domestic restructuring coupled with international pressures for change. While in the cases of agriculture and textiles the international pressure for change came directly from the GATT negotiations, in the cases of coal and steel the pressure came from the unfavourable international conjunctions facing the EC's industries at the beginning of the 1990s. Moreover, the EC's cautious offers can be seen, in all three cases, not as a proportional response to the 'threat' posed by the Association applicants, but instead, as having been dictated by the EC's involvement in other peripheral games. The prioritisation of these peripheral games over the EAs can be explained by a number of reasons. For instance, by the fact that the EC's economic stakes in some of these games were far greater than in the EA's (i.e. GATT); also, by the fact that the EC's opponents in these games were far too strong to be bullied into a 'convenient' deal (i.e. the Americans in GATT, or the agricultural lobby in the CAP reform); or by the fact that certain sectoral groups with a vested interest in a protectionist Association deal were able to penetrate successfully the EC decision making process and consequently shape the EC's negotiating position according to their own priorities (i.e. EUROFER in the case of steel).

The case of the free movement of workers, on the other hand, presented rather different characteristics. Unlike agriculture, textiles and coal/steel, the CEECs' 'threat' (in terms of the former communist countries being the biggest 'pool' of illegal migration into the EC) to the EC's interests was far greater, with serious political and economic ramifications. In this respect, the EC's refusal to accept a more generous arrangement regarding the free movement of workers can be better understood not in relation to the EC's peripheral games (although domestic economic difficulties clearly contributed towards the EC's scepticism), but rather in relation to the end of the Cold War in Europe and the dramatic increase in the number of CEE nationals seeking refuge in the EC member states.

'High politics' games

This chapter has so far concluded that a generous Association deal for the Visegrad applicants was often 'sacrificed' in order for the EC to maximise its payoffs in other peripheral games within the *Grand* game. However, most of the peripheral games already examined were of a predominantly economic nature[5] and as such they were played in areas of *low politics* (Hoffmann, 1966) where sectoral interests of all kinds had increased opportunities for intervention and influence. Nevertheless, not all peripheral games were played in areas of *low politics*. For this reason, the attention of the chapter will now shift to areas of the *Grand* game which were dominated by *high politics* issues and assess how the EC's involvement in these *high politics* games affected the CEECs' payoffs from the Association bargain.

The 'European security' game

Arguably, the most important of these *high politics* games relate to the new security arrangements in Europe following the collapse of the Berlin

Wall.[6] Clearly, in the new post-Cold War setting, the departure from its traditional 'political pygmy' profile became an urgent priority for the EC. The assertion of the EC's political role in the international and particularly in the European scene was encouraged by three main factors: firstly, by the CEECs' almost universal commitment to strengthening economic and political relations with the EC; secondly, by Gorbachev's idea of a 'common European home' (Gorbachev, 1988: 194-205) at the heart of which laid the USSR's decision to tolerate a more assertive EC role in Europe; and thirdly, by the US decision to allow the EC to assume the leadership in stabilising the situation in Eastern Europe.[7]

In fact, the need to reinforce Europe's security soon became amongst the more pressing priorities for the EC's leadership. Such a preoccupation was clearly reflected in the conclusions of the Strasbourg European Council where it was argued that "The changes and transitions which are necessary must not take place to the detriment of the stability of Europe but rather must contribute to strengthen it" (Doc/89/3, 9.12.89). While the aims and objectives of the new EC role in Europe remained unclear (see below), the strategy of how this new role would come about enjoyed an almost universal support amongst the EC member states; through the deepening of the EC's integration process. President Delors' speech before the Strasbourg Summit was revealing: "Since events are accelerating in the rest of Europe we must accelerate construction of the European Community" (Speech/89/87, 7.12.89).

The idea of closer political co-operation between the EC member states gained further impetus following the result of the election in Eastern Germany (18.3.90) which made clear that the process of German unification was irreversible. Increased insecurity in Eastern Europe, coupled with renewed fears over the future of Germany in the new Europe led to the conclusion that a new treaty on Political Union could serve a double purpose: ensuring coherent external action in Eastern Europe and elsewhere, while 'tightening' Germany within the process of European integration. Against this background, in April 1990 the German Chancellor Helmut Kohl and the French President Francois Mitterrand, building upon an earlier Belgian proposal, revealed their plans for a new IGC on Political Union to run in parallel with the one on Economic and Monetary Union (*Agence Europe*, 20.4.90).

The Franco-German proposal was initially discussed (and in principle agreed) by the extraordinary Dublin Summit of 28.4.90 (SN 46/3/90, 28.4.90), while in June 1990 it was finally agreed that the IGC on Political Union would start together with the IGC on EMU in December 1990 (SN 60/1/90, 26.6.90). Arguably, the most ambitious item on the

IGC's agenda was the plan for the establishment of a Common Foreign and Security Policy (CFSP) which would be incorporated into the new treaty. The EC's member states' decision to negotiate the creation of a Common Foreign and Security Policy (which had also been one of the main features of the Franco-German proposal) was yet the clearest manifestation of the EC's increasing assertiveness in the post-Cold War world and its determination to ensure stability in the eastern part of the European continent.

However, during the course of the IGC serious disagreements began to emerge amongst the EC member states. Attempts to create a truly supranational foreign policy was soon blocked by those member states (most importantly, Britain and France and to a lesser extent by Denmark and Portugal) who supported the continuation of the intergovernmental legacy on which the EPC was build (Ioakimidis, 1993: 250-283; Cloos *et al.*, 1994). Moreover, the negotiation of a 'European' defence and security policy inevitably raised questions about the future role of the US and NATO in Europe, with the EC member states broadly divided between those resisting any weakening of NATO (the so-called *Atlanticists* led by Britain) and those advocating a more independent European defence policy (the so-called *Europeanists* led by France) (on this, see Tiersky, 1992).

As Forster and Wallace argued (1996: 422), the debate surrounding NATO's security presence in Europe was conducted simultaneously in three different fora: the IGC on Political Union, the Western European Union (WEU) and, since April 1990, within the process of NATO's Strategic Review. The end result of this triple-faceted bargain was a compromise struck in two stages: firstly, in the NATO Rome Summit (7-8.11.91) when the alliance adopted its new 'strategic concept' which approved the development of European multinational forces, but reaffirmed NATO's primacy as the Western forum for defence co-operation (Forster and Wallace, 1996: 426); and secondly, in Maastricht where the EC member states 'promoted' the WEU as 'an integral part of development of the EU' (J.4.2.), but also acknowledged that the responsibilities emanating from NATO membership would be respected (J.5). As Forster and Wallace (1996: 428-433) concluded, however, the final compromise remained rather problematic, forcing both the EU and the NATO/US to embark on a process of 'learning by doing' which often proved detrimental to the efficiency of both sides' security policy planning and implementation.

Western disagreements over the future of NATO and the EC's new security role in Europe were further exacerbated by the vigorous efforts of the new democratically elected governments in Eastern Europe to integrate their countries into the Western security framework. A clear manifestation of East Europe's commitment to the West could be seen during the Iraqi crisis, when many East European governments volunteered non-combat troops in order to assist the Western allies' war efforts (Forster and Wallace, 1996: 422).

Nonetheless, the response to the East European aspirations for a rapid integration into the Western security structures was rather cautious. Arguably, at the time of the Visegrads' EA negotiations (January-December 1991), the question of NATO's eastwards enlargement had not yet been given serious consideration (the Warsaw Pact was not formally dissolved until July 1991). Despite the fact that during the Moscow coup in August 1991 the alliance declared that the security of the Visegrads was 'inextricably linked' to that of NATO, it made clear that neither membership nor security guarantees were on offer (Collinson *et al.*, 1993:42). Moreover, the alliance's decision to create the North Atlantic Cooperation Council (NACC) in which all former members of the Warsaw Pact were given consultative status, while constituting an important symbolic gesture, still felt short of a concrete security guarantee. Against this background, the security vacuum in Eastern Europe was left to be managed largely by the Conference of Security and Co-operation in Europe (CSCE), the co-operative security system created by the Helsinki Final Act. As Collinson *et al.* (1993: 43) pointed out however, the consensual character of the CSCE, as well as its heterogeneous composition, rendered it a rather weak executive regime with no means of enforcing its decisions other than peer pressure.

In fact, the negotiation of the Association agreements should not be seen in isolation from the EC's (and more generally the Western) inability to provide concrete security guarantees to Eastern Europe. Since agreement over the security map of the new post-Cold war Europe proved to be a far too 'hot potato' to handle at this stage, the conclusion of Association agreements with the more advanced countries of Eastern Europe could, in the meantime, serve as a relatively painless reaffirmation of the EC's commitment to act as a 'stabilising force' in the region. In August 1990, the Commission's Communication on the Association agreements had already highlighted the security implications of the EAs arguing that they were expected to strengthen "...the climate of confidence and stability favouring political and economic reform...and the foundations of the new European Architecture" (Commission of the EC, 1990f: 3). It was, therefore, not surprising that the new agreements would not be solely confined to regulating trade relations, but would also provide for new institutions to strengthen political dialogue and co-operation in foreign policy matters of common interest.

As the negotiations with the Visegrads got under way at the beginning of 1991, a number of external events further emphasised the need to use the Association agreements as a stabilising force in Eastern Europe. The first major challenge in this direction came from the Yugoslav crisis. While evidence for the eventual break up had become apparent long before, events in former Yugoslavia accelerated rapidly in the first months of 1991. Despite initial warnings by the EC leadership concerning the preservation of the status quo in the country, nationalist pressures continued to grow out of control leading to formal declarations of independence by Croatia and Slovenia on 25.6.91 (ELIAMEP, 1993: 102). The threat to European stability from what was now becoming a full scale civil war in Yugoslavia was coupled, on 19.8.91, with the coup in the Soviet Union. The overthrow of the Soviet leader Michael Gorbachev (who was always considered as a pair of 'safe hands') had a great impact upon the Western world. When he returned to Moscow, Gorbachev, whose authority had been seriously undermined as a result of the coup, was unable to contain nationalist tendencies within the Soviet Union and consequently the country entered the irreversible process of disintegration.

The events in Yugoslavia and the Soviet Union made it clear that new, firmer action was urgently needed on behalf of the EC in order to: (i) provide support and legitimisation to the democratically elected governments in the region, (ii) provide (or to be seen to provide) greater safeguards for the CEECs against an increasingly 'unpredictable' Soviet Union. (iii) respond to the increasing influence of communist and nationalist forces which appeared to benefit from the continuing political, social and economic crisis in most of the CEECs.

The developments over the Summer of 1991 and the deepening crisis in Eastern Europe had a positive impact not only on these CEECs which had already begun Association negotiations with the EC (i.e. Visegrads), but also for those who were trying enter the Association process (i.e. Bulgaria and Romania). As far as the Visegrads were concerned, the impact of the Yugoslav crisis and the Moscow coup was clearly reflected in the Commission's September Communication to the Council asking for greater 'flexibility' in order to allow the early conclusion (i.e. before the end of October 1991) of the EA negotiations with the first wave applicants (see chapter 2). The positive impact of security considerations on the progress of the Association negotiations has been stressed both by East European negotiators (Stawarska, 1992: 81-82;

interviews in the Bulgarian and Romanian delegations to the EU), and EC officials in Brussels (interviews in the Commission's DG IA and DG VI).

'The 'European Economic Area' game

The ongoing negotiations between the EC and the EFTA countries (Austria, Finland, Iceland, Norway, Sweden and Switzerland) for the creation of the European Economic Area (EEA) was another important parameter affecting the course of the Association bargain, in that they provided a good indication of how far the EC was prepared to go in its dealings with non-members who either aspired to accession into the EC or to closer links with the EC's internal market. Whilst the EC's member states and the EFTA countries often found themselves in stark disagreement over the extent and nature of the integration process in post-War Europe, economic ties between the two trading blocks had always been strong. Soon after France lifted its reservations over the EC's first enlargement, the prospective new member states (particularly the UK and Denmark who had been amongst the founding members of EFTA) put pressure on the EC for the swift conclusion of bilateral free trade agreements with the remaining EFTA countries. Indeed, the agreements between the EC and the EFTAns entered into force on 1.1.73, the same day as the UK, Denmark and Ireland officially entered the EC (Pedersen, 1994: 23).

Despite their cautious provisions in a number of sectors (e.g. agriculture and paper), the EC's agreements with the EFTA countries resulted in extensive liberalisation for industrial products and, more generally, created a stable foundation for the development of bilateral trade which, during the period 1972-1986, grew five-fold (de Lange, 1988: 311). Nevertheless, the relaunch of EC integration during the second half of the 1980s and in particular the EC's '1992 programme' offered EC companies substantial competitive advantages vis à vis their EFTA competitors, which now found themselves partially excluded (facing numerous non-tariff barriers) from the EC's lucrative single market (Baldwin *et al.*1992: 107).

The idea for closer multilateral dialogue between the EC and EFTA was first raised by Sweden in April 1984, during the first EC/EFTA inter-ministerial meeting in Luxembourg which convened to celebrate the successful implementation of the free trade agreements of the early 1970s. Sweden's initiative, which received a positive response from the EC and later formed the basis of what became known as 'the Luxembourg process', provided for, amongst other things: extended co-operation in research and development; co-ordinated action in relation to the international monetary disorder; co-operation with regard to the Third World and, most importantly, industrial co-operation aiming at the creation of a truly internal market (Pedersen, 1994: 27).

By 1987-88, however, 'the Luxembourg process' was criticised as deficient both in terms of its enforceability and coherence (Wallace and Wessels, 1989: 4). Responding to these criticisms, President Delors in his speech to the European Parliament in January 1989 (*Agence Europe*, 26.1.89) proposed a new framework for the EC's relations with the EFTA countries: the European Economic Area (EEA). The centrepiece of Delors' initiative was the extension of the four freedoms (goods, persons, services and capital) and flanking policies of the single market to the EFTAns, without them becoming full members of the EC. Following Delors' speech, a joint EC/EFTA high-level steering group was set up in April 1989 with the task of preparing the agenda for the EEA negotiations. Further exploratory talks were held during the first half of 1990, while formal negotiations did not start until June 1990 (Pedersen, 1994: chapter 4).

Despite early hopes that an EEA agreement could be clinched before the end of 1990, the negotiations proved to be both difficult and lengthy, with two issues causing the greatest difficulties: firstly, the participation (or not) of the EFTAns in the EC's decision making process for issues relating to the single market and, secondly, the composition and responsibilities of the EEA court which would be responsible for monitoring the implementation of the agreement (Collinson *et al.* 1993: 14-15). For the problem of the EFTAns participation in the EC's decision making process, a compromise was finally found during the EC/EFTA joint ministerial meeting on 13.5.91 which decided that the EFTA counties would not be able to opt out from future rules affecting the EEA, but they would be allowed to send experts to the proceedings of certain committees under the Commission (Pedersen, 1994: 53). In the same inter-ministerial meeting, agreement was also reached in relation to the EEA court. The new court would consist of five judges from the EC and three from the EFTA. Moreover, whist the EEA court would 'technically' be independent, it would remain functionally integrated into the EC's Court of Justice (Pedersen, 1994: 52). Despite the progress made in the May inter-ministerial meeting however, the negotiations were deadlocked in November 1991, when the ECJ ruled that a separate EEA court was incompatible with the EC treaties. As a result, a new compromise between the two parties was reached in February 1992 which allowed the conclusion of the negotiation in May 1992. According to the new compromise, the original idea of an EEA court was dropped altogether. Instead, the EFTA side would set up a counterpart to the EC's surveillance mechanism and Court of Justice which would have sole legal competence only in competition cases dealing with EFTA internal trade (Pedersen, 1994: 61).

The long and often torturous process leading to the EEA agreement provided some useful conclusions as to how far the EC was prepared to go in its partnership building with third parties. As the EC's determined position during the EEA negotiations highlighted, a meaningful participation of third countries in the EC's decision making process could not be possible without full EC membership (Baldwin *et al.* 1992: 50-51). Moreover, the negotiations showed that the preservation of the *acquis* remained the cornerstone of the EC's position vis à vis third parties and as such any partnership which would be likely to erode the EC's legal and institutional system became automatically unacceptable (Collinson *et al.*, 1993: 15).

On a different level, the EC's determination to preserve its internal coherence was yet another manifestation of the overwhelming victory of the EC's 'deepeners' led by the Delors' Commission and 'intergrationist' member states such as Germany and France. In fact, from the outset the whole EEA project was widely regarded as an attempt by the EC to avoid addressing the Austrian membership application (July 1989) while at the same time deterring other EFTA countries from doing so (Wallace, 1991: 270-272; Wijkman, 1991). The rationale behind such delaying tactics was simple: the EC would be able to complete the 1992 programme and negotiate Political Union and EMU, without the distraction of extending the single market or addressing the question of EFTA membership with all its financial and institutional implications. One may argue that the idea was largely successful: whilst the EEA did not, in the long run, deter the members of the EFTA from applying for full EU membership (Sweden applied in July 1991, Switzerland in May 1992 and Finland and Norway in November 1992), enlargement negotiations did not begin until February 1993, long after the bargain over the EC's deepening was over with the conclusion of the Maastricht treaty.

An assessment of the interdependence between the Association and the 'European security' and the 'European Economic Area' games

In assessing the EC's involvement in the 'European security' game and the effects of such an involvement on the CEECs' payoffs from the Association bargain, the following observation can be made. While in the cases of agriculture, textiles and coal/steel the Association game can be conceived as being 'nested' (in the sense that the EC's economic stakes in it were much smaller) within far greater games (i.e. GATT), in the case of the 'European security' game the CEECs clearly remained the protagonists. In this sense, the 'European security' game resembled the 'free movement of workers' game. However, unlike the case of the 'free movement of workers' game, for the 'European security' game a generous Association deal for the CEECs was considered to be supplementary, not detrimental, to the EC's wider security interests. That is to say, the more generous the EC's offers to the Association applicants, the less likely the CEECs would plunge into further economic and political crisis. In turn, the more stable the CEECs' economies and political systems, the fewer security risks were posed for the EC and its member states.

In this respect, it can be argued that the EC's security considerations in Eastern Europe were somehow contradictory to its economic interests in the Association game (on this, see Sedelmeier, 1994). While the stabilisation of Eastern Europe remained a top security priority for the EC, the pursuit of such an objective proved costly in the sense that it often carried the danger of undermining the EC's position vis à vis its major international competitors or upsetting important sections of its domestic audience. In fact, ever since the fall of the Berlin Wall and up to the present day the EC's strategy in the region has been shaped by a continuous and elusive struggle to reconcile these two contradictory elements (high security concerns vs limited economic interests). In the case of the Association negotiations with the Visegrads it can be argued that only when the Continent's security was seriously threatened in Summer 1991 (with the combined effect of the Yugoslav crisis and the Moscow coup), did the EC consider a serious improvement in its offers to the first wave applicants (through the September 1991 mandate). These improvements included, amongst others, greater trade concessions for agriculture, textiles and coal, as well as the decision to strengthen political co-operation with the Associated partners thus "...overcoming the sense of isolation felt in Central Europe against the background of turbulence in the Soviet Union and Yugoslavia, and creating a feeling of belonging" (*Agence Europe*, 7.9.91: 7).

However, the improvements included in the September 1991 mandate were by no means a radical change of the EC's strategy in the region. After all, such a radical change continued to be costly for the EC's interests in other peripheral games. Nonetheless, the incremental changes agreed by the EC in September 1991 were sufficient to bring the Visegrads 'back on track', unlock the first wave of Association negotiations (which had been deadlocked since June 1991) and preserve the EC's reputation as a stabilising force in the region. Moreover, this reputation was soon to be extended to other CEECs following the Council's decision to authorise the opening of Association negotiations with Bulgaria and Romania (*Agence Europe*, 28.9.91: 8).

The interdependence between the 'EEA' and the Association game, on the other hand, produced rather different results for the Visegrad applicants. Here, the EC's determination to preserve its internal coherence and concentrate its efforts on the process of deepening had led to a rather cool reception to the Austrian and later the Swedish applications for membership. In fact, the whole EEA project was regarded as an attempt by the EC to ease, at least temporarily, the pressures for widening. Against this background, the Visegrads' request that an explicit reference to future membership should be included in the Preamble of the Association agreements was doomed. At a time when the EC had given such a cool reception to the rich EFTAns request for membership, how could it justify a more generous wording for the Visegrad EAs in this field? With this in mind, it is hardly surprising that the Preamble of the Visegrad agreements made reference to future EU membership only as 'the ultimate objective' of the East European applicants, not as an EC objective or the natural progression of the Association agreements.

Conclusion

This chapter has addressed one of the most puzzling features of the Association process: why did the EC appear so cautious during the first wave of Association negotiations, despite the fact that, from an early stage, EC leaders had promised 'maximum help' for the newly emerged democracies and also despite the fact that this 'maximum help' (translated as fast track liberalisation for all products) constituted an almost insignificant threat to the EC's economy. If this paradox is viewed in isolation, two propositions emerge: that either the EC leaders simply lied to their Eastern counterparts when they promised 'maximum help' or that the EC's 'sensitivity' over trade liberalisation was an irrationally sub-optimal choice. This chapter argues that neither of these propositions (at least in their entirety) can provide a credible explanation of how the EC negotiating position was formed, as they are either impossible to prove or appear to be over-simplistic. Alternatively, it is argued that the EC's 'sensitivity' can be more accurately explained only if one looks at the 'broader picture' (what was described as the *Grand* game) in which the Association agreements were negotiated.

Using Tsebelis' concept of *nested games* (1988: 145-46), it was argued that the Association game was *nested* within the *Grand* game, a network of interdependent peripheral games with *variable payoffs* (1988: 145-46) in which the EC was involved at the time (see Figure 3.1.). It was precisely this variability of payoffs within the *Grand* game that bounds the EC's involvement in peripheral games inextricably with the proposed Association deal to the first wave applicants. In other words, when studied in isolation the EC's cautious offers to the CEECs during the Association negotiations seemed unnecessarily punitive behaviour and, as such, an almost irrationally sub-optimal strategy. Nevertheless, when the EC's involvement in other peripheral games are taken into consideration, such punitive behaviour might have been, after all, an optimal choice!

In order to clarify the argument further, the EC's *Grand* game cam be divided into three different *arenas:* the *Association arena*, the *Domestic arena* and the *International arena*. If a single issue dominated all three *arenas,* and the *Grand* game was viewed in isolation, its schematic representation could be as follows:

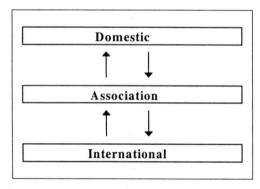

Figure 3.2 The *Grand* Game

While Figure 3.2. provides a useful framework for analysis, in identifying the *arenas* where the EC's payoffs were determined, its explanatory power remains limited, as the *Grand* game is simplistically represented as a single-issue game. The structure, therefore, needs to include more variables.

The *Association* arena, for example, consisted of a number of games, all of which emanated from the wide scope of the Europe agreements. Arguably, the most important of these games related to the free movement of people, political co-operation as well as to the gradual abolition of trade restrictions for textiles, industrial, agricultural and ECSC products. In this respect, the *Association arena* was itself an area of multiple games with *variable payoffs* as all games interacted and were interdependent with each other for they were all part of a *package deal* which had to be negotiated and 'ratified' as a whole. Schematically, the *Association arena* could be represented as follows:

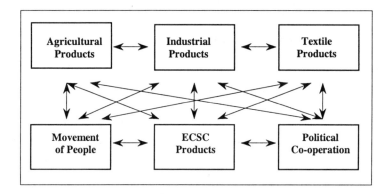

Figure 3.3 Multiple Games within the *Association Arena*

Similarly, the *Domestic arena* could also be considered as a network of games. As shown in this chapter, in parallel with the EA negotiations the EC was involved in the process of restructuring a number of its 'sensitive' industries (i.e. agriculture, textile etc.) as well as tackling the problems caused by economic recession (i.e. increasing unemployment and social security bills). Furthermore, the EAs were negotiated in parallel to the negotiation of the Maastricht treaty, in which (amongst others) the EC tried to redefine its role in the post-cold war world by developing a more active foreign and security policy. Some of the games within the *Domestic arena* appeared to be independent from one another (the development of the CFSP, for example, had little impact on the CAP reform and vice versa). Other games, nevertheless, appeared to be connected and interdependent (and thus with *variable payoffs*). For example, deterioration of living standards and rising unemployment (both caused by economic recession) was clearly affecting the way in which the EC was pursuing the restructuring of its agricultural, textile and coal/steel sectors.

Figure 3.4 provides a schematic representation of the multiple games (with *variable payoffs*) within the *Domestic arena*:

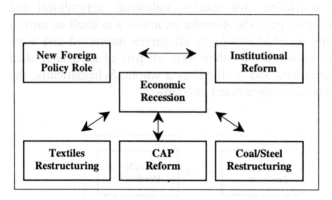

Figure 3.4 Multiple Games[8] within the *Domestic Arena*

Finally, the *International arena* could also be viewed as a broader network of games involving the EC and other international players. Figure 3.1 showed that the EA negotiations coincided with the EC/US bargain over GATT, the negotiations for the creation of the EEA as well as with major security risks in Eastern Europe. As was the case within the *Domestic arena*, some of the games within the *International arena* were inexplicably linked with each other as they were part of the same *package deal* (i.e. the bargain over textiles and agriculture within the Uruguay round), while others could be viewed separately (i.e. the game over Yugoslavia can be separated from the game over GATT). The schematic representation of the *International arena* could therefore be as follows:

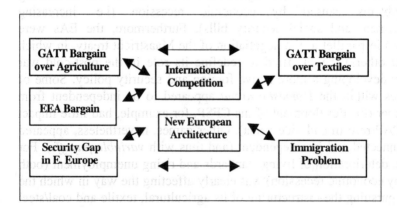

Figure 3.5 Multiple Games[9] within the *International Arena*

It has been argued, therefore, that in order to strengthen the explanatory power of the *Grand game* described in Figure 3.2, a number of new *nested games* would have to be inserted into the three *arenas* (*Domestic*, *Association* and *International*). It has also been argued that some of the games within these *arenas* were interdependent with one another and as such they constituted, what Tsebelis called (1990: 60), *multiple games* with *variable payoffs*. Payoffs, however, could vary not only as a result of changes in balance between *multiple games* within each *arena*, but also as a result of changes in payoffs in other *arenas*. In order to further clarify the interdependence of the payoffs that transcended different *arenas* and different games, the example can be cited of the three issues of the EA negotiations agenda: steel, agriculture and the free movement of people. As part of the EA package deal, all three issues were interdependent with each other. The EC's position on the free movement of people (*Association arena*) depended at the international level on the scale of the problem of illegal immigration to Europe (*International arena*), and at a domestic level on the level of unemployment within the EC (*Domestic arena*). The level of unemployment within the EC however, was linked to the process of reform in the EC's agricultural and steel sectors (*Domestic arena*), which in turn was affected by the ongoing GATT negotiations (*International arena*). Changes in the EC's payoffs in any individual game, had, therefore, a spill over effect on the EC's payoffs in all other games. Figure 3.6 provides a schematic representation of a game in *multiple arenas* with *variable payoffs*.

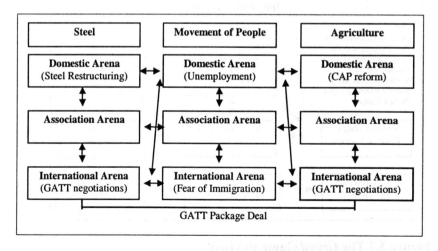

Figure 3.6 A Game in *Multiple Arenas* with *Variable Payoffs*

Having taken into account the multiplicity of the games within each of the three *arenas* (*Association, Domestic, International*) as well as the complex payoffs' interdependence between multiple games which sometimes transcends different *arenas*, the *Grand game* (which was simplistically represented in Figure 3.2) could take the following form:

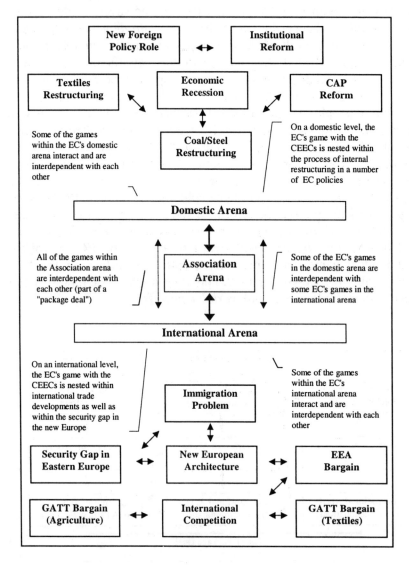

Figure 3.7 The *Grand* Game Revised

While Figure 3.6 provides a schematic representation of the EC's *Grand* game, a major question still remains unanswered: How was *equilibrium* reached within the *Grand* game? In other words, what were the factors that determined the EC's offers, and consequently the CEECs' payoffs, in the Association *arena*? Taking into account the large number of actors, but also the vast complexity of issues co-existing within the three *arenas* of the *Grand* game, it is clear that a 'scientific measurement' of each peripheral game's influence on the EC's negotiating position during the Association bargain is an impossibility. Even if one was able to locate every possible aspect of the EAs' interdependence with the EC's peripheral games, such a 'scientific measurement' would still have to face inescapable 'qualitative' difficulties. For example, how can one be sure that each individual negotiator (both at the EC and international level) was in a position to comprehend every possible detail of the *Grand* game? Moreover, how can one be sure that each individual negotiator valued the *Grand* game (and the interdependent peripheral games within it) in the same way?[10]

While the exact 'scientific measurement' of the interdependence within the *Grand* game remains impossible, it can still be argued that the EC's response to the CEECs' requests for a generous Association deal was determined by five main propositions:

- Proposition 1: *The larger the CEECs' payoffs from the Association arena the smaller the EC's payoffs in both the International and the Domestic arenas.*

This is the situation described in the case of agriculture. A generous offer to the CEECs would undermine the EC's negotiating position within GATT (*International arena*), but also upset the EC's domestic agricultural lobby which was already in disarray over the GATT and the proposed CAP reform (Domestic *arena*). Such a conjunction was amongst the most unfavourable for the CEECs' attempts to maximise their payoffs from the Association *arena*. Its implications can be seen in the final text of the EAs in which agriculture was altogether excluded from the proposed FTA.

- Proposition 2: *The larger the CEECs' payoffs from the Association arena, the EC's payoffs in both the International and the Domestic arena remained mixed.*

This is the situation described in the case of textiles. Here, the prospect of greater trade liberalisation with the CEECs (and for that matter with other international competitors within GATT) was opposed by a section of the industry (i.e. producers and employees), but favoured by another (i.e. commerce). As a result of this conjunction, the EC's protectionism against the CEECs was moderated. Textiles (unlike agriculture) was to be included in the proposed FTA, but (unlike industrial products) complete liberalisation would be accomplished in the second phase of the EAs transitional period.

- Proposition 3: *The larger the CEECs payoffs from the Association arena, the smaller the EC's payoffs from either the International or the Domestic arena.*

This is the situation described in the case of coal and steel as well as in the case of the EEA game. Here, in the absence of a major international (i.e. coal and steel) or domestic (i.e. EEA) bargain, the implications of a more generous Association deal for the CEECs were felt predominantly in *either* the EC's Domestic *or* International *arenas*. For example, how could the EC justify a generous deal for coal and steel in a period of severe crisis for its domestic industries? Moreover, what would be the implications of such generosity for the difficult (and expensive) process of restructuring the EC's coal and steel industries? On a different level, how could the EC make a concrete promise for membership to the CEECs when it had refused to do so to the economically and politically more advanced EFTA countries? As in the case of the textiles sector, the conjunction prevailing in the coal/steel sectors as well as in the EEA bargain resulted in what can be described as a form of 'moderated reluctance' vis à vis the Association applicants. Coal and steel were to be included in the FTA, but complete liberalisation would be accomplished in the second phase of the transitional period. Moreover, in the EAs' preamble, EU membership was recognised as the CEECs' ultimate objective, not as the agreements' natural progression.

- Proposition 4: *The larger the CEECs' payoffs from the Association arena, the smaller the EC's payoffs from the Association arena.*

This is the situation described in the case of free movement of workers. Here, a more generous deal for the CEECs was directly connected to the reduction of the EC's payoffs. In other words, whereas in other games the CEECs were considered a side issue, in this case they were the EC's 'main enemy'. Relaxation of travel and working restrictions for the CEE national was expected to aggravate the problem of immigration as well as to put more strain on the EC's declining economy. Alongside Proposition 1, this conjunction was the most harmful for the CEECs' Association payoffs; the EC's only concession in this direction related to the introduction of non-discrimination for those CEE nationals already legally working within the EC (only as far as contributory benefits were concerned).

• Proposition 5: *The larger the CEECs' payoffs from the Association arena, the larger the EC's payoffs from the Association arena.*

This is the situation described in the case of the 'European security' game. Here, a generous Association deal for the CEECs was considered as supplementary, not detrimental, to the EC's efforts to stabilise Eastern Europe. In addition to their decisive impact on the initiation of the Association process in the first place, security considerations often acted as a counterbalancing force against the EC's protectionism during the Association negotiations (i.e. in trade-related issues). In this respect, the 'European security' game was arguably the CEECs' greatest ally in their efforts to maximise their payoffs from the Association bargain. An example of such a positive impact can be seen in the improved EC offer to the Visegrads, following the 'hot' summer of 1991 which included the Moscow coup and the outbreak of hostilities in former Yugoslavia.

These five propositions can, therefore, serve as a broad explanatory framework for the EC's behaviour during the Association negotiations. Nevertheless, for a better understanding of the final *equilibrium* reached within the *Grand* game, a number of additional parameters also need to be taken into consideration:

(i) The size of the EC's payoffs from peripheral games

For example, if a generous Association deal for the CEECs undermined the EC's strategy in a peripheral game in which the EC's economic stakes were far greater, then it is clear that the latter would be given priority over the former and not the other way around. The limitations imposed by the EC's involvement in the GATT bargain over its ability to provide more generous offers to the CEECs in agriculture and textiles is a good example of this.

(ii) The strength of the EC's opponents within the International and Domestic arenas

Using the example of agriculture, it is clear that the need for a cautious Association offer to the CEECs would have been smaller had the EC been able to 'bully' its domestic (i.e. agricultural lobby) and international (i.e. the US) opposition into a more 'convenient' (for the EC) deal in order to compensate for its reduced payoffs in the Association *arena*. In this respect, the strength of the EC's opponents in peripheral games was detrimental to the CEECs' payoffs from the Association game.

(iii) The potential for future damage attributed to the CEECs

Despite their tiny share in the EC's external trade in 1990-91, the Association applicants were treated as countries with great export potential, an assumption based on their clear competitive advantage over the EC in labour-intensive sectors such as textiles, steel/coal and agriculture. While such fears were later proven unfounded, the CEECs' 'export potential' clearly contributed to the hardening of the EC's position during the Association negotiations.

(iv) The timing of the bargain

Often, the timing the CEECs requests for improved EC offers was an important parameter for the size of their payoffs. For example, the EC's concessions in relation to the question of membership were the result of the first deadlock in the first wave of Association negotiations in April 1991. Had these concessions been discussed in September 1991 (under the pressure of the crisis in Yugoslavia and the USSR), the Visegrads' chances of securing a better deal would have been considerably higher.

(v) The East European applicants' ability to resist the EC's offers

Two important aspects should be taken into consideration here; firstly whether the participants of each wave were able to remain united in their opposition against the EC's offers; and secondly, how far were they prepared to go in order to push the EC into more generous offers. Notwithstanding their limited negotiating power during the Association bargain, empirical evidence suggests that in the very few times[11] the Association applicants stood united and determined to block the negotiations (i.e. April and September 1991) - and consequently threatened the EC's image as Eastern Europe's 'caring Hegemon' - they did manage to secure an incrementally better deal.

Notes

[1] The Association game can also be conceived as being *nested* into the entire network of games in which the Association applicants were involved during the period 1990-92. The focus of this chapter, however, will only be confined to the EC.

[2] The term 'peripheral' will be used throughout this book in order to describe games within the *Grand* game other than the Association game. However, the term is used in relation to the focus of this book and does not imply that the Association game was 'superior to' or 'more important' than other peripheral games.

[3] The MFA has historically operated as an exception to the multilateral discipline of the GATT. Under the MFA, countries negotiate quotas bilaterally in narrowly-defined product categories. Exporting (developing) countries negotiate annual quotas for individual products with individual importing (developed) countries. These quotas are administered by the exporting countries themselves, subject to some form of control by the importing countries. Therefore, they function as a form of voluntary export restraint (VER). For more details on the functioning of the MFA see Commission of the EC (1994: 488-489).

[4] It is estimated that between 1980 and 1990, employment in the steel industry fell by more than 40%. The problem was aggravated further by the fact that the biggest share of job losses occurred in areas which already suffered from high unemployment as a result of the decline of the EC's 'traditional' industries. See Barnes and Barnes (1995: 236).

[5] The issue of 'free movement of people' could be seen here as a possible exception. This, nevertheless, does not undermine its important economic dimension.

[6] For some early reflections on the new security system in Europe see Ullman (1991) and De Gust (1989).

[7] See, for example, speech by the US Secretary of State, James Baker, in West Berlin as reprinted in *Agence Europe*, 15.12.89.

[8] This figure refers to a limited number of games within the *Domestic Arena* which appeared to be relevant to the Association bargain.

[9] This figure refers to a limited number of games within the *International Arena* which appeared to be relevant to the Association bargain.

[10] Within the wider game theoretic tradition, the problems relating to the different interpretations attributed by individual negotiators to the concept of self-interest have been raised by Putnam (1988: 457). Decision making theorists have also elaborated on the difficulties of ensuring that all the participants of the decision making process have access to the same information and conceive complex problems in the same way. See, for example, Lindblom (1959: 79-81) and Etzioni (1967: 385-386).

[11] For more details on the first wave applicants' inability to remain united during their Association negotiations with the EC see Mayhew (1998: 42). For more details on the Bulgarian and Romanian inability to remain united see chapter 6.

PART II

THE NEGOTIATION OF THE SECOND WAVE OF EUROPE AGREEMENTS

4 Bulgarian and Romanian Attempts to Enter the Association Game: The Response of the EC's Member States

Part I examined the evolution of the EC's Association strategy in Eastern Europe since 1990 (chapter 2) and continued with the negotiation of the first wave of Europe agreements between the EC and the Visegrad countries in 1991 (chapters 2 and 3). It was argued that throughout this period the EC's main actors displayed considerable unity over the basic principles of the Association strategy, while internal disagreements concentrated almost exclusively upon sectoral rather than substantive policy choices. As a result of such widespread consensus, it was also argued that political leadership (i.e. European Council and General Affairs Council) within the EC managed to maintain firm (and relatively unchallenged) control over the Association process, including devising the general principles of the EAs as well as selecting the Association applicants.

The normalisation and strengthening of bilateral relations with the EC member states was, therefore, a necessary pre-requisite for all CEECs aspiring to Association with the EC. For Bulgaria and Romania, the process of normalising bilateral relations with the EC's member states began soon after the collapse of the Zhivkov and Ceausescu regimes in late 1989, but their efforts in this direction clearly intensified following their official request to start Association negotiations in March 1991.[1] This chapter examines the evolution of such bilateral relations throughout what can be called the pre-negotiation phase, that is the period starting with the Bulgarian and Romanian requests for Association negotiations in March 1991 and ending with the actual opening of the negotiations with the two countries in May 1992.

It will be argued that the pre-negotiation period was characterised by a 'political' rather than an 'economic' bargain. For both the Bulgarian and the Romanian governments the 'prize' of this initial period was the agreement of the EC leadership, in principle, to grant them entrance to the Association game. The details of the agreement were to be the 'prize' of a later bargain, this time economic in nature, into which the two countries would enter with the Commission following the Council's in-principle agreement for the beginning of Association negotiations. In this respect, this chapter will look at the build up to the making of a *fundamental* (Etzioni, 1967: 389) or else a *history making* decision (Peterson, 1995: 72). According to EC practice, such decisions are made by the 'senior' Councils, either the European Council or the General Affairs, at a level that "transcends the EC's day to day policy process" (Peterson, 1995: 72). Precisely because such decisions have a long term perspective, "...details and specifications are omitted so that an overview is feasible" (Etzioni, 1967: 390).

The highly political nature of the decision to allow Bulgaria and Romania to begin Association negotiations, as well as the senior level at which the decision was made, were both critical features of the pre-negotiation bargain. It is argued that the political nature of the pre-negotiation bargain allowed the EC leaders to embark upon an overwhelmingly positive rhetoric vis à vis the second wave applicants, which was dominated by 'good intentions' and promises of 'maximum support'. The positive rhetoric of the EC's leadership however, was clearly not reflected in the 'economic' bargain that began with the opening of Association negotiations with the East European applicants. The long and painful negotiations with the Visegrads in 1991 (see chapter 2) and to a greater extent the restricted mandate for Bulgaria and Romania in 1992 (see chapter 6) are both good examples of this. As one official from the Commission's DG VI put it: "When you examine negotiations in a particular sector, generalisations based on political arguments are not very helpful" (interview in the Commission's DG VI, 20.3.97). In the highly technical phase of the formation of the EC's negotiating position what mattered the most was not the 'good intentions' expressed by the EC's political leadership, but rather the accommodation of the EC's member states' national interests (Moravcsik 1991, 1994) and the need to ensure that the EC's offers to the CEECs would enjoy *ratification* (Putnam, 1988) within the EC's member states' domestic fronts.

In this respect, the study of the EC's member states' domestic politics is important in understanding the EC's offers to East European applicants during the Association negotiations. This chapter argues that while the EC's leadership appeared ready to offer a generous deal for Bulgaria and Romania, a number of powerful groups within key EC member states were already beginning to oppose such a prospect. The highly political nature of the pre-negotiation bargain left little leeway for those protectionist forces to have a significant impact during this initial period. As soon as the negotiations entered the technical phase however, their voices were to be clearly heard either through their national organisations or through their pan-European associations.

A final theme to be addressed in this chapter is that of patronage. The term is used to describe the patron-client relationship which has been developing since 1989 between some of the EU member states and one or more of the CEECs. In such relationships, the patron, usually in the name of close historical links and cultural proximity, acts as the main advocate of its client's Association with the EC. In return, the client not only recognises the patron as a model for its economic and political reforms, but also makes sure that it faithfully represents its patron's interests at a regional level. Of course, similar patron-client relationships are not new in EC practice. Relations between Greece and Cyprus and more recently between Germany and the Visegrads are some indicative examples. The importance of a good patron could be crucial in two domains: firstly to ensure that the client is included in the Association game as soon as possible and secondly, to ensure that the client's requests for generous trade concessions find a sympathetic audience within the Council. As will be argued later in this chapter, the cause of the second wave applicants was significantly weakened by the absence of strong and willing patrons. In the case of Bulgaria, the special relationship with Greece proved to be somewhat dubious (considering the disagreement between the two countries over the recognition of FYROM) and, in any case, relatively insignificant given Greece's limited influence within the EC. Romania's patrons (France and, to a lesser extent, Italy), though powerful, remained 'constrained' by their own domestic audience which, for a number of reasons, opposed the prospect of more generous concessions to the East European applicants.

This chapter looks at the evolution of the pre-negotiation bargain through the examination of bilateral relations between the second wave applicants and the EC's big three, Germany, France and Britain as well as with the EC's Southern flank including Italy, Spain, Portugal and Greece (from now on collectively referred to as 'the South'). While the selection of seven out of the then twelve EC member states does involve a degree of simplification, it is hoped that the analysis provided in this chapter excludes neither any EC member state with a special interest in the

Romanian and Bulgarian EAs nor any of those actors which, due to their relative power, acquired an exceptional importance for the EC's Association strategy in Eastern Europe.

Germany: second class applicants?

Amongst all the EC member states, Germany remained arguably the most ardent and consistent supporter of the CEECs' efforts to ensure speedy and far-reaching Association with the EC. The German government's commitment to strengthening the EC's links with Eastern Europe was based on the country's close historical ties with the region and also on the conviction that the CEECs integration into the EC was a historic necessity for guaranteeing security and prosperity in the post-Cold War Europe. Bonn's enthusiastic approach to the prospect of East European Association to the EC was backed not only by the fact that Germany remained by far the EC's largest investor (European Commission, 1994: 139) and trade partner in Eastern Europe (see Table 4.1), but also by a considerable cross-party consensus on this issue as well as by public opinion, which remained overwhelmingly sympathetic to the CEECs' cause (see Table 4.2).

Against this background, the Bulgarian and Romanian requests for the opening of Association negotiations were compatible with Bonn's vision of the 'new European architecture'. Moreover, the outbreak of the Yugoslav war and the need to avoid a wider regional conflagration further advanced the two Balkan applicants' cause in Germany. On the other hand, the Bulgarian and Romanian appeal in Germany continued to be weakened by the lack of geographical proximity, their modest progress towards reform as well as by their relative (in comparison to the Visegrads) insignificance to the German economy.

Table 4.1 Trade Between EU and Eastern Europe, 1991

	Exports (ECU millions)				Imports (ECU millions)			
	D	F	UK	I	D	F	UK	I
Poland	6,361	911	495	671	5,421	751	448	490
Czechoslovakia	3,720	606	184	353	3,805	465	187	479
Hungary	3,156	392	188	490	3,199	517	148	651
Romania	916	326	84	211	906	386	84	274
Bulgaria	598	237	51	193	399	125	53	135
All 5 CEECs	14,751	2,473	1,002	1,918	13,731	2,245	920	2,029
% World Total	3.0	0.9	1.5	1.4	2.8	0.8	1.8	1.38

Source: FMI, Direction of Trade Statistics, Washington 1995

Table 4.2 Opinions on EC's Assistance to Eastern Europe, December 1990

	D		F		UK		I		E		GR		P		EC-12	
	-	+	-	+	-	+	-	+	-	+	-	+	-	+	-	+
Speed up integration	13	74	14	72	20	64	5	85	8	67	8	74	8	72	13	71
Increase EC budget	23	62	31	56	22	64	15	72	14	60	15	67	13	66	22	62
Give EC Benefits	22	63	15	73	16	71	14	71	6	66	13	67	11	70	15	69
Offer Assoc/ Coop. treaty	14	68	21	64	17	64	16	64	11	59	16	60	15	60	16	64
Allow EC membership	16	66	21	62	14	69	9	74	5	65	11	68	15	60	15	66

Source: Eurobarometer (1990).

Normalising relations with Bulgaria and Romania

The collapse of communism and the achievement of re-unification opened a whole new chapter in the relations between Germany and Eastern Europe. While initial fears of the restoration of a new *Mitteleuropa* (Hauner, 1994: 27-34, Handl, 1993: 45-51) based on the development of bilateral relations with the CEECs outside the EC framework did cast some doubts over the future direction of the new Germany, it soon became apparent that the principle of *multilateralism* (Bulmer, 1996: 10-13), the cornerstone of German foreign policy throughout the post-war period, continued to dominate Bonn's strategy policy in Eastern Europe. Based on the conviction that the newly emerged democracies in the region needed to be institutionally linked within a multilateral framework, Germany soon emerged as the leading advocate of East European Association and entry into the EC.

The German policy of speedy EC Eastern enlargement was the product of four inter-related factors. Firstly, because of the strong historical and cultural links between Germany and the CEECs (especially the Visegrads) which had been violently interrupted by the Cold War. Secondly, by the huge economic potential of the region (both in terms of trade and investment opportunities) which in the past had been the centre of economic activity for German industrialists. Thirdly, by the belief that prolonged economic decline in the region could have serious security implications. As one senior official in the German Permanent Representation in the EU put it: "You cannot have for a long time countries on your borders that are economically disadvantaged" (interview, 21.3.97). Finally, and most importantly, by the conviction that "the unification of Germany is part of a wider process of the unification of

Europe" (interview in the German Permanent Representation to the EU, 21.3.97). As Chancellor Kohl put it, these two processes are: "...two sides of the same coin" (quoted in Ruhl, 1995: 33). In addition to the political support for the CEECs' cause within the EC, the importance of the German economy to the process of economic transition in Eastern Europe was also of fundamental importance. In 1991, Germany was the largest trade partner in Eastern Europe (see Table 4.1) while in 1992 37.4% of total EC foreign direct investment (FDI) in those countries came from German companies (European Commission 1994: 139).

German interests in Eastern Europe, and the key role that the German government had acquired in the development of East-West relations, were realised by both the Bulgarian and Romanian governments which soon sought to re-establish good relations with Bonn. Their strategy was based upon two basic considerations: firstly, that their countries should be rapidly granted associated status as a means of strengthening their economies and political systems and consequently act as stabilising factors in the troubled Balkans (the first signs of the Yugoslav tragedy were already visible); secondly, that Bulgaria and Romania should not be separated from the Visegrad countries and be treated as 'second class' applicants by the EU.[2] The period April 1991-May 1992 was therefore characterised by intense diplomatic activity aimed at full normalisation of relations between Bonn, Sofia and Bucharest.

In the case of Bulgaria, President Zhelyu Zhelev, accompanied by his Foreign Minister Victor Vulkov and other officials, paid a four-day visit to Germany on 2.9.91, where he held talks with the German President Richard von Weizsäcker, Chancellor Helmut Kohl and Foreign Minister Hans-Dietrich Genscher. The visit was perceived by the Bulgarian President as being extremely successful:

> What we were promised here exceeded our expectations. We are going home absolutely pleased *(BBC SWB*, 11/9/91: A1/3-4).

Indeed, the Bulgarian side had every reason to be happy. Germany had promised full support to the Bulgarian efforts to be admitted as a full member in the Council of Europe, to expand its co-operation with NATO, and most importantly, to begin negotiations for an Association agreement with the EU. Furthermore, the two countries agreed to sign a Treaty of Friendship and Co-operation by the end of October that same year. By the end of 1991, relations between Germany and Bulgaria continued to improve. As scheduled in the Bonn meeting, Hans-Dietrich Genscher visited Sofia on 9.10.91 for the formal signature of the 'Treaty of Friendship and Cooperation' in which the German commitment to support

Bulgarian incorporation into the European structures was repeated (*BBC SWB*, 11.10.91: i). Meanwhile, the Bulgarian election on 13.10.91 left scope for further improvement. The new government, led by Philip Dimitrov, was the first to be formed without the participation of the former Communist Party (now renamed the Bulgarian Socialist Party). The new government soon turned to Bonn for support. Foreign Minister Stoyan Ganev visited Germany on 13.1.92 where he held talks with his German counterpart and once again managed to assure support for the speedy conclusion of an Association agreement with the EU (*BBC SWB*, 24.1.92: A1/1).

In the Romanian case, relations with Bonn proved somewhat more difficult. In the first meeting between the Romanian Foreign Minister Adrian Nastase and Hans-Dietrich Genscher on 3.4.91 (*BBC SWB*, 6.4.91: A1/3), discussions were focused on the issue of the German minority in Romania and little was said about Romania's Association with the EU. Relations were further strained following the miners' strike and the demonstrations in Bucharest in September 1991, which finally led to the fall of Petre Roman's government and left the country in a deep political crisis (*BBC SWB*, 28.9.91 and Shafir, 1992).

However, the new government under Theodor Stolojan managed to temporarily stabilise the political climate, whilst the adoption of a new constitution in late November further assisted Romania to improve its international image. These positive developments in Bucharest seemed to please Germany and, on 12.3.92, a 'Treaty of Friendship and Co-operation' between the two countries (similar to that signed with Bulgaria and other East European countries) was initialled in Bonn (*BBC SWB*, 17.3.92: A1/3). In his official visit to Bucharest on 21.4.92 for the signature of the new treaty, Hans-Dietrich Genscher, following his meetings with the Romanian leadership, spoke positively for the first time about the prospect of a Romanian Association agreement with the EU:

Following the fall of the Iron Curtain there should not be a new frontier of poverty across Europe (*BBC SWB*, 25.4.92: A1/3).

The Romanian Foreign Minister Nastase was also optimistic:

...we rely on Germany's full assistance in our efforts regarding Romania's association with the European Community and the West European Union...and in general regarding our country's integration in European structures...(*BBC SWB*, 25.4.92: A1/3).

The domestic scope for German policy

On its domestic front, the German government's line on Eastern Europe faced little challenge. One year after his re-election as the 'Chancellor of unification', Helmut Kohl strongly committed himself to the effort of re-integrating Eastern European countries into the EU structures and enjoyed the full backing of the CDU/CSU coalition. The government's enthusiasm for this issue also extended to other political parties including the SPD and especially the FDP whose leader, and long-serving Foreign Minister of the Federal Republic, Hans-Dietrich Genscher, became one of the key actors in formulating German policy towards Eastern Europe (Bulmer and Paterson, 1996: 24; interview in the German Permanent Representation to the EU, 21.3.97) .

This broad consensus among German political parties reflected the mood of the German public opinion which, despite its enthusiasm for the process of 'deepening' EC integration, remained also overwhelmingly supportive of the prospect of the EC's 'widening'. According to data provided by Eurobarometer, in December 1990 the German public's support for the granting of Association status to the CEEC's was the highest within the EC, while eventual East European membership into the EC also received a positive reception within Germany (see Table 4.2). What is all the more astonishing however, is the fact that such a level of support was provided during a period of financial difficulty for the newly re-united Germany and the despite the country's position as the largest net contributor to the EC budget.

Clearly, the Bulgarian and Romanian efforts for Association with the EC were also assisted by the fact that the outbreak of hostilities in the former Yugoslavia quickly became a highly emotive issue for German public opinion and thus brought Chancellor Kohl under significant pressure to assert German foreign policy in order to stabilise the wider Balkan region. As a German official put it:

> It is true that the war in Yugoslavia drew more attention to these countries. Our concern then was to avoid the spreading of war to the neighbouring countries (interview in the German Permanent Representation to the EU, 21.3.97).

Central to this idea was the assumption that the stabilisation of the Balkans would ease the pressure of economic and political migration from Central and particularly Southeastern Europe which, in 1992, threatened to develop into a major socio-economic problem for the German Federal government (Marshall, 1992: 124-134).

Whilst on the political level the support for the EC's Eastern enlargement remained undisputed, *domestic ratification* (Putnam, 1988) for the strengthening of the EC-CEECs relations was not unconditional in all sections of German society. This was especially true for the German coal and steel industries. These sectors, already under pressure from rationalisation plans (e.g. 'the contract of the century'- Jahrhundertvertrag- resulting in 30,000 redundancies in the coal extraction sector alone) (*Agence Europe*, 12-13.11.91: 15), did not share their government's enthusiasm for rapid trade liberalisation with countries which had the potential for cheap coal and steel exports to the EC market. The support for a gradual and 'safeguarded' liberalisation process with the CEECs on behalf of the German metal workers was confirmed by senior European trade unionists (interview in the ETUI, 18.3.97) while a similar position on this issue can also be found in the speeches of the President of the German Steel Federation, Ruprecht Vondran (*Agence Europe*, 8.3.91: 13-14 and 28.5.92: 16).

Similar concerns were also voiced by agricultural groups, especially within highly concentrated agricultural regions such as Lower Saxony and Bavaria (interview in the German Permanent Representation to the EU, 21.3.97). The size of the German farming community, which in 1991 amounted to just under 1 million people (The Commission of the EC, 1993b), should not be underestimated. Nor should its political strength, especially in Bavaria, which was the constituency of the federal minister for agriculture Ignaz Kiechle and the power base of the governing coalition's junior partner, the Christian Social Union (CSU). As one official from the Commission's Directorate General for Agriculture put it:

Germany at a political level was very pushy, but when it comes to trade concessions, Germany is a country of farmers (interview in the Commission's Directorate General for Agriculture, 20.3.97).

It is therefore not surprising that, despite the commitment of the leadership to fast track trade liberalisation with the associated CEECs, German officials argued alongside the more protectionist delegations within the Council on several occasions. The imposition of safeguard measures against Czechoslovakian steel imports in August 1992 (see chapter 6) and also the deadlock of the Visegrad Association negotiations in September 1991(see chapter 2) are two indicative examples. The high degree of decentralisation and departmentalisation of the German policy making process (Bulmer and Paterson, 1996: 12, Philip, 1997: 4) did, of course, provide fertile ground for domestic protectionist forces to penetrate and influence the government's policy on sectoral issues (Sedelmeier, 1995: 16).

Conclusion

In an overall assessment of the period April 1991-May 1992, it can be argued that the Bulgarian and Romanian requests for Association agreements with the EU found a sympathetic audience within the German political leadership which had long argued in favour of the rapid integration of the CEECs into European structures. However, rather than being based on 'positive' political and economic incentives to integrate, as in the case of the Visegrads, support for Bulgaria and Romania mainly reflected concerns over potential negative 'externalities' (Cooper 1986: 292-293) that destabilisation in the two countries could produce i.e. the spreading of the Yugoslav war to the volatile wider Balkan region and further migratory pressures on the West.

In purely economic terms, the two Balkan countries had little appeal within German economic circles. German trade with Bulgaria and Romania for 1992 accounted for only 10% (see Table 4.1) of that conducted with the Visegrad three (Poland, Hungary and Czechoslovakia), while German investment in the two countries for 1992 amounted to 15 million DM, a tiny fraction of the Visegrad figure which for the same period exceeded 1.5 billion DM (UN ECE, 1994). The relatively insignificant economic interaction between Germany and the two Balkan countries, combined with the already existing (since the first wave of EAs negotiations) opposition of some domestic groups (i.e. coal and steel associations) to the prospect of fast track liberalisation did, of course, limit the enthusiasm of the German government over the prospect of the Bulgarian and Romanian Association to the EC, but not to the extent of threatening Bonn's decision to allow the two applicants to enter the Association game. The impact of domestic pressures as well as the absence of a significant incentive (i.e. large volume of trade or investment) for fast track trade liberalisation was to be seen more clearly in the position of the Germans during the elaboration of the EC's negotiating position vis à vis the second wave applicants and particularly in the insistence of the German delegation on the inclusion of a specific safeguard clause against steel imports from the two countries (see chapter 6).

It can, therefore, be argued that the Bulgarian and Romanian pre-negotiation strategy vis à vis Germany was only partially successful. The two Balkan countries did manage to secure Germany's approval for their entrance into the EC's Association game and by 1992 bilateral relations between Bonn, Sofia and Bucharest had been fully normalised. On the other hand however, neither the Bulgarian nor the Romanian governments were successful in persuading German policy makers to put their countries on an equal footing with the Visegrad three. After all, economic and political reforms in Central Europe were far more advanced whilst geographical and cultural proximity proved to be a strong incentive for the development of closer relations. The relegation of Bulgaria and Romania into 'second class' applicants was most clearly reflected in the words of the German Foreign Minister, Hans-Dietrich Genscher who, in March 1992, was predicting full EC membership for the Visegrad 'darlings'[3] before the turn of the century, whilst for the two Balkan applicants he reluctantly suggested that "...the door should be open for later membership" (*The Financial Times*, 23.3.92).

France: the reluctant patron

The French policy vis à vis the CEECs shared little of the German enthusiasm and from an early stage gave a rather lukewarm (if not hostile) reception to calls for the speedy integration of the former communist countries into the EC. On a political level, the French President had invested much of his personal prestige in the relaunch of EC integration and the EMU project to allow them to fall 'victims' of a carelessly prepared 'widening'. Moreover, the anxieties generated by the events of 1989 and the German unification reinforced Mitterrand's conviction that the new European challenges (as well as the French national interest) could only be met through the deepening of co-operation between the existing EC member states. Mitterrand's reluctance over more generous EC concessions to the CEECs' appeared to be in accordance with the scepticism of the French public opinion (see Table 4.2), while the majority of the French political elite effectively supported (though often not publicly!) his commitment to a 'deeper' rather than a 'wider' EC.

Economically, the French stakes in Eastern Europe were also limited. Investment (European Commission, 1994: 139) and trade (see Table 4.1) with the CEECs were rather moderate, while certain 'sensitive' sections of the French economy (i.e. agriculture) were expected to be hit hard by the trade liberalisation envisaged in the EAs. Amongst the second wave of Association applicants there is little doubt that Romania, in both political and economic terms, remained a much more 'useful' ally to France than Bulgaria. However, wider French reservations over the EC's relations with the CEECs clearly restricted the Romanian government's ability to exploit the full potential of its special relationship with Paris and advance further its Association aspirations.

Normalising relations with Bulgaria and Romania

The dramatic changes in Eastern Europe following the collapse of the Berlin Wall in 1989 shocked some of the fundamental principles which guided French foreign policy for most of the post-war period. The Franco-German axis, the cornerstone of the French policy in Europe, was now facing the prospect of a united Germany, freed from the constraints of the Cold War and seemingly ready to reassert its traditionally close relations in Eastern Europe. Moreover, calls for a fast-track eastwards EC enlargement threatened to derail plans for the deepening of co-operation amongst existing EC members which had been a top priority for French foreign policy since the mid-'80s (*Financial Times*, 17.6.91).

Driven by its relatively low-levels of economic penetration in Eastern Europe and the conviction that closer relations with the newly emerged democracies in the region should not jeopardise the process of the EC's deepening, France soon emerged as the leading force against the rapid eastwards EC enlargement, acting as a counterweight to the political impetus provided in this direction by Germany and Britain (each for different reasons). As such, the French government was a key actor for the timing and terms under which the CEECs' would become associated to the EC. This was realised by both the Bulgarian and Romanian governments which soon moved towards normalising their relations with Paris.

In Romania, President Iliescu viewed the strengthening of bilateral relations with France as one of his government's main foreign policy priorities and as the first step towards his country's rehabilitation following a long period of isolation under the Ceausescu regime. In fact, Bucharest's efforts to revitalise the traditionally close relations between the two countries found a receptive audience in Paris. Roland Dumas was the first EC Foreign Minister to visit Romania in January 1990 (*Financial Times*, 12.1.90), while a few months later President Mitterrand was the first Western leader to visit the country after the 1989 revolution promising his full support for both the process of political and economic reforms and the newly formed NSF (National Salvation Front) government.

Meetings between the political leadership of the two countries continued on a regular basis throughout the period March 1991-May

1992. In his second visit to Bucharest on 18-19.4.91, President Mitterrand met both the Romanian President Iliescu and Prime Minister Roman, and good relations between Paris and Bucharest were once again reaffirmed. In the same visit, important meetings also took place between Romanian officials and the French Minister Delegate for European Affairs Elisabeth Guigou, as well as between the two Foreign Ministers Nastase and Dumas, who discussed the possibility of the signing of a 'Friendship and Co-operation Treaty' later the same year (*BBC SWB*, 24.4.91: A1).

Further French assistance was also promised in July 1991 during the visit of the Romanian Prime Minister Petre Roman to Paris where he held meetings with the French leadership, including President Mitterrand, Prime Minister Edith Cresson and Foreign Minister Roland Dumas. The issue of the EC-Romanian Association Agreement was also discussed and Roman urged for solid French support. Interestingly, the Romanian Premier in his interview on French TV, tried to connect the achievements of his country with those of the Visegrad countries and not with those of Bulgaria (despite the fact that the EC's institutions and most EC's member states were treating Bulgaria and Romania as a 'group' with different characteristics from that of the Visegrad countries):

> Our countries - Poland, Czechoslovakia, Romania - had after all made enormous steps towards a market economy and in economic reform and it would be a pity, if not dangerous, to forget us at the very moment when our economic reforms are bearing fruit (*BBC SWB*, 25.7.91: A2-3).

Relations between France and Romania reached their peak on 20.11.91 when the two countries signed a 'Treaty of Friendship and Co-operation' in Paris (4 months earlier than a similar agreement was signed by Romania and Germany). This new treaty not only strengthened the already close ties between Paris and Bucharest and provided for regular top-level meetings, but most importantly committed France "to favour the development and deepening of the relations between Romania and the European Community" and "to back the conclusion of an agreement of association of Romania with the EC" (*BBC SWB*, 27.11.91: A1/2).

Relations between Paris and Sofia, on the other hand, remained on a relatively good level throughout the period March 1991-May 1992, but top level contacts were not as frequent as in the case of Romania. The visit of the Bulgarian Premier Popov to Paris on 4.6.91 for example, was rather undermined by the French leadership, as the Bulgarian Prime Minister was seen neither by the French President nor by Prime Minister Cresson (*BBC SWB*, 7.6.91: A1/1). The first top-level contact did not take place until 21.2.92 when the Bulgarian President Zhelev visited Paris (accompanied by his Foreign Minister Ganev), and met with the French leadership, including President Mitterrand and Prime Minister Cresson. During the visit a 'Treaty of Friendship and Cooperation' was signed, similar to those signed between France and other Eastern European countries, including Romania just three months before. The treaty, as expected, fully normalised relations between the two countries and stated French commitment to assist "the early conclusion of an association agreement between Bulgaria and the European Community" (*BBC SWB*, 21.2.91: A1/1). The optimism surrounding relations between France and Bulgaria was reflected in Mitterrand's statement after the signature of the treaty that the two nations were again good neighbors just as at the time of Charlemagne, and were "...citizens of one homeland, the homeland of freedom" (*BBC SWB*, 21.2.91: A1/1).

The domestic scope for French policy

The normalisation of relations between France and the two Balkan countries in question created a climate of optimism, leading to the signature of the Co-operation and Friendship treaties in which Paris was committed to assisting both Bulgaria and Romania in their efforts for a rapid conclusion of their Association agreements with the EC. However, the supportive declarations of the French leadership hardly reflected the country's readiness to accept the political and economic consequences of East European Association to the EC.

The French government continued to be fully committed to the process of EC deepening and naturally remained sceptical towards widening (Kramer, 1993: 221-22). President Mitterrand himself on many occasions warned that EC integration should not be "diluted" (*Financial Times*, 20.9.91) by enlargement, whilst making it clear that he would not allow the "Community to become a vague free trade area, as certain Community countries wanted from the first day" (*Financial Times*, 13.9.91). In fact, Mitterrand's scepticism over the prospect of a speedy EC eastwards enlargement had become apparent since an early stage. Launching his idea of a pan-European Confederation on New Year's Eve 1989, the French President argued along the lines of Gorbachev's 'common European home', where Eastern and Western Europe would unite "in a joint and permanent organisation of exchange, peace and security". His design, however, made no mention of the CEECs' entry into the EC. Instead, the project would be based on the 1975 Helsinki Final Act, with the participation of all 35 signatories including the USSR as well as the US and Canada (*Financial Times*, 2.1.90).

The idea of a pan-European Confederation was re-launched by the French President in June 1991 during the Prague Conference (*The Financial Times*, 12.6.91). Once again the plan remained ambiguous since the exact purpose and institutional design of the Confederation were never really clarified. Initial reports suggested that the proposal was inspired by the 1948 Hague Conference (in which Mitterrand himself was among the participants) which eventually led to the creation of the Council of Europe. Critics, however, argued that the proposal went no further than mentioning areas in which ad hoc co-operation between European governments was possible and which, when added together could be called a European Confederation. Not surprisingly, Mitterrand's idea (at the heart of which lay his commitment to the uninterrupted completion of the EC's deepening process) never really took off the ground since it was met with suspicion by the CEECs which, particularly after the August coup in Moscow, remained resolutely opposed to any proposal not leading to eventual full EC membership (*The Financial Times*, 12.6.91).

The scepticism of the French President over the CEECs relations with the EC was fiercely criticised by his domestic opponents. Jacques Chirac, the leader and presidential candidate of the Gaullists (RPR), attacked Mitterrand for replacing the Berlin wall "...by a new wall made of money" (*The Financial Times*, 13.9.91), while Alain Juppe, Secretary General of the RPR, referring to Mitterrand's response to the Moscow coup stated that the French President "...simply isn't up to it" (*Keesing's Record of World Events*, 38445). Despite the attacks against Mitterrand however, neither Jacques Chirac (leader of the RPR) nor Giscard d' Estaing (leader of the UDF) seriously challenged the basic principles of the French policy in Europe. This was demonstrated by the two men's backing of the "yes" vote in the French referendum over the Maastricht treaty, despite serious divisions within their own parties (*Keessing's Record of World News*, 39081-2). Moreover, the sincerity of Chirac's and Giscard's commitment to Eastern Europe can also be brought into question given the fact that the two leaders gave their full personal backing to the farmers' demonstrations over reduced CAP subsidies in Paris in September 1991 (*Keessing's Record of World News*, 38466), while both their parties opposed the Socialist government's decision to reduce protection for the French farmers through GATT and the CAP reform (Assemblé Nationale, 1992a: 509-516; 1991a: 2378-2380 and 1992c: 1723-1728).

Alongside with France's mainstream political parties, French members of the European Parliament also demonstrated a low level of interest over the strengthening of the EC's relations with the CEECs (interview in the European Parliament, Directorate General 2, 20/3/1997). It is indicative that by the end of 1992, none of the seven major Inter-Parliamentary Delegations of the EP dealing with Eastern Europe was chaired by a French MEP.[4]

Arguably the politicians' indifference to, if not scepticism over, the CEECs' Association with the EC was in line with the country's more general attitude towards Eastern Europe. French public opinion remained amongst the most reluctant in the EC regarding the prospects of closer co-operation with the CEECs. 21% (the highest amongst all EC member states) of the French population opposed the idea of granting Association status to the CEECs, while only 61% (the second smallest after Portugal) supported eventual East European membership into the EC. The scepticism regarding the strengthening of the EC's relations with the CEECs was clearly associated with the wider French sensitivities over the unification of Germany. Moreover, 31% (the highest amongst member states) of the French public opposed the prospect of increasing the EC budget in order to support the newly emerged democracies in Eastern Europe (see Table 4.2). In short, while public mood in France, like in Germany, remained overwhelmingly positive towards the 'deepening' of EC integration, the French did not share the view of their German neighbours that the EC's 'deepening' and 'widening' could proceed as two parallel processes.

In economic terms, France's penetration of Eastern European markets was also limited. By the mid 1993, French investment in the Visegrad countries was less than half of that of Germany, accounting for 13.8% of the EC total (European Commission, 1994: 139). Moreover, in 1991 the 5-CEECs shared less than 1% of the total French foreign trade, whilst French exports to these countries for the same period amounted to 2.4 billion ECUs, a figure almost six times smaller than that of Germany (see Table 4.1). With particular reference to the two Balkan applicants, it can be argued that while Bulgaria and Romania accounted for 25% of French trade with the 5-CEECs (compared with only 10% in the case of Germany), their overall economic significance for France was hardly noticeable. Despite the fact that France ranked third amongst foreign investors in the two countries, the total French capital invested was, by mid-1993, a moderate $78 million (EKEM, 1993).

Calls for the strengthening of the EC's relations with the CEECs, therefore, found a rather sceptical audience among France's political leadership, while the appeal of the region to the French public and the country's industrialists was also limited. The prospects of domestic ratification (Putnam, 1988) of a generous Association deal for the CEECs were hindered further by the opposition of key interest groups within the French economy, especially that of the farming lobby. While by 1992 only 5.3% of the working population was employed in agriculture (European Commission, 1993b: T20-21), the strength of the French farming lobby remained undisputed. Its 200,000 strong demonstration in Paris on 29.9.91 and the continuous disruption caused by the FNSEA (Federation Nationale des Syndicats d'Exploitants Agricoles) throughout October 1991 brought the Socialist government under great pressure to protect the income of rural France (*Keesing's Record of World Events*, 38446; 38544; 38942).

Domestic pressure by the farming lobby was soon translated into the hardening of the French position at a European level, as was clearly shown on at least three occasions during the last months of 1991: firstly, when France vetoed the proposals for more generous agricultural concessions to the Visegrad Association applicants in September 1991 (see chapter 2); secondly, when in the same month the French government vigorously opposed the proposals of Commissioner Mac Sharry for the reform of the Common Agriculture Policy (CAP) (see chapter 3); and finally, in December 1991, when the French Agriculture Minister Louis Mermaz denounced the Dunkel document[5] concerning the conclusion of the Uruguay Round as being "the ruin of European agriculture" (*Keesing's Record of World Events*, 38746).

Conclusion

Summarising the pre-negotiation bargain between Paris, Sofia and Bucharest, it can be argued that by early 1992, both Balkan applicants had fully normalised their bilateral relations with France and had secured Paris' agreement in principle for their entry into the Association game. The same period however, is also characterised by the gradual 'hardening' of French policy in relation to the EC's Association strategy in Eastern Europe. Mitterrand's relaunch of the proposal for a European Confederation in June 1991 revealed the growing French scepticism about the drive towards widening which was boosted (even though not designed for) by the EC's decision to grant associated status to the CEECs. Further evidence of Paris' reluctance came to light in September 1991 with the decision to veto further trade concessions to the Visegrads, only weeks after the dramatic events in Moscow and despite widespread opposition within the EC.

Concerns over the impact of the changes in Eastern Europe on the balance of power within the EC, limited economic interaction with the countries in the region, as well as significant domestic opposition against the prospect of fast-track trade liberalisation with the CEECs lay at the heart of French policy vis-à-vis Eastern Europe during the second half of 1991. In this respect, the French reluctance over the strengthening of the CEECs' relations with the EC was inseparably linked with the question of German unification and its feared effects on the Franco-German axis which, for many decades, had been the cornerstone of the French European policy. In economic terms, the relatively small volumes of French trade and investment in the region failed to provide a strong incentive for co-operation, whilst militant opposition against the liberalisation of agricultural trade by the farming lobby further reduced the appeal of Eastern Europe amongst French policy makers.

Whilst these concerns never really escalated so as to threaten the French government's decision to give its in principle agreement for the Bulgarian and the Romanian bids for EC Association, they nevertheless deprived the two Balkan applicants from a powerful ally which could advance their cause within the EC in a similar manner to Germany's patronage of the Visegrad applicants. This is particularly true for Romania, which based on close historical, cultural and economic links with France, relied heavily on Paris' support in order to improve its image in the West. While the frequency and closeness of bilateral contacts at the highest level reveals the willingness of the French leadership to undertake the role of the patron for its "Latin Sister",[6] Paris' support for Romania's Association bid, being inevitably limited by a number of political (e.g. absolute priority given to EC deepening) and economic (e.g. opposition of the farming lobby) considerations, could hardly match that provided by Germany for the first wave applicants.

Britain: a selfish but welcomed ally

Alongside Germany, Britain was arguably the most enthusiastic supporter of the CEECs' Association and early entry into the EC. The support provided by the two governments for the CEECs' cause, however, was based on rather different considerations. Britain, in comparison to Germany, had limited historical bonds with Eastern Europe, while its economic involvement in the region during the post-communist period was modest (see Table 4.1). Moreover, unlike the German government, which largely saw the processes of the EC's widening and deepening as supplementary (rather than mutually exclusive), the Conservative British government sought to use widening as a tool for resisting what it saw as an unwanted drive towards the creation of a European super-state.

The British government's enthusiasm for the EC's widening was further assisted by a predominately Eurosceptic public opinion (see Table 4.2), by the relatively weak opposition of sectoral interest groups to the prospect of fast track trade liberalisation with the CEECs, and also by the agreement of all political parties in the House of Commons about the need for a speedy and far-reaching integration of the former communist countries into the EC. As far as the second wave applicants were concerned, both Bulgaria and Romania proved rather unpopular (as compared with other CEECs) for British exporters and investors (see Table 4.1 and EKEM, 1993). Nevertheless, both countries' requests for entry into the Association game clearly benefited by the British government's commitment to the EC's widening.

Normalizing relations with Bulgaria and Romania

Soon after the collapse of the Berlin Wall, Britain emerged as one of the keenest supporters of East European Association with the EC. As early as September 1990, and despite the initial reluctance by most of her EC counterparts, British Prime Minister Margaret Thatcher had already gone beyond the Association Agreements by proposing entry of CEECs into the EC at the earliest possible date (*Financial Times*, 6.9.90). The British position remained unchanged under John Major's leadership, following Mrs Thatcher's resignation in November 1990. During his visit to Germany in June 1991, the new Prime Minister, talking to the CDU headquarters, followed his predecessor's rhetoric:

> ...outside our Community the strongholds of Communism in the East have crumbled...Hungarians, Poles, Czechoslovaks, Bulgarians and others look to our European Community for inspiration, hope and support. They must not, and I trust will not, look in vain."(*European Access*, 1991(3): 7-9).

The British leadership confirmed the pursuit of the widening agenda even in front of the unsympathetic French audience:

> We in the European Community cannot say: 'Here is our club, we have made the rules, and we will make new rules regardless of your interests' (*Financial Times*, 13.9.91).

Indeed, a quick Eastern European Association and eventual entry into the EC was compatible with London's long-term economic and political objectives: in the sphere of economics, the EAs were moving towards the elimination of trade barriers between the East and West. Britain, being one of the biggest trading powers in Europe but also led by a neo-liberal Conservative government, had long ago expressed its determination to fight the protectionist tendencies within the EC. Signs of this long term British strategy can be traced back to the early and mid '80s and can be seen in all major international negotiations including the Single European Act, the Maastricht Treaty, the reform of the Common Agricultural Policy (CAP) and the GATT.

On a political level, the Association agreements were seen by British foreign policy as the first step towards future EC Eastern enlargement. The possibility of a Community comprising 20-25 member states could only be attractive to the British policy makers, since it would inevitably slow down the process of 'deepening' and bring the EC closer to the British vision of an extended free trade area based on intergovernmental co-operation. Relations between the UK, Bulgaria and Romania for the period under examination (March 1991-May 1992) continued to improve steadily, despite the fact that the British Prime Minister did not meet with any of the leaders of the two Balkan countries.[7] During his official visit to Britain on 7-11.5.91, the Romanian Foreign Minister Nastase not only denied that relations between Bucharest and London were under strain, but appeared rather optimistic: "...I think that there is an openness which will have effects not only on a political but also on an economic plane" (*BBC SWB*, 16.5.91: A1/2.).

Similarly successful was the visit of the British Permanent Under-secretary of State for Foreign and Commonwealth affairs Sir David Gillmore to Bulgaria on 18.6.91. The Foreign Office official held meetings with the Bulgarian leadership (including President Zhelev, Prime Minister Popov, and Foreign Minister Vulkov) and after recognising "that the Bulgarians had a strong will for change", promised further development of bilateral relations (*BBC SWB*, 25.6.91: A1/2). Furthermore, during the first six months of 1991 both Bulgaria and Romania were included in the British 'Know How' funds, offering assistance towards effective management, banking reform, and privatisation. Finally, close co-operation was also developed in the field of defence following the visits of British military delegations to the two Balkan capitals in February 1992 (*BBC SWB*, 6.2.92: A1/6 and 13.2.92: A1/2).

The domestic scope for British policy

On the domestic front, the British government's policies towards Eastern Europe faced little opposition. In January 1990, initial discussions in the House of Commons concerning the revolutions in Eastern Europe revealed a broad consensus amongst the major political forces over the need for closer relations between the EC and the CEECs. The Conservative Minister of State for the Foreign and Commonwealth office, Francis Maude was keen to leave the door to EC enlargement open:

> I do not think that the Community can insist forever that Europe will be divided between its present 12 members and others. If others wish to join and can meet the Community's demanding standards, we should not prevent them (*The House of Commons Parliamentary Debates*, 31.1.90: 339).

The Labour spokesman George Foulkes on the other hand, while not as enthusiastic as the Conservative FCO Minister on the issue of enlargement, did nevertheless argue for the need of the CEECs to become associated with the EC:

> ...in Eastern Europe democracy will need to be established and consolidated and economies developed and stabilised before integration into the Community can be contemplated. Clearly other forms of association are both possible and desirable (*The House of Commons Parliamentary Debates*, 31.1.90: 342).

Perhaps the most overwhelming support for the CEECs was given by the Social and Liberal Democrats which at the time represented the most pro-European forces in the House of Commons. Arguing along the German line that the widening and deepening of the EC were complementary rather than mutually exclusive Paddy Ashdown (LP) was already contemplating the establishment of a free trade area, while David Owen (SDP) suggested that the Visegrad countries could become full EC members by the end of the decade (*The House of Commons Parliamentary Debates*, 31.1.90: 331 and 348).

The widespread support for the CEECs' requests for ever-closer relations with the EC was restated by all major political forces in Britain in early 1992, during the House of Commons discussion of the EC Association agreements with the Visegrad countries (*The House of Commons Parliamentary Debates*, 17.2.92: 126-152). The FCO Minister Tristan Garel-Jones, despite criticisms from Eurosceptics of his own party (i.e. Sir Teddy Taylor and Phillip Oppenheim) that John Major's government did little to stop protectionist tendencies within the EC, insisted that the EAs were a step in the right direction, while also praising "British leadership ...in setting up the Association agreements...and pushing for them within the Community". (*The House of Commons Parliamentary Debates*, 17.2.92: 131). The Labour Party spokesman George Robertson on the other hand, departing from the slight caution with which his party treated the prospect of eastwards EC enlargement back in 1990, was now calling the trade provisions envisaged by the EAs "too conservative", whilst urging that the EC "...shall have to go well beyond the measures in the agreements to ensure that full membership is attainable and possible" (*The House of Commons Parliamentary Debates*, 17.2.92: 131-134). Indicative of the overall consensus on the principle of East European Association with the EC is the fact that the motion urging for early ratification of the Visegrad EAs received a unanimous vote in the House of Commons.

This broad parliamentary support for the EAs was hardly surprising. In addition to serving the British government's political objective of weakening the drive towards further EC integration, closer relations with the CEECs made economic sense too. In the aftermath of the conclusion of the First Generation agreements between the EC and the five CEECs, the British trade balance in the region rocketed to a surplus of 468 million ECUs in 1992 (from a deficit of 122 million ECUs in 1989) (FMI, 1995). Domestic ratification (Putnam, 1988) of generous EC concessions to the associated CEECs was also facilitated for two more reasons. Firstly, because the farming lobby did not forcefully object to the prospect of trade liberalisation within the context of the EAs. While the Ministry of Agriculture, Fisheries and Food (MAFF) did come under pressure to take action against cheap imports in certain product categories (*The House of Commons Parliamentary Debates*, 17.2.92: 148-152), the overall opposition to the agreements by the National Farmers Union (NFU) was hardly comparable to that of its counterparts in France, the EC's South or even Germany. This lack of significant domestic opposition can be explained by the small number of people employed in agriculture as well as by the historically high competitiveness of the British farming industry which, in the early 1990s, remained largely supportive of the Conservative government's determination to reform the CAP and liberalise world trade in agriculture (*Financial Times*, 1.5.91).

The second reason facilitating domestic ratification (Putnam, 1988) of a generous EC offer vis à vis CEECs relates to the British coal and steel industries. Unlike most of its European counterparts, the British government had already embarked upon radical rationalisation plans in both industries since the mid-1980s involving widespread privatisations and the curtailing of trade union powers. As a result, by the early '90s the voices which could have potentially opposed rapid trade liberalisation within the EAs' framework had been significantly weakened, thus leaving the British position on this matter to be almost fully dominated by the free trade agenda pursued by the Department of Trade and Industry (DTI) (Sedelmeier, 1995: 9-10).

Conclusion

On a political level, Britain remained one of the most ardent supporters of the CEECs' Association and early accession into the European Community. The British position on this matter, shaped by Margaret Thatcher in late 1989, was followed with equal zeal by John Major when he succeeded her in late 1990, but also enjoyed considerable support by all major political forces within the House of Commons. However, the supportive declarations by the British political elite hardly matched the level of economic inter-penetration between Britain and Eastern Europe. The figures in this respect are revealing. In 1991, British exports to the 5-CEECs reached a moderate 1,002 million ECUs (see Table 4.1), a figure which was smaller than that of France or Italy and less than 10% of the German total. Moreover, by 1993, British foreign direct investment (FDI) accounted on average for only 3.3% of the total amount invested in the same five countries. This share was five times smaller than that of Germany, one third of the Italian and half of that of France (European Commission, 1994: 137-139). Finally, for the period 1990-91 within the framework of the G-24 assistance to Eastern Europe, Britain spent less on grants to the region than Denmark or Netherlands, while British overall assistance to the CEECs over the same period, as a percentage of the donors' GDP, was only greater than that of the EC's three poorest member states, Ireland, Portugal and Greece (see Table 4.3).[8]

All evidence, therefore, suggests that the enthusiasm of the British government over the prospect of the CEECs Association to the EC was neither in proportion to its willingness to increase public expenditure, nor to the performance of Britain's exporters to the region. Instead, this enthusiasm can be better understood in relation to the impact of the EC deepening process on British politics. It is clear that the Conservative government, deeply divided at that time over Europe, sough to use the EC-CEECs relations as the Trojan horse which would redirect the EC's agenda away from the undesirable and domestically damaging drive towards EMU and Political Union. The Conservative government's enthusiasm over CEECs Association was, indeed, facilitated by the lack of significant domestic constraints (i.e. farming lobby), but also by the fact that the Labour party also remained sceptical about the process of EC deepening and therefore did not seriously challenge the government's policy.

Table 4.3 G-24 Assistance for Central and Eastern Europe, 1990-1991

	Total Assistance	Grants ECU million	%	Credits ECU million	%	Assistance/ GDP
EC/ECSC/EIB	6,994.20	1,521.7	21.8	5,472.50	78.2	-
Belgium	165.88	0.00	0.0	165.88	100.0	0.104
Denmark	320.77	268.67	83.8	52.10	16.2	0.302
France	1,798.36	215.98	12.0	1,582.38	88.0	0.186
Germany	6,224.48	2,477.57	39.8	3,746.91	60.2	0.490
Greece	31.56	6.19	19.6	25.37	80.4	0.057
Ireland	0.90	0.90	100.0	0.00	0.0	0.003
Italy	1,345.38	424.66	31.6	920.72	68.4	0.146
Luxembourg	22.50	2.10	9.3	20.40	90.7	0.308
Netherlands	296.39	77.07	26.0	219.32	74.0	0.128
Portugal	2.00	0.00	0.0	2.00	100.0	0.004
Spain	476.92	4.41	0.9	472.51	99.1	0.112
UK	671.40	39.61	5.9	631.79	94.1	0.080
Total Community	18,350.74	5,038.86	27.5	13.311.88	72.5	0.362

Source: European Commission (1992a)

As far as British relations with Bulgaria and Romania are concerned, it is arguable that while bilateral relations did improve steadily during the period March 1991-May 1992, the two Balkan applicants remained in a second, slower track compared to the Visegrad countries. On a political level, the British government's preoccupation with first wave applicants was reflected by the decision not to include Bulgaria and Romania in Margaret Thatcher's (*Financial Times*, 17.9.90) and John Major's (*BBC SWB*, 29.5.92: A1/1-4) East European tours in September 1990 and May 1992 respectively, but also by the infrequent meetings between the British political leadership with their Romanian and Bulgarian counterparts. In economic terms, the second wave applicants were also of limited importance for Britain. While Romania did attract relatively more attention than Bulgaria for British investors, Britain's combined FDI in the two countries by mid-1993 was a moderate $81 million (EKEM, 1993). Moreover, in 1991 Bulgaria and Romania accounted for just over 10% of British exports to the 5-CEECs, while for the same period, Britain's trade surplus with the Visegrads (Poland,

Hungary and Czechoslovakia) reached 83 million ECUs as compared with the 2 million ECUs deficit with the two Balkan countries (see Table 4.1).

Nevertheless, the priority given to the Visegrad group did not jeopardise the Bulgarian and Romanian Association bids. On the contrary, the British government's determination to use Eastern Europe as a tool for directing the EC's attention away from the deepening process, meant that all CEECs Association applicants would enjoy London's blessing. In this respect, both Bulgaria and Romania found in Britain a selfish, yet welcome ally.

The southern member states: a coherent group?

The reaction of the Southern EC member states to the prospect of closer cooperation between the EC and the CEECs has not been a uniform one. It is true that the trade liberalisation envisaged by the Association agreements with the CEECs did present the South with certain common problems, particularly in the sensitive sectors of steel, textiles and, above all, agriculture. Moreover, in the longer term, an eastwards EC enlargement could prove threatening for the South's institutional position within the EC (e.g. the issue of 'flexibility') as well as for the commitments available to it from the EC's Structural Funds

On the other hand, each of the Southern EC member states shared considerably different degrees of economic and political interest in Eastern Europe. These differences were even more striking in the case of the second wave of Association applicants. For example, the Spanish and Portuguese involvement in the two Balkan countries was limited in both economic and political terms. On the contrary, Bulgaria and Romania remained important economic partners for Greece and, to a lesser extent, Italy (see Table 4.4).

Table 4.4 EC's South Trade with Bulgaria and Romania, 1991-1992

	South's Exports (ECU mil.)				South's Imports (ECU mil.)			
	Bulgaria		Romania		Bulgaria		Romania	
	1991	1992	1991	1992	1991	1992	1991	1992
Italy	193.0	169.0	211.0	385.0	135.0	180.0	274.0	280.0
Greece	71.0	129.0	68.6	83.0	126.0	124.3	74.5	52.4
Spain	9.4	13.6	24.1*	21.9	19.8	29.2	54.6*	51.9
Portugal	4.0	5.6	5.0*	3.5	3.0	3.4	1.2*	1.8

Source: Eurostat, 1994a   *1990

Most importantly however, the two countries possessed significant geo-strategic value for both the Italian and the Greek policies in the fragile Balkans; a link which clearly influenced Rome's and Athens' responses to the Bulgarian and Romanian requests for entry into the Association game.

Normalizing relations with Bulgaria and Romania

During the period March 1991-May 1992, the Bulgarian and Romanian leaderships held numerous meetings with their 'Southern' counterparts. These contacts provided the two Balkan countries with the opportunity to either fully normalise bilateral relations (as in the case of Spain and Portugal) or to sign 'Friendship and Co-operation' treaties (as in the case of Italy and Greece) in which they received reassurances of support for their Association bids.

Although relations with Spain developed at a relatively slow pace, by May 1992 they had reached a satisfactory level, and both the Bulgarian and Romanian Foreign Ministers managed to secure Madrid's support for the beginning of EA negotiations with the EC.[9] The case of Portugal is also of interest, as Lisbon acquired an exceptional importance to the two Balkan applicants since it held the EC presidency for the first half of 1992, a period in which the decision for the beginning of the negotiations was finally taken. First to meet the Portuguese Foreign Minister and forthcoming President of the General Affairs Council, Pinheiro, was the Romanian Foreign Minister Nastase during his visit to Portugal on 6.12.91. In addition to the discussions about the bilateral relations between the two countries, the agenda also included the issue of Romanian Association with the EC, and Foreign Minister Pinheiro promised that the negotiations would start during the Portuguese presidency (*BBC SWB*, 11.12.91: A1/2). The visit of the Bulgarian Foreign Minister Ganev to Portugal on 28-29.4.92 was equally successful, during which he received reassurances regarding full Portuguese support for Bulgaria's efforts to conclude its Association Agreement with the EC (*BBC SWB*, 2.5.92: A1/2-3).

Good relations with Rome were also one of the top priorities for both Bulgarian and Romanian foreign policy. Italy was amongst the biggest investors and trade partners in Southeast Europe (see Table 4.4 and EKEM, 1993) as well as an influential player within the EC. The improvement in bilateral relations, which had grown steadily since 1989, reached its climax in July 1991 and January 1992 when Italy signed 'Friendship and Co-operation' treaties with Romania and Bulgaria respectively. On both occasions the Italian Foreign Minister De Michelis praised Sofia's and Bucharest's policies towards the Yugoslav problem, urged for a more equal treatment of all CEECs by the EC, and promised Rome's full support in their efforts to integrate into the European structures.[10]

Finally, in Greece, the process of full normalisation of bilateral relations with the two Balkan applicants, especially with Bulgaria, proved somewhat more difficult. Indeed, Bulgaria's early commitment to recognise the former Yugoslav Republic of Macedonia (FYROM) under the name Macedonia initially jeopardised relations with Greece. The two countries however, gradually managed to set aside their differences over FYROM and soon developed close co-operation at all levels. Indicative of these good bilateral relations is the fact that, during the second half of 1991, the Greek Prime Minister Mitsotakis met with his Bulgarian counterpart Popov on at least three occasions[11] and the two countries signed a 'Friendship and Co-operation Treaty' on 7.10.91, in which Greece stated its full support for Bulgarian Association with the EC (*BBC SWB*, 12.10.91: A1/1).

Greek-Romanian relations on the other hand proved to be less turbulent, mainly due to Bucharest's 'understanding' of Greek reservations about the recognition of FYROM (*Eleftherotipia*, 23.4.91).[12] Therefore, despite the fact that Greece signed a 'Friendship and Cooperation Treaty' with Romania much later than it did with Bulgaria (late 1992), relations between the two countries continued to grow rapidly and by April 1992 Greece was fully supportive of Romania's request for inclusion into the association game. The good climate in Greek-Romanian relations which, was reaffirmed in every major meeting,[13] was also reflected in the words of the Romanian President Iliescu during his visit to Athens on 10.4.91:

...today we note that there is a favorable climate for and a mutual interest in the development and diversification of links on all planes- political, economic, cultural, scientific, human...(*BBC SWB*, 21.4.92: A1/3).

The domestic scope for the policies of the EC's southern member states

While at a senior level, the Bulgarian and Romanian requests for the opening of Association negotiations secured the in-principle agreement of the EC's South, domestic, political and economic considerations in those countries significantly limited the ratification prospects of a generous Association deal for the second wave applicants. Several factors pointed in this direction. Firstly, the importance of agriculture for the South's economy both in terms of employment and contribution to the GDP. In

1992, the share of agricultural employment in Italy, Spain, Portugal and Greece was almost 13%, a figure more than double the EC average (European Commission, 1992). Secondly, the proximity of Bulgarian and Romanian agricultural exports to the EC with the main product categories produced by the EC's South. Wine, fresh fruits and fresh vegetables for example, which contributed almost 40% to the Bulgarian and 26% to the Romanian total agricultural exports to the EC (Tracy, 1994: 72 and 80), also accounted for 30% of the South's total agricultural production (European Commission, 1993b: T22-23). Thirdly, the importance of other 'sensitive' sectors, already under pressure from domestic reform and international competition, to the South's economy. According to data provided by Eurostat, steel, textile and clothing sectors absorbed on average 8.5% of the South's total workforce (Eurostat, 1993).

The Southern EC member states' determination to resist the relaxation of trade protection in 'sensitive' sectors such as agriculture, textile/clothing and steel had been made clear long before the Bulgarian and Romanian requests for the opening of Association negotiations. Spain, for example, had been among the EC countries which, in November 1988, blocked the conclusion of GATT's Mid-Term Review due to its opposition to the proposed liberalisation of agricultural trade (Woolock and Hodges, 1996: 311), while Italy and Portugal did the same in April 1989 over trade in textiles (*Agence Europe*, 19.11.88). Moreover, the South, and Italy in particular, was also against the Mac Sharry plan for the reform of the CAP (*Agence Europe*, 15-16.7.91: 6).

As far as the ongoing Association negotiations with the Visegrads were concerned, the South was, in most cases, among the leading forces of the EC's protectionist group which argued against fast track trade liberalisation for 'sensitive' products. To this end, one should mention the Portuguese, Italian and Greek objections to more generous EC concessions on textiles (*Agence Europe*, 9-10.9.91: 9 and 30.9.91: 7); the Italian backing of the French veto of the Commission's proposals to increase the quantities of agricultural imports from the Visegrads (*Agence Europe*, 7.9.91: 8); as well as the Spanish fury over the Commission's decision not to include a specific safeguard clause against steel imports into the EAs (*Agence Europe*, 21.11.91: 9).

In addition to trade related issues, domestic ratification (Putnam, 1988) of more generous Association deals for the CEECs on behalf of the South was further restricted by other economic and political considerations relating to the overall rationale of the EC's widening process. The South's concerns about this direction concentrated on two major issues: the future funding of the EC's regional policy and the reform of the EC's institutional framework in order to accommodate Scandinavian and Eastern enlargements. In relation to the EC's regional policy, the stakes for the Southern member states were particularly high, since during the 1980s the Structural and Cohesion Funds had provided substantial resources for tackling long-lasting social and infrastructure-related problems (see, for example, Buzelay, 1989: 124).

As far as the prospect of institutional reform is concerned, proposals for a more 'flexible' EC in order to accommodate future enlargements, could only be alarming news for the Southern member states which felt threatened that an enlarged Community would almost certainly result in their 'relegation' to a 'second speed' group and consequently limit their bargaining power vis à vis the EC's 'core'. While it is true that back in 1991-92 neither the question of flexibility nor that of structural funds reform had yet topped the EC agenda, it is clear that these issues could not have been absent from the Southern member states' long-term strategy over the question of EC widening, an integral part of which were the Association agreements with the CEECs.[14]

Conclusion

The similarity of problems facing the EC's South as a result of the process of CEECs Association and eventual membership into the EC did not lead Italy, Spain, Portugal and Greece to act as a coherent group during the formation of the EC's Association strategy. In fact, each Southern EC member state displayed significantly different levels of economic activity in Eastern Europe and shared different geo-political interests in the region. These differences were even more striking in the case of the second wave applicants. In 1991, for example, the combined Spanish and Portuguese exports to Bulgaria and Romania were five times smaller than that of Greece and ten times smaller than that of Italy (see Table 4.4). Moreover, while Italy and Greece, by mid-1993, were the largest foreign investors in Romania and Bulgaria respectively, neither Spain nor Portugal registered any significant investments in the two Balkan countries (EKEM, 1993).

In geo-political terms, the wider Balkan region presented little interest for either Spain or Portugal. For Italy and Greece on the other hand, the only EC member states directly neighbouring the Balkans, the stakes in the region were much higher. For Rome, the end of the Cold War and the arrival of Gianni De Michelis as Foreign Minister in July 1989 marked the beginning of a more energetic policy towards the Balkans, keen to present Italy as the main counter force to German influence in the region (*Financial Times*, 6.8.91). At the forefront of such a policy stood the Italian design for regional co-operation known as Quadrangorale (involving Austria Hungary and Yugoslavia),[15] the efforts to rebuild the Albanian state and economy and, most importantly, the capitalisation on the cultural and religious ties with the seceded Yugoslav republics of Croatia and Slovenia (Greco, 1994: 81-92).

For Athens, the end of the Cold War coincided with a prolonged period of domestic political instability characterised by polarisation and introversion. Confusion over the country's Balkan policy continued even after the formation of the New Democracy (ND) government following the April 1991 election.[16] The new Centre-Right government led by Prime Minister Costantinos Mitsotakis, torn by its own divisions and restricted by its slim parliamentary majority, found it increasingly difficult to control domestic nationalist tendencies (which it had itself previously unleashed for electoral gains) and soon engaged in a bitter dispute with FYROM over the right of the newly independent republic to be called Macedonia. The 'Skopjenisation' of the Greek foreign policy during the period 1991-92, as well as the long-standing confrontation with Turkey and the renewed tension with Tirana over the treatment of the Greek minority in Southern Albania, left little room for the development of a 'positive' Balkan policy (Couloumbis, 1992; Ioakimidis, 1992; Veremis, 1992, 1993; Cofos, 1992 and Pettifer, 1993.

The exhaustive analysis of Athens' and Rome's overall Balkan policy is well beyond the scope of this chapter. What does become clear however, is that both Bulgaria and Romania, as an integral part of the 'Balkan puzzle', did acquire great significance for the realisation of the Italian and Greek objectives in the region. In this respect, contrary to their limited economic and political weight for the Iberian EC member states, the two Balkan applicants could expect to find a more sympathetic audience in Athens and Rome for their requests to begin Association negotiation with the EC.

The different degrees of economic and political significance attributed to Bulgaria and Romania by different Southern EC member states, undermined the South's ability to act as a unitary block either 'in favour' or 'against' a generous Association deal for the second wave applicants. Without a doubt, voices resisting a fast track trade liberalisation in 'sensitive' sectors continued to be strong in all four countries. That was clearly demonstrated on several occasions during the negotiations with the Visegrads (see chapter 2), but also later in 1992 when the Association bargain with Bulgaria and Romania entered its technical phase (see chapter 6). The highly political nature of the pre-negotiation bargain however, provided to those Southern EC member states with a vested interest in the wider Balkan region, such as Italy and Greece, the opportunity to assume the role of a 'bridge' between the European Community and the second wave applicants. In this respect, Italian and Greek patronage, although often impaired by the two countries' domestic difficulties, did make an important contribution to Romanian and Bulgarian efforts to enter into the Association game.

Conclusion: the relegated applicants

This chapter examined the evolution of bilateral relations between the second wave applicants and the EC member states during the pre-negotiation phase which began with the Bulgarian and Romanian requests for Association in March 1991 and ended in May 1992 with the opening of the official EA negotiations between the two countries and the EC. At one level, it can be argued that the strategy of the two Balkan applicants during this period has been a largely successful one. By May 1992 bilateral relations with all EC member states were fully normalised, whilst the rhetoric of most European leaders underlined the EC's commitment to assist the process of political and economic reform in the two countries. Most importantly, if one considers that what was at stake during this highly political pre-negotiation bargain was the EC's *history making* (Peterson, 1995) decision on whether to allow Bulgarian and Romanian entry into the Association process, then the two Balkan applicants appeared to have achieved most of their fundamental objectives.

Yet, despite their eventual inclusion into the Association process neither Bulgaria nor Romania could claim to have caught up with the Visegrad countries (Poland, Hungary and Czechoslovakia) in the pyramid of EC preferences and priorities in Eastern Europe. Both countries continued to offer little 'positive' economic incentives for integration with the EC. Their record of economic reform continued to be far poorer than that of the Visegrad countries. Political uncertainty and economic mismanagement has led to very low levels of foreign investment. Moreover, the small volume of trade with the EC and the limited purchasing power in both countries offered little compensation to most EC member states to counterbalance the negative effects of rapid trade liberalisation. Therefore, rather than being dictated by economics, Bulgaria's and Romania's inclusion into the Association process seemed to be more connected with high politics considerations and, in particular, with the rapidly deteriorating security environment in Southeast Europe. This lack of 'positive' economic incentives for integrating the two Balkan countries into the EC could also help to explain the EC's more protectionist attitude (than the one displayed during the first wave of EA negotiations) vis-à-vis Bulgaria and Romania during the negotiation of the second wave of Association agreements (see chapter 6).

Bulgaria's and Romania's relegation into second class applicants was also apparent in political terms. Both the Bulgarian and Romanian requests for fast track integration into the EC lacked consistent and powerful patronage by any of the big EC member states. This stood in sharp contrast to the experiences of both the Visegrad and the Baltic group whose Association and, later, membership strategies received powerful support by Germany and the Nordic EU member states. In the case of Romania, the special relationship with France could not be exploited to its full potential given Paris' overall scepticism about the process of EC widening. Italy on the other hand, while keen to assume the role of the patron for the two Balkan applicants (particularly Romania), lacked the necessary credibility, mainly due to its unstable governmental coalitions and the problems relating to the so-called sensitive sectors of the Italian economy. The same can also be argued for Greece, whose patron credentials were further limited by its small influence within the EC as well as by the shortcomings of its policy over 'Macedonian issue'. The lack of effective patronage, which contributed to the relegation of Bulgaria and Romania into the second wave of Association applicants, was to be felt even more throughout the negotiation and ratification process of their Association agreements with the EC.

Notes

[1] The two Balkan countries first requested the opening of Association negotiations with the EC during Commissioner Andriessen's East European tour of 6-12.3.91. The Bulgarian request was also repeated on 29.4.91 during Prime Minister Popov's visit to Brussels, while the Romanian government on 30.5.91, restated its determination to conclude an Association agreement with the EC during the inaugural meeting of the EEC/Romanian Joint Committee within the framework of the 'First Generation' agreement. For more details see *Agence Europe*, 29-30.4.91: 11 and 1.6.91: 8.

[2] In his official visit to Brussels for example, the Bulgarian prime-Minister Popov urged that Bulgaria "should not be treated in discriminatory fashion compared to the more economically advanced countries such as Czechoslovakia and Hungary in negotiations in view of an association agreement". See *Agence Europe*, 29/30.4.91: 11.

[3] Expression used by a senior Romanian official in London during an informal personal conversation on 2.12.95.

[4] The seven Inter-Parliamentary Delegations Committees were: Delegation for Relations with Hungary, Delegation for Relations with Poland, Delegation for Relations with Czechoslovakia, Delegation for Relations with Albania, Bulgaria and Romania, Delegation for Relations with Estonia, Latvia and Lithuania, Delegation for Relations with the CIS, and Delegation for Relations with the Yugoslav Republics.

[5] In December 1991 the then Director General of the GATT, Arthur Dunkel, presented the EC and the USA (but also all other participants in the GATT negotiations) with a final draft agreement in agriculture. This came to be known as the Dunkel document. For the first reaction of the EC's Agriculture ministers to the Dunkel document see *Agence Europe*, 23-24.12.91: 6.

[6] Expression used by the rapporteur of the Foreign Affairs Commission, Jean Marie Daillet, during the discussion within the French National Assembly for the ratification of the treaty of Friendship and Co-operation with Romania. See Assemblé Nationale, 1992b: 1273-1275.

[7] The Bulgarian President Zhelev did, however, visit Britain in late February 1991, where he met with John Major and signed an agreement promoting cultural co-operation between the two countries. The visit was described by British officials as "highly successful". For more details see The House of Commons Parliamentary Debates (1991: 36).

[8] "Ludicrously miserable" was the description given by the Labour MP George Robertson to the sum allocated by the Know- How Fund for the assistance of the CEECs since 1989. See House of Commons Parliamentary Debates (1992: 134).

[9] For more details see statement by the Bulgarian Foreign Minister Ganev after his meeting with his Spanish counterpart Francisco Fernandez-Ordonev on 30.4.92 (*BBC SWB*, 6.5.92: A1/4). See also similar statement by the Romanian Foreign Minister Nastase after his visit to Spain on 5-6.2.92 (*BBC SWB*, 8.2.92: A1/3).

[10] For the Friendship and Cooperation Treaty between Italy and Romania see *BBC SWB*, 27.7.91: A1/2-3. For the Friendship and Cooperation Treaty between Italy and Bulgaria see *BBC SWB*, 15.1.92: A1/1-2. See also the same references for statements by the Italian, Bulgarian and Romanian Foreign Ministers. For more contacts between the Italian and the Romanian political leadership see visit of Romanian Prime Minister Stolojan in Italy. *BBC SWB*, 7.12.91: i.

[11] See Popov's visits to Athens on 27.7.91 (*BBC SWB*, 30.7.1: i) and 24.9.91 (*BBC SWB*, 7.10.91: A1/1). See also Mitsotakis' visit to Sofia on 7.10.91 (*BBC SWB*, 12.10.91: A1/1). For more top level contacts see Prime Minister Mitsotakis' meeting with Bulgarian Deputy Premier Tomov on 17.6.91(*BBC SWB*, 25.6.91: A1/1) and talks between the Greek and Bulgarian Foreign Ministers Ganev and Samaras on 6.12.91 (*BBC SWB*, 11.12.91: A1/1).

[12] See, for example, interview of the Romanian President Ion Iliescu given to a Greek newspaper in which he argued that the Greek position vis à vis Macedonia was "reasonable". *Eleftherotypia*, "Logiki I Thesis sas gis ta Scopia [Your position is reasonable over Skopje]", 23.4.91.

[13] For some examples of this favorable climate see visit by the Greek Minister Tzitzikostas to Bucharest on 3.5.91 (*BBC SWB*, 8.5.91: A1/2) and talks between the Romanian Foreign Minister Nastase and the Greek Prime Minister Mitsotakis in Greece on 19.3.92 (*BBC SWB*, 31.3.92: A1/4).

[14] The South's categorical opposition to the reduction of the structural funds or change of the constitutional position of the 'small' EC member states as the result of Eastern enlargement took a more concrete form a few years later within the context of the IGC for the revision of the Maastricht treaty. For more details on the South's position on the issue of Eastern enlargement and institutional reform see European Parliament (1996).

[15] Later renamed Hexagonale with the inclusion of Czechoslovakia in 1990 and Poland in 1991. For details see *The Financial Times*, 6.6.91.

[16] The divisions between the hard-liner Foreign Minister Samaras and other more moderate elements of Mitsotakis' cabinet over the 'Macedonian issue' offer a good example of this.

5 Relegation Confirmed: The Response of the EC's Institutions to the Bulgarian and Romanian Attempts to Enter the Association Game

Chapter 4 examined how the efforts of the Bulgarian and Romanian governments to re-invent their bilateral relations with 'key' EC member states contributed towards the Council's decision to allow their entry into the Association game in May 1992. It was argued, however, that the success of the two Balkan governments was only partial since both Bulgaria and Romania failed to attract the same level of support enjoyed by their Visegrad neighbours and consequently were relegated into second wave applicants. Chapter 4 identified several reasons for Bulgaria's and Romania's relegation: their sluggish progress in economic and political reforms in the post-1989 period; their inability to attract foreign investment and their insignificant trade exchanges with the EC's partners; as well as the unwillingness of the EC's 'big' member states to provide effective patronage for the two Balkan applicants' Association bids.

Following the examination of the progress towards normalising relations with the EC's member states, the attention of this chapter shifts onto the two applicants' relations with the EC's institutions, in particular, the Commission and the European Parliament. Chapter 2 argued that both EC institutions displayed limited entrepreneurship in the shaping of the EC's strategy in Eastern Europe. Nevertheless their significance for the CEECs' drive towards Association remained crucial since both EC institutions held extensive powers over the pace and terms of the EC's rapprochement with Eastern Europe. For the Commission, these powers included the co-ordination of the G-24 Assistance, its role as policy initiator within the EC as well as its role as the EC's external negotiator.

121

The European Parliament's involvement in Eastern Europe, on the other hand, was secured through its influence over the EC budget (which partially financed the Phare programme) as well as through its constitutional right to ratify the EC's Association agreements before these could enter into force. In this respect, the 'selling' of their democratic and free market credentials to the Commission and the European Parliament as a means of securing a sympathetic hearing for their Association bids within these institutions, was a crucial part of the pre-Association strategy that none of the CEECs could afford to miss.

With particular reference to Bulgaria and Romania, it can be argued that the process of normalising relations with the EC's institutions was distinctively more difficult than that experienced by the Visegrad countries. Added to their inability to foster powerful coalitions with the EC's member states, Bulgaria's and Romania's failure to 'sell' their democratic and free market credentials to the EC institutions was clearly a decisive factor in their exclusion from the first wave of Association applicants. For Romania, in particular, the rapprochement with the EC institutions was exceptionally turbulent. While the country was the first CEEC to sign a trade agreement with the EC in 1980, relations with both the Commission and the EP in the post-1989 period remained poisoned by accusations of human rights abuses and the lack of economic and democratic reforms. In fact, the process of Romania's 'return to Europe' which started slowly in early 1990 was effectively frozen for the second half of that year, while it was only after the Moscow coup in August 1991 that the country's Association application gathered enough momentum to secure a cautious welcome by the EC institutions.

Bulgaria, on the other hand, enjoyed a relatively more sympathetic hearing amongst the Commission and the European Parliament and, unlike Romania, its democratic credentials were, by the end of 1990, largely undisputed. Nevertheless, Bulgaria's Association request failed to gather enough support and consequently the country was 'relegated', alongside Romania, into a group of second wave applicants. It will be argued that Bulgaria's exclusion from the Visegrad group was closely connected with the EC's institutions' growing scepticism over the strength of the local Communist party (the first exclusively non-communist government was formed in late 1991) as well as with the fact that the selection of first wave applicants in August 1990 coincided with a period of prolonged domestic uncertainty in what was until then Bulgaria's worst political crisis since 1989.

On a more general level, it will also be argued that the widespread consensus enjoyed by the Commission and the EP over the early development of the EC's strategy in Eastern Europe (see chapters 1 and 2), was comfortably extended over the Bulgarian and Romanian Association requests. The decision to freeze the EC's relations with Romania during the second half of 1990 as well as the view that the country was unsuitable to be granted Associated status was actively supported by both institutions. Moreover, the EP's request for the strengthening of the conditionality principle - largely inspired by its concerns over Romania's human rights record - was zealously taken on by the Commission and incorporated into the EC's position during the Association negotiations with the second wave applicants. Perhaps the only seeds of disagreement between the Commission and the EP can be found in the case of Bulgaria, particularly in late 1990 when the EP appeared to favour Bulgaria's inclusion into the first wave applicants. Nevertheless, the consensus between the two institutions was quickly restored in early 1991 when the EP fully subscribed to the Commission's proposals for a Visegrad-only first wave of Association applicants.

The reaction to the Romanian Association request: from outright rejection to a cautious welcome

Whilst Romania was the first Eastern European country to establish contractual relations with the EC in 1980, the Ceausescu regime's appeal in Brussels was significantly diminished during the second half of the 1980s as a result of the East/West rapprochement that followed Gorbachev's rise to power. Moreover, the intensification of human rights abuses in Romania in the late 1980s led to the further isolation of the Ceausescu regime and brought the special treatment that the country had enjoyed for most of the Cold War period to an end.[1] Romania's fiercest critic during that period was the European Parliament which, by early 1989, was campaigning to break off negotiations between the EC and Romania for the signing of a Trade and Co-operation agreement (to replace the 1980 agreement) which had begun in April 1987 (OJ C 096/137, 16.3.89). Alarmed by the practices of the Ceausescu regime, the Commission responded positively to the EP's calls and, in April 1989, suspended the ongoing negotiations with the Romanian government. Moreover, in December 1989, in retaliation to the Romanian government's brutal suppression of the Timisoara demonstrations, the External Relations Commissioner Frans Andriessen announced additional sanctions against Romania including the freezing of the 1980 agreement, the cancellation of the Commission's technical missions to the country as well as Romania's exclusion from further EC trade concessions to the CEECs (IP/89/1001, 20.12.89).

Following the collapse of the Ceausescu regime on 22.12.89, the Commission was very quick indeed to establish contacts with the provisional NSF government. Within three days of the execution of Nicolae and Elena Ceausescu, a Commission delegation visited Romania in order to evaluate the situation in the country and discuss the possibility of granting humanitarian aid to the new government. In his report to Commissioner Andriessen, the Phare adviser Herman de Lange stressed the fluidity surrounding the NSF take-over in Romania, but nevertheless, argued for the granting of humanitarian aid "...without any preconditions whose observation was, at that time, impossible" (EC Mission to Romania, 1990: 8). Indeed, in his Communication to the Council on 17.1.90, the External Relations Commissioner Andriessen, who had meanwhile visited Bucharest on 14.1.90, reported that although "...the possibility of set-backs remains in Romania", "sympathetic consideration" should be given to the country's request for inclusion into the Phare programme whilst he urged the Council to allow the resumption of negotiations for the conclusion of a Trade and Co-operation agreement "...during the first half of the year [1990]" (Commission of the EC, 1990b: 8).[2]

The overthrow of the Ceausescu regime was also welcomed by the EP which, in its January 1990 Resolution, was now supporting the "rapid conclusion" of a Trade and Co-operation agreement with Romania (OJ C 38/96, 18.1.90). The "honeymoon" period between the EP and Romania, however, was soon to end following fresh allegations of human rights violations by the NSF government. In the period between February and May 1990, the EP passed two more resolutions condemning the practises of the Iliescu regime while human rights abuses also became the subject of numerous written questions by MEPs of all political groups.[3] By May 1990, Romania was the only CEEC with which the EP had not yet held an Inter-parliamentary meeting. The situation deteriorated further following the EP's condemnation of Romania's first multi-party election on 20.5.90. In its resolution on the election, the EP called the Council of Ministers to make it clear to the Romanian authorities that the EEC would not provide economic and technical aid unless the country engaged in serious political reform. (OJ C 149/124, 17.5.90).

Despite the concerns voiced by the European Parliament, however, relations between the Commission and the Romanian government continued to improve during the first months of 1990. The Commission's Phare delegation which visited Romania on 14-16.3.90 in order to hold exploratory talks with the Romanian government, concluded that political reforms had made "considerable progress" and that "the principle of market economy was now beyond question" (IP/90/263, 27.3.90), while the country was also included in the Commission's 'Phare-Action Plan' for the beneficiaries of the G-24 assistance (Commission of the EC, 1990d). Moreover, the EC-Romania Joint Committee (provided for in the 1980 agreement) convened in Brussels on 19.3.90 and reconfirmed the mutual interest for the resumption of trade negotiations which had been suspended in April 1989. Following this meeting on 18.4.90, the Commission requested a new negotiating mandate for a Trade and Co-operation Agreement with Romania from the Council.

The violent suppression of the student demonstrations in Bucharest on 13-15.6.90, however, aggravated fears concerning the reform process in Romania. On 14.6.90, in his speech to the European Parliament Commissioner Bruce Millan announced the effective freezing of relations with the Iliescu regime until "...the achievement of an economic and political system founded on the same principles prevailing within the Community" (*Debates of the EP*, 14.6.90: 290-291). The EP, on the other hand, in its Resolution on Romania (July 1990) congratulated the blocking of the signature of the Trade and Co-operation agreement[4] and called for the Commission "...not to resume technical assistance to Romania, with the exception of humanitarian aid administered through recognised organisations" (OJ C 231/36, 10.7.90)

The effects of the EC's sanctions against Romania were indeed severe. The Trade and Co-operation agreement was not forwarded to the Council for signature, the country was excluded from the Phare programme (Commission of the EC, 1990e), while the extension of the European Investment Bank's loans to Romania was made conditional on a future decision by the Council (IP/90/694, 8.1.90). Most importantly, however, the freezing of EC/Romanian relations effectively killed the country's aspirations to be included amongst the first wave of Association applicants. In its crucial Communication to the Council and the EP (August 1990) on the general outline of the Association agreements with the CEECs, the Commission identified Poland, Hungary and Czechoslovakia as the countries to form the first wave of Association applicants, while for Romania and Bulgaria "...the Community will continue to monitor the situation...with a view to opening explanatory conversations as soon as the necessary conditions have been established" (Commission of the EC, 1990f: 2).

Romania's exclusion from the first wave of Association applicants was particularly welcomed by the EP. In October 1990, while urging the Commission "to speed up" the process leading to Association for Poland, Hungary and Czechoslovakia, the EP expressed its concern about Romania and called on the Commission and the Council "to make clear that any hesitation on the road towards achieving democracy and respect of human rights and the rights of minorities will lead to counter-measures on the part of the Community" (OJ C 284/140, 11.10.90). An even clearer message was sent to the Romanian government one month later, in November 1990, when on its Resolution on the Association agreements with the Visegrads, the EP specifically indicated that it "considers the negotiation of a Europe agreement with Romania to be inappropriate until such time as the Parliament's reservations about the Trade and Co-operation agreement have been dispelled when developments in Romania with regard to democracy and a market economy finally follow a similarly positive path to those in other Central and Eastern European countries" (OJ C 324/341, 23.11.90).

Meanwhile, the severe deterioration of Romania's economic situation and the almost certain humanitarian crisis forecast for the winter of 1990, combined with the absence of a serious political crisis in the country, began to shift the EC's attitude towards the Iliescu regime. Despite the fact that the Council of Ministers on 17.9.90 had rejected Romania's request for inclusion in the Phare programme, the conclusions of the G-24 meeting in October 1990 noted that "...encouraging progress had been recorded" (as quoted in A3-0021/91/PartB, 12.2.91: 5).[5] Moreover, on 22.10.90, the Council lifted its reservations and signed the First Generation agreement with Romania, while on 12-16.11.90 the first Inter-Parliamentary meeting between the EP and Romania was held in Brussels (Bull-EC-10/90).

Against this background of overall improvement in Romania's image in Brussels, the European Parliament debated the ratification of the Romanian Trade and Co-operation agreement in February 1991. In her report to the EP, Mrs A. Aglietta (MEP) stated that "...despite the remaining inconsistencies, the political, economic and social development of Romania has begun to achieve progress..." and urged the EP to ratify the agreement (A3-0021/91/Part B, 12.2.91: 5). The Aglietta Report on the approval of the Romanian Trade and Co-operation agreement with the EC represented the EP's first major attempt to influence the rules of the Association regime. Apparently alarmed by the dubious progress of reforms in Romania, the EP was now arguing for the strengthening of the conditionality principle for the second and subsequent waves of Association applicants:

With a view to preparing future Association agreements, attention should be given to the possibility of drawing up a 'democratic clause' that affirms in the most decisive way possible the central importance attached to the protection of human rights and democratic principles in the Association relationship between the Community and its partners (A3-0021/91/Part B, 12.2.91: 8).

The EP's proposal for 'improved' conditionality on future Association agreements was later adopted by both the Commission and Council and, as will be shown in chapter 6, finally led to one of the biggest policy changes in the EC's Association strategy from the first to the second wave of EA's negotiations.

The ratification (*Debates of the EP*, 19.2.91: 66-70; OJ C 72/192, 22.2.91) of Romania's First Generation agreement however, did not ease the EP's doubts about Bucharest's Association credentials. In its Resolution on the general outline of the Association agreements with the CEECs, the EP was still critical about the pace of democratic reforms in the country:

Political reform is lagging. It is still not clear whether the revolution was not, in fact, a coup. The new government, the NFS, consists mainly of ex-Communists. There are doubts as to the freedom of the elections last year. Democratisation of the decision making process has not yet been achieved and human rights are still being violated (A3-0055/91, 13.3.91: 24).

A similar degree of scepticism was also shared by the Commission's officials. In November 1990, Commissioner Andriessen had promised that the EC was prepared to open Association negotiations with Bulgaria, Romania and Yugoslavia "...in the not too distant future" (*Debates of the EP*, 22.11.90: 280). Nevertheless, throughout the first half of 1991 the Commission refused to undertake a clear commitment as to when Association negotiations with Bucharest would begin. Responding to the repeated requests of the Romanian leadership during his visit to Bucharest on 11-12.3.91, Commissioner Andriessen dismissed the opening of Association negotiations as "...premature to discuss at the moment" (*BBC SWB*, 19.3.91: A1/4), while similar Romanian claims during the inaugural meeting of the Joint Committee (under the new Trade and Co-operation agreement) on 31.5.91, received the reply that, due to lack of personnel, the Commission would be unable to start exploratory talks with Romania before the Visegrads' EAs were concluded (*Agence Europe*, 1.6.91: 8).

The August Moscow coup, however, and its deep impact within both Eastern and Western European capitals forced the EC to re-examine some of the basic principles of its policy towards Eastern Europe.[6] In its Communication to the Council on 4.9.91, the Commission was now proposing a new package of measures for all CEECs including greater EC concessions for the ongoing Association negotiations with the Visegrads (see chapter 2), strengthening of relations with Albania and the Baltic states and also the opening of exploratory talks with both Romania and Bulgaria aimed at beginning official Association negotiations with the two countries as soon as possible (*Agence Europe*, 5 and 7.9.91: 7). However, the political turmoil caused by the miners' demonstrations in Bucharest and the subsequent collapse of the Roman government on 27.9.91 threw the Romania's efforts to begin Association negotiations with the EC into disarray. On 30.9.91[7] the Council instructed the Commission to open exploratory talks with the Bulgarian government, but urged that similar talks with Romania could only begin "once the political situation had been normalised" (Bull 9-1991).

Meanwhile, the appointment of Theodor Stolojan as the new Romanian Prime Minister in October 1991 brought back some sort of normality to the country's political landscape. For its part the European Parliament, despite some sporadic accusations made by individual MEPs (OJ C 227/25, 1991; OJ C 126/52, 1992) against the Romanian government, also appeared ready to 'soften' its position vis à vis the prospect of the Romanian Association to the EC. The 'softening' of the EP's position was demonstrated by both the smooth running of the second Inter-parliamentary meeting with Romania on 18-22.11.91 (*Agence Europe*, 28.11.91: 6) and the ratification of the EC's medium-term financial assistance to Romania (OJ C 158/253, 1992) as well as by the country's inclusion in the so-called 'triangular operations' (OJ C 280/178, 1992). As a result the Council on 16.12.91, authorised the opening exploratory talks and the first meetings between the new Romanian government and Commission officials began in January 1992, leading to the official opening of the Association negotiations in May 1992.

The reaction to the Bulgarian Association request: good, but not good enough

Until June 1988 Bulgaria's political and economic dependency on the USSR had left practically no room for co-operation with the EC. However, the EC/Comecon Joint Declaration in June 1988, combined with the USSR's growing inability to absorb Bulgarian exports and provide low-cost energy to the country, forced Theodore Zhivkov's regime to re-examine its foreign policy priorities. In fact, soon after the 1988 EC-CMEA Joint Declaration the Bulgarian government sought to strengthen its relations with the EC institutions. Links with the European Parliament, in particular, grew rapidly in late 1988 and despite some concerns over human right abuses in the country (European Parliament, 1988: 11 and OJ C 47/133, 19.1.89), the first Inter-Parliamentary meeting was held in Sofia on 22-27.4.89 (almost 18 months earlier than the first EP meeting with Romania). During the same month negotiations also began between the Commission and the Bulgarian government for the conclusion of a Trade and Co-operation agreement (Commission of the EC, 1990a: 2).

These early successes of the Bulgarian government however, were soon to be tainted by renewed accusations concerning the treatment of the Muslim minority (Swain and Swain, 1993: 209). In response to these allegations the Commission in May 1989 suspended the negotiations for a Trade and Co-operation agreement with Bulgaria and relations with Sofia remained effectively frozen until Zhivkov's resignation in November 1989.[8] The new Bulgarian government, although still fully dominated by the Communist Party, moved fast to restore good relations with the EC. In his letter to Jacques Delors on 1.12.89, the Bulgarian Prime-Minister Atanasov informed the Commission's President about his government's measures for the restitution of the Turkish minority and asked for the resumption of negotiations for the conclusion of a Trade and Co-operation agreement with the EC (Commission of the EC, 1990a: 2). The Bulgarian request met a sympathetic audience in both the Commission (Commission of the EC, 1990b: 7)[9] and the EP (OJ C 38/96, 18.1.90). As a result, negotiations between the Commission and the Bulgarian government resumed in March 1990 and the country's Trade and Co-operation agreement with the EC was finally initialled on 3.4.90 (IP/90/291, 3.4.90) alongside those of the GDR and Czechoslovakia.

Despite the initiation of the First Generation agreement, relations between the Bulgarian government and the EC's institutions were about to enter a turbulent period. In its May Resolution, the European Parliament severely criticised the practices of the Lukanov government against the opposition parties during the build up to the 10.6.90 elections and urged the Council to make the strengthening of Bulgaria's relations with the EC conditional upon democratic reforms in the country (OJ C 149/124, 17.5.90). Moreover, the electoral victory of Bulgaria's Socialist Party (BSP),[10] coupled with the political instability that followed President

Mladenov's resignation on 6.7.90, cast further doubts over the progress of reforms in the country. These doubts became all the more apparent in July 1990 when the EP (following the demands of certain political groups such as the EEP, the LDR and the ED) postponed the debate for the ratification of Bulgaria's Trade and Co-operation agreement until the political situation in the country became more stable (*Debates of the EP*, 10.7.90: 29-41).

The more the political crisis in Bulgaria deepened during summer 1990, the more the country slipped towards the 'second tier' of the CEECs' Association applicants, away from the GDR, which in November 1990 was absorbed by Germany, and Czechoslovakia which under the leadership of Vachlav Havel was now moving ever closer to the 'first tier' alongside Poland and Hungary. The clearest manifestation of this division came with the Commission's August 1990 Communication on the Association agreements. Predictably, what was now becoming the 'Central European' group (Poland, Hungary and Czechoslovakia) was chosen as the first wave to negotiate Association agreements with the EC, while a clearly 'relegated' Bulgaria was to join the second wave alongside Romania whose relations with the EC at that time were effectively frozen.

The period following Bulgaria's exclusion from the first wave of Association applicants was characterised by the gradual improvement of the country's image in the EC's institutions. In September 1990 the EP ratified the Bulgarian First Generation agreement (*Debates of the EP*, 13.9.90: 204-210; OJ C 260/162, 13.9.90) – a ratification which came 5 months earlier than the Romanian one. The resignation of Andrei Lukanov in November 1990 and the creation of a new reform-minded government under Dimitri Popov along with the election of the UDF leader Zhelyu Zhelev as the first non communist President of Bulgaria for 50 years, further boosted the country's reform credentials. Under the new circumstances, the EP was now ready to re-examine its position vis à vis Bulgaria's request for Association. In its new Resolution on the Association agreements with the Visegrads in November 1990, the EP called "...for the possibility of Association agreements with other CEECs to be considered before the mandate is granted." (OJ C 324/341, 22.11.90), while Bulgaria was no longer to be grouped together with Romania (for which the opening of EA negotiations was labelled 'inappropriate').

However, the hopes of the Bulgarian government of being included amongst the Visegrads in the first wave of Association candidates did not materialise. The Randzio-Plath report on the Commission's proposed general outline for the EAs, while acknowledging the progress made in certain areas of reform, concluded that "...the restructuring of society is still being slowed down by political instability" (A3-0055/91, 13.3.91: 25). Moreover, during the debate of the report in the Plenary Session, none of the speakers challenged the Council/ Commission's wisdom in selecting the Visegrads as the first wave of Association applicants, or the conclusions of the Radzio-Plath report concerning Bulgaria (*Debates of the EP*, 14.4.91: 253-262). Despite its exclusion from the first wave, nevertheless, Bulgaria's relations with the EC's institutions continued to improve steadily throughout 1991. Indeed, following Frans Andriessen's visit to Sofia on 11-12.3.91, the Commission backed Bulgaria's request for medium-term financial assistance (Commission of the EC, 1991 and OJ L 174, 3.7.91), while during his visit to Brussels in April, the Bulgarian Prime Minister Popov received assurances that the opening of Association negotiations during the next few months was "perfectly feasible (*Agence Europe*, 29-30.4.91: 11).

As in the case of Romania, Bulgaria's request for the opening of Association negotiations with the EC received a major boost as a consequence of the August 1991 coup in Moscow. The deepening of Bulgaria's relations with the EC, which was signalled by the beginning of exploratory Association talks in October 1991, was clearly reinforced by the UDF's electoral victory on 13.10.91[11] as well as by President Zhelev's visit to the Commission on 15.11.91 (*Agence Europe*, 16.11.91: 5). Moreover, in the same month the European Parliament also concluded that Bulgaria was now "...on the road to genuine democratisation and a market economy...." (OJ C 326/252, 22.11.91). As a result, following the conclusion of the Visegrad EAs negotiations on 13.2.92 (Bull 1/2-1992, point 1.4.7), the Commission requested a negotiating mandate from the Council, and official Association negotiations with the second wave applicants began in May 1992.

Conclusion: relegation confirmed

This chapter examined the evolution of Bulgaria's and Romania's relations with the EC's institutions from the EC/Comecon Joint Declaration in 1988, through to the end of 1991 when the Commission and the EP consented to the inclusion of the two Balkan countries into the Association game. It was argued that while the progress shown by the Bulgarian and Romanian governments was 'sufficient' to secure their entry into the Association game, both countries failed to persuade the Commission and the EP that they had advanced sufficiently down the path of economic and political reform to be placed among the first wave of Association applicants. Doubts expressed by the EC's institutions over the two Balkan applicants' reform credentials, coupled with Bulgaria's and Romania's inability to foster powerful coalitions with key EC member states (see chapter 4), therefore came to finalise the compartmentalisation of CEECs Association applicants, with Poland, Hungary and Czechoslovakia forming the first wave and the two Balkan countries being relegated to 'second class' applicants (see Figure 5.1).

	Poland	Hungary	CSFR	Bulgaria	Romania
Ratification of 1st Gen. Agreement	25.10.89 (OJ C 304/48)	26.10.88 (OJ C 309/33)	19.9.90 (OJ C 260/163)	19.9.90 (OJ C 260/162)	22.2.91 (OJ C 72/192)
Assessment of first multi-party election	15.9.89 "EP expresses its confidence to the new government and assures it of its support in pursuing its difficult task"* (OJ C 256/154) * In this election, Solidarity was not allowed to contest all parliamentary seats	13.9.90 "The EP welcomes the emergence of a peaceful transition... consolidated by the first free multi party elections... and the first free government for 45 years" (OJ C 260/163)	13.3.91 "Political reform has made further progress with parliamentary elections [June 1990]" (A3-55/Randzio-Plath Report)	17.5.90 Observers to be sent "...not only on the day of the election but also during the election campaign...". Observers to "...have access to polling stations when votes are counted" (OJ C 149/125)	17.5.90 "EP condemns all intimidation of opposition parties and their candidates..." "The EP calls for the equal access to the media and balanced media election coverage in Romania and Bulgaria" (OJ C 149/125)
Assessment of respect of human and minority rights	15.2.90 "The EP is convinced that the new Polish government will respect the rights of minorities living on what is now Polish territory" (OJ C 68/148)	14.9.89 The opening of borders with the GDR marks "...a great advance in respect of human rights..." (OJ C 256/116) 13.9.90 "The EP is noticing that human rights are once again being respected..." (OJ C 260/165)		18.1.90 "The action of the new government in favour of the Turkish minority is welcomed " (OJ C 38/97) 13.3.91 "...restructuring of society is being slowed down by political instability..." (A3-55/Randzio-Plath Report)	5.4.90 "The EP insists on the duty of the Romanian authorities to protect the rights of all citizens..." (OJ C 113/139) 10.7.90 Guarantees to be given "...that the human rights of all citizens are respected fully." (OJ C 231/37)
View on the opening of EA negotiations	11.10.90 "The EP holds the view that the sooner these three countries [Poland, Hungary and Czechoslovakia] conclude European agreements with the Community the better for the security and prosperity of the whole continent" (OJ C 284/140)	11.10.90 "The EP holds the view that the sooner these three countries [Poland, Hungary and Czechoslovakia] conclude European agreements with the Community the better for the security and prosperity of the whole continent" (OJ C 284/140)	11.10.90 "The EP holds the view that the sooner these three countries [Poland, Hungary and Czechoslovakia] conclude European agreements with the Community the better for the security and prosperity of the whole continent" (OJ C 284/140)	11.10.90 The situation to be "...monitored carefully" (OJ C 248/140). 23.11.90 "...possibility of EA with other CEECs to be considered..." (OJ C 324/342) 3.3.91 Consent to exclusion from first wave. (A3-55/Report)	11.10.90 The situation to be "...monitored carefully" (OJ C 248/140). 23.11.90 "The EP considers the negotiation of a 'Europe' agreement to be inappropriate..." (OJ C 324/342)

Figure 5.1 Relegation Confirmed: The EP's Assessment of the Reform Process in the Five Association Applicants, 1989-1990

For Romania, the reasons behind such a relegation were clear. The country's appalling image during the last years of the Ceausescu era was only temporarily improved in early 1990. Soon after, the new Romanian government's relations with the EC's institutions were once again strained following widespread accusations of further human rights abuses and a lack of democratic and economic reform. At the forefront of such accusations stood the European Parliament, whose increasing hostility towards the Romanian government had a decisive influence on the Commission's decision to freeze the EC's relations with Bucharest for the second half of 1990. Under these circumstances the exclusion of Romania from the first wave should not, therefore, come as a surprise. In fact, if it had not been for the deep impact of the Moscow coup (August 1991) on the EC's strategy in Eastern Europe, it is arguable whether Romania would have managed to gather enough support, especially within the EP, for its inclusion even in the second wave of Association applicants.

For Bulgaria on the other hand, the reasons behind its exclusion from the first wave seemed to be related to the timing of events in the country and, in particular, with the fact that the Commission's August 1990 Communication, in which the composition of the first wave of Association applicants was announced, coincided with a period of prolonged political paralysis in Bulgaria. Moreover, the fact that the local communist party (BSP) emerged victorious from the June 1990 election did little to reassure the EC's institutions that economic and political reforms in the country would continue. Despite the political stalemate during the summer of 1990, however, by the end of that year Bulgaria had managed to make considerable progress down the path of political and, to a lesser extent, economic reforms. As such, Bulgaria's exclusion from the first wave of Association applicants was less clear cut than Romania's. After all, by November 1990, the country had a coalition government under a non-communist Prime Minister, while by Autumn 1991, it was the only Association applicant to have held two largely fair parliamentary elections (Poland, at that time, had not yet held a free parliamentary election). As far as political reform was concerned, Bulgaria was the first CEEC to adopt a democratic constitution (July 1991), while by November 1991 the Turkish minority party (MRF) was a partner in the country's coalition government. Czechoslovakia, at that time, was heading towards disintegration.

The contrast between the EP's treatment of Bulgaria and Czechoslovakia is indeed revealing. Both countries signed Trade and Co-operation agreements with the EC in May 1990. However, while

Czechoslovakia was, in October 1990, split from the EP's delegation for relations with Eastern Europe II (in which it was part, alongside Bulgaria and Romania, since 1987) and became a separate delegation on its own (as was indeed the case for Poland and Hungary), Bulgaria was grouped in a single delegation with Romania (whose relations with the EC at that time were frozen) which was later (February 1991) enlarged to include also Albania (which had just came out of 50 years of Stalinist isolation). Whilst these divisions might have little or no direct impact on Bulgaria's exclusion from the first wave of Association applicants, they do, nevertheless, offer an interesting insight on the way in which the administration of the EC's institutions perceived and 'grouped' the CEECs (see Figure 5.2).

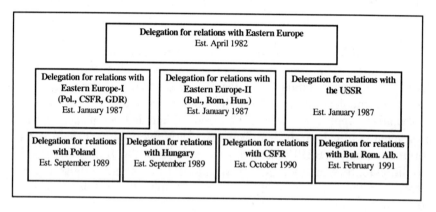

Figure 5.2 Evolution of the EP's Relations with the CEECs, 1982-1991

On a more general level, this chapter has also argued that the attempts of the Bulgarian and Romanian governments to enter the Association game, did not pose a major challenge to the consensus built, since the early post-1989 period, between the Commission and the EP over the EC's strategy in Eastern Europe (see chapters 1 and 2). Both institutions continued to favour the 'safe approach' based on the conviction that the EAs with the CEECs should be negotiated with a small group of applicants at the time and, preferably, on a 'region by region' basis. This consensus was only temporarily disturbed in late 1990, when the EP appeared to favour Bulgaria's inclusion into the first wave, but was quickly restored in March 1991, when through the adoption of the Randzio-Plath report, the EP embraced the Commissions proposals for a Visegrad-only first wave of Association applicants.

The consensus amongst the two institutions was also extended over the question of 'improved' conditionality for the second and subsequent waves of EAs applicants, an issue raised by the European Parliament during the ratification process of the Romanian Trade and Co-operation agreement in early 1991. The strengthening of the conditionality principle with the insertion of a clear reference to the protection of human rights, was arguably the EP's most important (and successful) attempt to act as a policy entrepreneur in the EC's strategy in Eastern Europe and decisively influence the 'rules' of the Association regime. The EP's proposal, which was clearly based on its growing concern over the protection of human rights by the two Balkan applicants (especially Romania), was soon to be taken on by the Commission and, following the Council's agreement, constituted the single most important change in the EC's negotiating position during the second wave of EAs negotiations (see chapter 6).

Notes

[1] For the EP's reaction to these abuses see Resolution on Romania, OJ C013/101, 18.1.88; Resolution on new measures liquidating villages in Romania, OJ C 235/104, 12.9.88; Resolution on the situation of Protestant Christians, OJ C 290/115, 14.11.88; and Resolution on the fate of Mrs Doina Cornea, OJ C 012/151, 16.1.89.

[2] Both of the Commission's proposals for resumption of Trade and Co-operation negotiations with Romania and its inclusion into the Phare programme were agreed by the Council on 5.2.90 and the G-24 meeting on 16.2.90 respectively.

[3] See, for example, resolutions OJ C 068/136 (on Romania) and OJ C 113/139 (on Transylvania) on 5.4.90. See also written questions on bilateral relations with Romania (OJ C 069/30) and on the detention of Csaba Szilagyi (OJ C 069/43).

[4] Negotiations for the conclusion of a Trade and Co-operation agreement with Romania had resumed in February 1990 and the agreement was initialled by the Commission and the Romanian government on 8.6.90. See IP/90/459, 11.6.90.

[5] The G-24 finally approved the inclusion of Romania into the Phare programme on 30.1.91.

[6] In its meeting in Luxembourg on 28-29.6.91,the European Council had already invited the Commission to examine the possibility of strengthening the EC's relations with the CEECs. As far as the Balkan countries (including Bulgaria and Romania) were concerned, the European Council stated its hope that "... conditions permitting reinforcement of [their] links with the Community will soon be obtained". See DOC/91/2, 29.6.91.

[7] The Council's initial decision to authorise the opening of exploratory talks between the Commission and the Romanian government was scheduled for 7.9.91, but had to be deferred to 30.9.91 due to the member states' inability to agree on trade concessions for the Visegrads which was also part of the Council's agenda. For more details on this issue see chapter 2.

[8] Theodore Zhivkov was replaced on 10.11.90 by his former Foreign Minister Petar Mladenov who assumed the role of the President. In February 1990, Andrei Lukanov replaced Gueorgui Atanasov as the country's Prime Minister.

[9] Bulgaria was also accepted into the Phare programme on 4.7.90. For more details see European Commission (1990e).

[10] Bulgaria's former Communist (now renamed Socialist) Party (BSP) won 47% of the vote and 211 seats in the Assembly, while the opposition Union of Democratic Forces (UDF) won 36% of the vote and 144 seats in the Assembly.

[11] The UDF victory in the October 1991 elections led to the establishment of Bulgaria's first exclusively non-communist government under Philip Dimitrov who enjoyed the support of the UDF and the Turkish minority party, MRF.

6 Explaining the Outcome of the Second Wave of Association Agreements: The Effects of Bargaining in an Iterated Game

Chapters 4 and 5 examined how Bulgaria and Romania managed to normalise their relations with the EC (its institutions and its member states) and eventually secured approval to begin Association negotiations in May 1992. The Bulgarian and Romanian Association game was the second in the sequence of a series of Association games played between the EC and the CEECs during the period 1991-1995. As such, the Bulgarian and Romanian game was very much dependent on the results of the first wave of Association agreements with Poland, Hungary and Czechoslovakia. The importance of the precedent set with the Visegrad EAs was already known to all sides as early as 1990, since the Commission had proposed that the basic framework of the Association agreements as well as the main principles of trade liberalisation should remain the same for all applicants.

In addition to their dependence on the first wave of EAs, the Bulgarian/Romanian game was also linked to other Association games that the EC was expected to play with CEECs in the future. By mid-1992 it was already becoming clear that new Association agreements would have to be negotiated with the two republics of the former Czechoslovakia, while the Baltic states and Slovenia were also considered as possible Association candidates. The EC, which participated in *all* different waves of the Association negotiations, was, therefore, the only actor subjected to the advantages and disadvantages of the game's iterated nature. On the other hand, the East European applicants entered the

Association game *once*, at a time dependent on the wave in which the EC had classified them (see Figure 6.1).

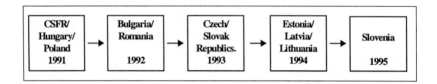

Figure 6.1 The Iterated Nature of the Association Game

The effects of such *iteration* on the actors' strategies constitutes the main focus of this chapter. It will be argued that the second wave of Association agreements provided the EU with a good opportunity to adjust its Association strategy so as to take into account the experience gained in negotiating the Visegrad agreements, alongside other important internal and international developments such as the signature of the Maastricht treaty and the deterioration of the situation in former Yugoslavia.

On a theoretical level, similar to the *multiple games*-based analysis of chapter 3, it will be argued that some of the EC's choices during the second wave of Association negotiations can be better explained, not so much by the direct 'threat' posed by Bulgaria and Romania, but rather as part of a strategy designed for and influenced by the iterated nature of the EC's Association game. To this end, much of this chapter's conclusions will be based on Tsebelis' observation that when actors:

> ... enter into repeated interaction, they are interested in maximising their payoffs during the entire period of their interaction. Therefore, they may choose sub-optimal strategies in the one-shot game if such strategies increase their payoffs over repeated play (Tsebelis, 1990: 73).

Moreover, Axelrod's emphasis on the actor's *reputation* during a repeated interaction is also of great relevance in explaining the EC's position:

> When third parties are watching, the stakes of the current situation expand from those immediately at hand to encompass the influence of the current choice on the reputations of the players (Axelrod, 1990: 151).

Unfortunately, the existing game theory literature, which focuses on the effects of *iterated games* on the actors' negotiating strategies, can offer little help in the case of the Association agreements. This is because most of the conclusions reached on this matter were based on the study of either iterated prisoners' dilemma games (Luce and Raiffa, 1957, Axelrod, 1981, 1990) or of non co-operative games (Friedman, 1971), none of which capture the dynamics of the EC-CEECs interaction within the Association game.

For the Bulgarian and Romanian one shot games with the EC, the iterated nature of the EC's Association game in Eastern Europe introduced two crucial factors:

- The first can be called the *'equal treatment'* factor. Taking into consideration that the main features of the Association game had already been decided in the negotiations with the first wave applicants, the optimum result for both Bulgaria and Romania in their negotiations with the EC would be to preserve 'equal treatment' with the Visegrad countries.
- The second can be called the *'catch up'* factor. This relates to the CEECs' conviction that the conclusion of the EAs would mark the opening of the process which would eventually lead to full EU membership (Stawarska, 1992: 79; interviews in the Bulgarian and Romanian Missions in the EU, 21.3.97). The optimum result for the second wave applicants in this respect, would be a speedy conclusion of the Association negotiations as a means of reducing the time deficit between the first and the second wave of Associated members in order that the latter would not miss out to the former in the EU membership race.

Both factors (equal treatment and catch up) were almost by their nature contradictory. For example, the tactic of forcefully insisting on equal treatment with the first wave would inevitably delay the Association negotiations, a development apparently at the expense of catching up with the Visegrads in the membership race. On the other hand, the tactic of insisting on the speedy conclusion of the EA would inevitably result in a worse deal from the Association negotiations.

This chapter will argue that the Bulgarian and Romanian positions during the EA negotiations were the product of a compromise between these two contradictory factors, both emanating from the iterated nature of the EC Association game in Eastern Europe. The different strategies finally followed by the two delegations during their Association negotiations are a reflection of their different perception and understanding of *iteration* as well as of the different prioritisation which they gave to the 'equal treatment' and the 'catch up' factors.

The EU's strategy: continuity and change

The conclusion of the first wave of Association agreements with the three Visegrad states in December 1991 paved the way for the beginning of substantive talks between the EC and the second wave of Association applicants. In fact, Bulgaria and Romania had already 'qualified' as the second group of CEECs to be granted such a status since early September 1991, but the decision to begin exploratory talks with the two governments was postponed following the complications of the EAs negotiations with the Visegrads (see chapter 2).

The Council finally authorised the Commission to start explanatory discussions with the Bulgarian government on 30.9.91 (*Agence Europe*, 28.9.91: 8), while similar talks with Romania did not begin until December 1991 due to a prolonged period of domestic instability following the collapse of Petre Roman's NSF government in late September 1991 (*Agence Europe*, 16-17.12.91: 9). Exploratory talks with the two governments both finished in early January 1992 and on 13.2.92 the Commission requested the opening of official negotiations from the Council for the conclusion of an Association agreement between the EC and the two countries (*Agence Europe*, 14.2.92: 5). Following the Council's approval on 11.5.92 (IP/92/389, 15.5.92), the first round of negotiations with Bulgaria and Romania began on 14 and 19.5.92 respectively. The Romanian agreement was finally initialled on 17.11.92, following six rounds of negotiations, while the Bulgarian agreement was initialled on 22.12.92, following seven rounds of negotiations. The negotiations were thus concentrated in a period of six to eight months across the summer break.

The second wave of Association negotiations attracted little EC attention at the time. The relatively small economic and political 'weight' of Bulgaria and Romania and also the EC's early commitment that the basic EA structure agreed in the first wave would remain the same for all subsequent CEECs applicants, clearly contributed to this attitude. The Bulgarian and Romanian agreements therefore, were largely treated as 'procedural'. As one senior official from the European Parliament put it:

> The first wave of EAs was a more substantial issue...Nobody seriously questioned that since the precedent with Poland was set everybody would have a similar treatment (interview, 20.3.97).

While not of great value in themselves, the Bulgarian and Romanian agreements nevertheless provided the EC with a useful opportunity to adjust certain elements of its Association strategy. In this respect, the fact that the Bulgarian and Romanian Association was, for the EC, part of an *iterated game*, rather than an 'independent' one-shot game, is crucial. Having already negotiated the first wave of EAs as well as having collected more information about the region, the EC was in a position to 'correct' earlier 'mistakes'. Furthermore, by incorporating such changes into the second wave of EAs, the EC could present future applicants with a *fait accompli*.

With particular reference to the Bulgarian and Romanian cases, the EC's negotiating position in 1992 appeared distinctively different in four main areas from the one followed with the Visegrads in 1991, all of which shall be assessed in this chapter. The first two referred to the Preamble and Final Provisions of the agreements and included: (i) a specific reference to the protection of human rights and minority groups within the Associated countries and (ii) a clause which would permit the possibility of an automatic suspension of the agreement in the event that either Party failed to meet its obligations. The last two areas subjected to a tougher EC negotiating mandate were trade-related and included (iii) the introduction of a specific safeguard clause against steel imports from Bulgaria and Romania and (iv) the reduction of the quantities of fruit and vegetables which qualified for improved access to the EC markets.

Returning to the *multiple arenas* framework of analysis provided in chapter 3, the next section will look at the evolution of games within the EC's *Domestic* and *International Arenas* and try to establish how changes in peripheral[1] games affected the EC's position in the second wave of Association negotiations.

Human rights and unilateral suspension clauses

The insistence on the inclusion of a specific human rights clause in the Association agreements was the biggest policy change in the EC's Association strategy from the first to the second wave of EAs negotiations. While the agreements with the Visegrads included no specific reference to human rights and the respect of minorities, the EC's position on this matter became significantly tougher in late 1991. During the exploratory talks the Commission was instructed to present the new EC position on human rights, but its proposals met strong opposition from the Bulgarian and Romanian governments.[2]

One day before the official opening of Association negotiations with the two countries however, the General Affairs Council restated its insistence on the inclusion of such a clause in the new agreements:

The Council underscores that the respect for democratic principles and human rights as defined in the Helsinki Final Act and the Charter of Paris for a new Europe, as well as the principles for a market economy, constitute essential elements of the Co-operation or Association agreements between the Community and its CSCE partners. The Commission is urged to act accordingly to ensure the inclusion of an appropriate and operational mechanism in the event of an emergency, which includes provisions related to a failure to fulfil obligations, in the agreements to be concluded by the Community (*Agence Europe*, 14.5.92)

The Council's statement was of double importance. The EC would insist not only on the inclusion of a reference to the respect of human rights, but most importantly, on the inclusion of an 'automatic' clause which would permit the two parties to suspend the agreement unilaterally in an event of an emergency.

The EC's determination to include clauses of, what Guggenbuhl (1995: 240) called, 'improved' conditionality in the second wave of Association agreements, left little scope for discussion. Negotiators from both the Bulgarian and Romanian delegations insisted that the Commission's attitude on this matter during the negotiations was on a 'take it or leave it' basis (interviews in the Bulgarian and Romanian Missions to the EU, 21.3.97). As a result, the Preamble of both the Romanian and Bulgarian Association agreements included a firm declaration in relation to the protection of human rights:

Considering the firm commitment of the Community and its member states and of Bulgaria to the rule of law and human rights, including those of persons belonging to minorities and to the full implementation of all other principles and provisions contained in the Final Act of the Conference on Security and Co-operation in Europe (CSCE), the concluding documents of Vienna and Madrid, the Charter of Paris for a new Europe, as well as to the principles and provisions of the European Energy Charter (Commission of the EC, 1992b: 3).

In relation to the unilateral suspension clause, Article 118 (par. 2) of the Final Provisions provides for:

If either Party considers that the other Party has failed to fulfil an obligation under the Agreement, it may take appropriate measures. Before so doing, except in case of special urgency, it shall supply the Association Council with all relevant information required for a thorough examination of the situation acceptable to the Parties (Commission of the EC, 1992b: 51).

The EC's determination for 'improved' conditionality can be explained by a number of factors that relate both to treaty changes and the 'peculiarity' of the second wave applicants as well as to important international developments.

The impact of Maastricht and the 'peculiarity' of the second wave applicants. The Association negotiations with the second wave applicants begun a few months after the signing of the Maastricht treaty. While the new treaty on European Union did not enter into force until 1993, it was apparent that the text agreed in Maastricht would have a crucial effect upon the EC's negotiating position vis à vis third countries. One of the novelties of the new treaty was the incorporation of Article F stating the commitment undertaken by the member states to respect fundamental rights "...as guaranteed by the European Convention for the Protection of Human Rights and Fundamental Freedoms signed in Rome on 4.11.50 and as they result from the constitutional traditions common to the member states, as general principles of Community law". Article F, in conjunction with the determination of the EC member states "...to maintain in full the *acquis communautaire* and to build on it" as stipulated by Article B, had important implications for the EC agreements with third countries. Since the *acquis communautaire* provided the basis of the EC's position during the negotiations and since the protection of human rights was part of this *acquis*, Association applicants would also have to accept it (interview in the Commission's DGIA, 24.2.97).

The seeds of the EC's new approach to the conditionality principle can be found in the European Parliament's resolution on the Romanian Trade and Co-operation agreement in February 1991 (see chapter 5). Ever since, the EP remained one of the most ardent advocates of 'improved' conditionality, thus reaffirming its long-standing reputation as the most sensitive EC institution regarding human rights violations. As far as Bulgaria and Romania are concerned, chapter 5 revealed the EU's institutions' scepticism (especially regarding Romania) over the treatment of ethnic minorities and the respect of fundamental rights in the two countries. At the time of the initial Council discussions on the strengthening of the conditionality principle (early April 1992), neither Bulgaria nor Romania were yet full members of the Council of Europe and as a result neither of the two countries had yet ratified the European Convention of human rights.[3] Thus, by early 1992 while the political situation in both countries had improved considerably, their democratic credentials were not yet undisputed. Against this background, both the Commission and the EP remained fully committed to the strengthening of the conditionality principle for the second wave of Association applicants (interviews in the EP, 20.3.97 and in the Commission's DGIA, 24.2.97).

The effects of the crises in Yugoslavia and Czechoslovakia. Chapter 4 examined how the Yugoslav crisis served as a very effective factor in persuading the EC member states to begin Association negotiations with Bulgaria and Romania as a means of preventing the war spreading to the wider Balkan area. While 'useful' for the initial decision to select Bulgaria and Romania as Association applicants however, the war in former Yugoslavia had a rather different impact on the interests of the two countries as soon as the actual EA negotiations began. The barbarity of the wars in Croatia and Bosnia had a profound effect on both the European public opinion and the EC policy makers. Above all, the escalation of the Yugoslav drama highlighted the need for a strong human rights component to the EC's strategy in Eastern Europe.

In addition to the need to ensure the protection of minority rights in Eastern Europe, the war in former Yugoslavia affected one more important change in the second wave of Association agreements. This was the introduction of a unilateral suspension clause. The Socialist Federal Republic of Yugoslavia was the first Communist country to sign a preferential Trade and Co-operation agreement with the EC in 1980 (OJ L 41, 14.2.83). Based on Article 238 of the Treaty of Rome, this agreement provided not only for improved market access, but also for the creation of common institutions responsible for ensuring the uninterrupted implementation of the agreement's provisions. Most importantly, the EC-Yugoslav agreement was concluded for an unlimited period of time, while there was no mechanism for rapid unilateral suspension in cases of urgency.

The absence of such a rapid suspension clause in the Yugoslav agreement proved to be very costly when the crisis in the country escalated in early 1991. Unable to use the rapid suspension of the agreement as a negotiating weapon for the preservation of the Yugoslav state, the EC found itself offering all the benefits emanating from the 1980 agreement to a country that was engaged in a full scale civil war. It is indicative that the Council was finally able to suspend all EC agreements with Yugoslavia in November 1991 (Bull-EC, 11-1991), six months after Slovenia and Croatia had already declared their independence[4] and a few weeks before the EC itself formalised the death of Yugoslavia by recognising the republics that had seceded.[5] Apparently, in the second wave of Association agreements, the EC was not prepared to repeat the mistake made with Yugoslavia. As a result, violations of human rights and repression of ethnic minorities were, from now on, to be sufficient reasons for the rapid unilateral suspension of the EC's Association agreements.

In addition to the Yugoslav crisis, the deteriorating situation in former Czechoslovakia can also be considered as one of the factors contributing to the strengthening of the conditionality principle. As shown in chapter 2, former Czechoslovakia had been one of the countries included in the first wave and was generally viewed as one of the most 'promising' Associated partners. The country was however, suffering from a deeply rooted suspicion between the Czech and Slovak communities. While nationalistic tendencies faded into the background during the early post-Communist period, in early 1992 those political forces- mainly situated in Slovakia- favouring the radical amendment of the federal constitution had grown significantly (Wightman, 1993).

While the disintegration of former Czechoslovakia was described as a 'velvet divorce', it nevertheless created further insecurity over the stability of the whole Central European region and most importantly, raised questions over the treatment of Hungarian and Czech minorities in the new Slovak state. Taking into consideration the iterated nature of the EC Association game in Eastern Europe, the strengthening of the conditionality principle in the second wave would, therefore, have a double positive effect. On the one hand, it would 'improve' the EAs' human rights provisions for Bulgaria and Romania, whilst on the other, it would set a strong precedent for Meciar's 'unreliable' Slovakia which (together with the Czech republic) was expected to form the third wave of EAs applicants re-negotiating the 1991 Czechoslovak agreement with the EC.

Steel safeguard clauses

Chapters 2 and 3 looked at how domestic and international pressures finally led the EC to exclude the ECSC products from the fast track liberalisation of the Association agreements with the Visegrads. Having been one of the most controversial issues during the first wave of EA negotiations, it was finally agreed that barriers in the trade of coal and steel were to be abolished by 1996 and 1998 respectively (see Table 6.1). The deal, however, left some EC member states (e.g. Spain) complaining that the EC markets were not sufficiently protected against cheap imports from the Associated partners (*Agence Europe*, 21.11.91: 9). Their demands for the introduction of a safeguard clause specifically designed for steel imports was rejected by the Commission (*Agence Europe*, 11.12.91: 7) on the basis that the existing general safeguard clause laid down in Article 30 offered sufficient protection. Arguing along a similar line the Commission was also able to defend its position against the increasingly sceptical EC steel producers who soon after the conclusion of the Visegrads EAs began to demand tough measures in order to tackle what they described as 'chaos' in the EC-CEECs steel trade (*Agence Europe*, 11.1.92: 8; 29.1.92: 13).

Table 6.1 Tariff Reduction for Industrial Products[a] from the CEECs

Product Group	1992/93[b]	Further Steps	Complete Elimination	
			Visegrads	Bulgaria, Romania
Basic Products				
(Annex IIa)	-50%	-50% following year	1.1.93	1.1.94
(Annex (IIb)	-20%	-20% each subsequent year	1.1.96	1.1.97
Sensitive Products				
Within limits of quotas and ceilings	-100%	Augmentation of quotas and ceilings by 20% per year	1.1.97	1.1.98
(Hungary)	(-100%)	(Annual increase by 15%)		
Quantities in excess	-15%	Annual reduction of 15%	1.1.97	1.1.98
(Hungary)	(-10%)	(Annual reduction of 10%)		
Textiles[c]				
(Protocol No. 1)	2/7	-1/7 each year, starting at the third year	1.1.98	1.1.99
ECSC Coal[d]				
(Protocol No. 2)	-	-50% 1994; -50% 1996	1.1.96	1.1.96
(CSFR, Poland)	-	(-100% 1993, Spain & Germany 1996)		
ECSC Steel				
(Protocol No. 2)	-20%	Three times -20% per year & then twice -10%	1.1.97	1.1.98
(Bulgaria)	(-20%)	(Four times -20%)		
Other Industrial Prod.				
	-100%	-	1.3.92	1.5.93[e]

a. Chapters 25-97 of the Combined Nomenclature except some products (Annex I) considered agricultural products.
b. 1.3.92: CSFR, Hungary and Poland; 1.5.93: Romania; For Bulgaria the date is assumed here to be 1993.
c. Tariff reductions apply to all textiles within Chapters 50-163 of the Combined Nomenclature. New quotas have been agreed in December 1992 for 1993and following years. For re-imports after processing, duties are abolished at the time of the entry into force of the agreement (concerning products covered by quotas)
d. All quantitative restrictions are abolished one year after the entry into force of the agreements, in Germany and Spain after four years at the latest.
e. Bulgaria: 31.12.93
Source: European Commission 1994

By May 1992, it became apparent that the most serious threat to the EC steel industry was coming from Czechoslovakia, the steel exports of which according to EUROFER's figures increased more than 180% during the period between January and February 1992 (*Agence Europe*, 1-2.6.92: 9). As a result, in the summer of 1992, the Commission came under pressure to utilise the general safeguard clause of the Czechoslovak agreement. Following a period of indecision and internal deliberation over the best way of protecting the EC's steel industry, the Commission finally 'gave in' to the demands of France, Germany and Italy and on 31.7.92[6] decided a selective application of the general safeguard clause, limited only to certain categories of products (coils, cold-rolled sheets, machine wire etc.) and to certain member states (France, Germany and Italy) which were particularly affected by the Czechoslovak steel exports (*Agence Europe*, 8.8.92: 4).

This decision, in addition to the timing of the utilisation of the EA's safeguard clause against Czechoslovak steel exports, received a hostile reception in Eastern Europe and raised further fears about the EC's protectionist tendencies (Drabek, 1993: 87-104 and Winters, 1992). Critics argued that Czechoslovakia's very small share (approx. 3.5%) of the total EC steel imports could not inflict 'serious injury' to the EC markets mentioned in Article 30 of the EAs (Van Den Hende, 1997: 149), while the utilisation of the safeguard clause without prior or subsequent public investigation and without prior consultation with the Czechoslovak authorities within the Joint Committee (*Agence Europe*, 21-22.9.92: 13), was regarded as a disproportionately harsh reaction to the danger posed by Czechoslovak exports.

The problem of increased steel imports from Eastern Europe, leading to the EC's measures against Czechoslovakia in August 1992, was an undesirable development for Bulgarian and Romanian interests in the EA negotiations. Those EC member states such as Spain and Italy (backed also by the German, French, Belgian and Portuguese delegations) which had been arguing for the inclusion of a specific safeguard clause for ECSC products since the first wave of EA negotiations (Agence Europe, 8.11.91: 9), now had a strong case for seeing their proposals applied to the second wave. Indeed, the protectionist tendency was once again able to overcome the reservations of the Commission and the more liberal member states (e.g. Britain and the Netherlands).

As a result, the Council's negotiating directives given on 12.5.92 left the Commission with a noticeably more cautious mandate than the one offered for the first wave.[7] The EC's sensitivity was clearly reflected in the final text of the EAs with Bulgaria and Romania. While the timetable for tariff reductions remained the same as that of the first wave applicants (complete elimination within 5 years, see Table 6.1), the Bulgarian and Romanian agreements were to include a specific safeguard clause for ECSC products. Article 5 of the second Protocol provided for:

> If, during a period equal to the derogation for subsidies under Article 9.4 and given the particular sensitivities of the steel markets, imports of specific steel products originating in one Party cause or threaten to cause serious injury to domestic procedures of like products or serious disturbances to the steel markets of the other Party, both Parties shall enter into consultations immediately to find an appropriate solution. Pending such a solution and notwithstanding other provisions of the Agreement and in particular Articles 31 and 34, when exceptional circumstances require immediate action, the importing Party may adopt forthwith quantitative or other solutions strictly necessary to deal with the situation, in accordance with its international and multilateral obligations.

Having learned from the 'mistakes' made in the first wave (e.g. Czech imports) as well as responding to new international (e.g. troubles with the American markets) and domestic (e.g. restructuring of the Spanish state-owned CSI) pressures, the EC was therefore, able to proceed with the necessary 'improvements' of its Association strategy. However, unlike the strengthening of the conditionality principle, 'improvements' in the steel sector did not constitute a major policy U-turn. In this case, attention was given to effective protection in cases of market disturbances, rather than altering (for the worse) the quantities or the timetable for liberalisation for the second wave of Association applicants.

Agriculture

The EC's sensitivity over agricultural products had already been clearly demonstrated since the first wave of Association negotiations. The idea of a free trade area for agricultural products was rejected at an early stage while the EC member states repeatedly refused to grant generous concessions in agricultural products which were already in surplus in the EC markets such as cereals, beef, sugar and dairy products (see chapter 2). The hard EC line on these products showed no signs of relaxation during the negotiations with Bulgaria and Romania. There were several reasons for this:

- The high political cost that the EC had paid in order to defend such a hard line during the negotiations with the Visegrads. Having already suffered the consequences (in terms of bad publicity) of the September 1991 deadlock over concessions for beef and cereals, in mid-1992 the EC had no reason to soften its position for Bulgaria and Romania. The continuation of the exaggerated rhetoric concerning the 'great export potential' of the CEECs, as well as the very limited negotiating power the second wave of Association applicants actually had, preserved the tough EC position regarding these products.
- The Council's approval of the CAP reform in May 1992. Following almost a year of internal deliberations and disagreements, Commissioner Mac Sharry's plan for reforming the CAP included, amongst others, drastic cuts to beef and cereal prices despite opposition from the agricultural lobby of the EC's north (Rieger, 1996: 97-125). Having already upset farmers over the CAP reform, and with the conclusion of the GATT negotiations (involving an inevitable compromise with the Americans over agriculture) scheduled for the end of the year, the EC's cautious position on meat, cereals and dairy products would be unlikely to change specifically for Bulgaria and Romania.
- The referendum for the ratification of the Maastricht Treaty in France scheduled for 23.9.92. The French vote on the TEU came to dominate the European agenda not only because it followed soon after the shock of the 'No' vote in Denmark (June 1992), but also because President Mitterrand connected the outcome of the French referendum with his own political survival. The predicted close outcome of the vote made it clear that the French government could not afford to 'irritate' the large and powerful farming lobby by further concessions to Eastern Europe. It is indicative that one day after the French 'Yes' vote, Commissioner Martin Bangemann admitted that the French Referendum forced the EC to be "...very cautious about expansion...[but] now the French vote should give us a green light again." (*BBC SWB*, 24.9.92: A1/3).

In addition to the reaffirmation of the EC reluctance to open up its markets for cereal, beef and dairy imports from Eastern Europe, the second wave of Association negotiations gave the EC the opportunity to clarify its position towards fresh fruit and vegetable imports from the CEECs. These product categories had not been contentious during the negotiations with the Visegrads mainly because of the limited exported quantities from these countries. For Bulgaria and Romania on the other hand, fresh fruit and vegetables were the biggest export categories, representing almost 20% of the total agricultural exports in both countries (Commission of the EC, 1995a and 1995b). The relatively strong export potential in fruit and vegetables of the second wave applicants (especially of Bulgaria) however, meant that unlike the Visegrads, Bulgaria and Romania were competing directly with the EC's south (see chapter 4) which produced similar products and which has always been very keen to support a high-level of EC protection for its farmers (as a result of the large share of agricultural employment and the strength of the farming trade unions).

In fact, the export potential of the second wave applicants for fruits and vegetables did not go unnoticed by the EC's southern member states. When the Council met in early October 1992 (*Agence Europe*, 7.10.92: 8) in order to specify the EC's negotiating position during the fifth round of the negotiations with Bulgaria and Romania (in which agriculture was top of the agenda), the mandate was clearly restricted as the Council decided to reduce the 'basic quantities' for fruit and vegetables by almost 25% and consequently limited all concessions based on these quantities (see Table 6.2).[8]

Table 6.2 Provisions on Agriculture: Bulgarian and Romanian EAs

	1992/1993	Further Steps
Quantitative Restrictions	Removed	-
Basic Quantities (eligible for concessions)	Average exports to the EC during the period 1988-90 (Bulgaria, 89-91) (Romania, 88-89)	10% annual increase for the first 5 years of the agreements
Products of Annex XIa (subject to max. quotas)	50% levy reduction	-
Products of Annex XIb (unlimited quotas)	Preferential Rates of Duty	-
Products of Annex XIIa[a] (subject to max. quotas)	Levy reduction -20%	Second Year: -40% Third Year: -60% Fourth/Fifth Year: Frozen
Products of Annex XIIb[b] (subject to max. quotas)	Duty reduction -20%	Second Year: -40% Third Year: -60% Fourth/Fifth Year: Frozen
Products of Annex XIII[c] (subject to max. quotas)	Tariff reduction -5%	Second Year: -10% Third Year: -15% Fourth/Fifth Year: Frozen
Products of Annex XIVa[d] (subject to max. quotas)	Tariff reduction -10%	Second Year: -20% Third Year: -30% Fourth/Fifth Year: Frozen

a. Annex XIIIa for Bulgaria; b. Annex XIIIb for Bulgaria; d. Applied only for Bulgaria
Source: Tracy, 1994

While the Visegrad and the Bulgarian/Romanian protocols on agriculture are very hard to compare due to the complexity of the liberalisation procedures and the large number of products involved, the reduction of the basic quantities for fruit and vegetables constituted a clear discrimination against the second wave applicants. It is also widely recognised that the overall deal on agriculture was less generous than the one offered to the first wave. This view was held by Guggenbuhl (1995: 241), Sukova-Tosheva (1994: 81) and Ibanescu (1994: 75), but is also clearly reflected in Andriessen's statement following the Council mandate on 7.10.92 in which the Commissioner for External Relations accused the EC member states of granting smaller concessions to the two countries than they have done for the Visegrads (*Agence Europe*, 8.10.92: 8).

The 'tightening' of agricultural concessions for Bulgaria and Romania is yet another manifestation of the opportunities offered by the iterated nature of the EC's Association game in Eastern Europe. As in the cases of human rights and steel, the second wave of Association negotiations provided the EC with a chance to 'improve' its Association strategy in the region, this time with agriculture. Of course, all such changes are to be dictated by the strongest actor (the EC) and are designed so as to fit its needs and priorities at the time of the negotiation. In the case of the second wave, continuation of unnecessarily protectionist practices (Bulgarian and Romanian agricultural exports to the EC in 1991 represented 0.4% of the total EC agricultural imports) can be justified as part of an 'already established' strategy, while marginal 'improvements' of the EC's strategy are made in the name of 'new circumstances' or 'internal difficulties'.

The Bulgarian strategy: the predominance of the 'equal treatment' factor

Since March 1991 when it requested the beginning of Association negotiations with the EC, the Bulgarian government's strategy had been one of arguing for the benefits of an early Association while at the same time reassuring the EC member states that the country was firmly committed to its 'European' future. In a statement following his victory in the 1992 election, the Bulgarian President Zhelev insisted:

Europe: This is the priority of our foreign policy. Our goal is Europe, and I will never get tired repeating: Europe, Europe, Europe (*BBC SWB*, 21.1.92: B/3).

The determination to have a fast and, if possible, complete Bulgarian integration into the European structures enjoyed an almost universal acceptance in the Dimitrov's UDF-dominated government[9] and was also supported by the considerable majority of politicians across the political spectrum, including the Bulgarian Socialist Party (BSP) whose government had submitted Bulgaria's Association application in early 1991. For the Bulgarian President Zhelev the beginning of Association negotiations with the EC was both an important political signal and a major incentive for speeding up reforms in order to make up for "the time lost" and increase the country's chances "...of catching up with Poland, Hungary and Czechoslovakia in the next few years.." (*Agence Europe*, 16.11.91: 5 and *BBC SWB*, 21.1.92: B/3).

Soon after the negotiations opened in May 1992 however, the first signs of a changing Bulgarian strategy became apparent. Now that the main political objective of getting the country in the Association game was accomplished and the negotiations focused on technical issues, the Bulgarian delegation toughened its position. While the Bulgarians showed signs of flexibility over the EC's reference to human and minority rights, Deputy Prime Minister Eskenazi (co-ordinator of all Bulgarian ministries involved in the negotiations) insisted after the completion of the first round that the EC should be more flexible over the free movement of people and, most importantly, it should align Bulgaria's liberalisation timetable with that of the Visegrad countries:

If the term for liberalisation of custom duties is five years, Bulgaria will insist that in its case it be reduced to four years. Otherwise we will lag not one but four or five years behind the other three countries (*BBC SWB*, 27.5.92: B/3).

The Bulgarian demands for an identical liberalisation timetable with that of the Visegrads were not accepted by the EC (interview in the Bulgarian Mission to the EC, 21.3.97). By August 1992, following the end of the third round, it was becoming clear that the negotiations were running into difficulties. Despite the fact that most issues relating to Political Dialogue were almost resolved, the timetable of liberalisation caused friction, while the articles on unilateral suspension and the steel safeguard clause also continued to be contested. Bulgarian dissatisfaction over the course of the negotiations was indicated by the letter of the Bulgarian Foreign Minister Ganev to the President of the Foreign Affairs Council, Douglas Hurd, in which the Bulgarian side asked for political intervention in order to facilitate the conclusion of the agreement:

The Bulgarian side believes that liberalisation of the EC markets is a more effective support for Bulgaria's economy than direct financial aid. That is why it is a cause of particular concern that even after the third round, trade negotiations are still in an initial phase. Bulgaria hopes to be treated as favourably as Poland, Hungary and Czechoslovakia (*BBC SWB*, 1.9.92: A1/3).

Moreover, departing from the early official position of 'catching up' with the Visegrads, the Bulgarian Foreign Minister was now arguing that:

What matters is reaching an agreement under which Bulgaria will be treated as an equal partner...a possible delay in Bulgaria's admittance to associated membership in the EC would be unimportant (*BBC SWB*, 15.8.92: B/2).

The resumption of the negotiations following the summer break was marked by a significant change. Having faced repeated EC refusal, the Bulgarian delegation decided to drop the demand of aligning the Bulgarian liberalisation timetable with that of the Visegrads and embarked on a new strategy which called for a "non-less favourable treatment". As a senior Bulgarian negotiator put it:

We amended our mandate and started demanding not less favourable treatment; that is compensating one thing for another. In the overall package to achieve an agreement that would be comparable to that of the other countries, we accepted less favourable treatment in some sectors and in other sectors we tried to negotiate a better deal (interview in the Bulgarian Mission to the EU, 21.3.97).

The new Bulgarian position helped the fourth round of negotiations to finish with relative success. Outstanding disagreements from the third round such as the Preamble and the unilateral suspension clause were mostly resolved, while the Chapters on services and economic co-operation were also finalised. The discussion on the substantive issues of trade on agriculture, textile and steel however, was transferred to the fifth round as both the Commission (as the EC's negotiator) and the Bulgarian delegation waited for further clarification from the Council of Ministers which would debate these questions on 6.10.92.

However, the new offers of the Council disappointed Bulgarian expectations. Despite the fact that some modest concessions were given for textiles,[10] the EC position remained unchanged for trade in ferrous metals, while the quotas for agriculture were significantly reduced. As a result, progress in the fifth round was modest. With the Bulgarian delegation effectively rejecting the new EC's offers, the protocols on agriculture, textiles and ECSC products as well as those on rules of origin and trans-border waterways were left to be re-examined at the next round. Apparently, the stalemate embittered Bulgarian officials who nevertheless insisted on their "non-favourable treatment" strategy. Deputy Prime Minister Eskenazi argued that:

> Bulgaria should seek to receive maximum concessions for the Bulgarian producers of textile and farm produce and then think about the general political effect of such agreement...despite the political and economic importance for Bulgaria of the association with the EC, this country should not join the European economic structures on its knees (*BBC SWB*, 17.10.92 and 12.11.92: A1/3).

As a result of the disagreements between the two parties, two more rounds[11] (a total of seven compared with the six for Romania) of negotiations were needed before the agreement was initialled on 22.12.92 (*Agence Europe*, 23.12.92: 7; Figure 6.2). Bulgarian demands for more concessions in agriculture as well as for the inclusion of the country in the diagonal cumulation of the rules of origin were rejected by the EC.[12] Moreover, the final agreement included a specific steel safeguard clause.[13] In return, the EC decided to reduce import duties on ECSC products for a year (see Table 6.1) as well as to insert a Joint Declaration that the steel safeguard clause (Art. 5 Protocol 2) would not be considered as a precedent in Bulgaria's negotiations to enter GATT.[14] Finally, the EC assured the Bulgarian side that it would receive equal treatment to that granted to the Visegrads in relation to trade in textiles.[15]

First Round (14-15.5.92)
EC delegation led by Mr. Benavides-Salas (Director in DG I).   Bulgarian delegation led by Mr. Ganev (Foreign Minister).   **Agenda**: General principles, Commercial aspects, Competition, Approximation of legislation
Second Round (16-17.6.92)
EC delegation led by Mr. Guggenbuhl (Head of Unit in DG I).   Bulgarian delegation led by Mrs. Daskalov (Deputy minister of Trade), Mr. Dobrev (Deputy Foreign Minister).   **Agenda:** Consensus on General Principles, Measures accompanying trade provisions, Economic Co-operation and Political Dialogue. First examination of textiles, transport, protocol on trans-border rivers, unilateral suspension clause.
Third Round (9-10.7.92)
EC delegation led by Mr. Guggenbuhl (Head of Unit in DG I).   Bulgarian delegation led by Mrs. Daskalov (Deputy minister of Trade), Mr. Dobrev (Deputy Foreign Minister) and Mr. Baichev (Foreign Ministry Director).   **Agenda**: Agreement on asymmetric concessions on industrial products, Measures accompanying trade provisions, Political Dialogue, Preamble, General principles, Economic co-operation. First examination of rules of origin, customs co-operation, agriculture, wine. Draft protocol on trans-border rivers. New Bulgarian proposals on suspension clause of the agreement.
Fourth Round (24-25.9.92)
EC delegation led by Mr. Guggenbuhl (Head of Unit in DG I).   Bulgarian delegation led by Mrs. Daskalov (Deputy minister of Trade), Mr. Dobrev (Deputy Foreign Minister).   **Agenda**: Final agreement on the Preamble, General Provisions on Trade agreed in principle. Progress on concessions on industrial products. Final agreement on services, Agreement in almost all provisions on economic co-operation. Progress on trans-border rivers.
Fifth Round (15-16.10.92)
EC delegation led by Mr. Guggenbuhl (Head of Unit in DG I).   Bulgarian delegation led by Mrs. Daskalov (Deputy minister of Trade).   **Agenda**: Agreement on Economic Co-operation, Trade of industrial products, and non-fulfilment of obligations. Modest progress on textiles, ECSC, and agriculture. Bulgaria asked for the same treatment as the Visegrads.
Sixth Round (10-11.11.92)
EC delegation led by Mr. Guggenbuhl (Head of Unit in DG I).   Bulgarian delegation led by Mrs. Daskalov (Deputy minister of Trade).   **Agenda**: Progress on trans-border rivers, transit, body of text. Some progress on the Rules of Origin, Agriculture and Wine. Problems in Steel and Textiles.
Seventh Round (3-4.12.92)
EC delegation led by Mr. Guggenbuhl (Head of Unit in DG I).   Bulgarian delegation led by Mrs. Daskalov (Deputy minister of Trade).   **Agenda**: Decisive progress in all remaining matters. No need for other session.   **22.12.92** : The Bulgarian Europe agreement initialled.   **8.3.93**: The Bulgarian Europe and Interim agreements signed.   **6.12.93**: The Bulgarian Interim agreement concluded.   **1.2.95**: The Bulgarian Europe agreement enters into force.

Source: Agence Europe (various issues), BBC Summary World Broadcast (various issues), Personal interviews.

Figure 6.2 Negotiating Rounds of the Bulgarian Europe Agreement

The 'tough' line followed by the Bulgarian delegation during the Association negotiations can be explained by a number of reasons relating to the economic situation in the country following the collapse of the Communist regime:

- *The desperate need to find new markets for Bulgarian products.* Throughout the Cold War period, Bulgaria had been amongst the most loyal allies of Moscow. In return, the USSR played a crucial role in Bulgaria's foreign trade. By 1990, the Comecon accounted for more than 73.7% of Bulgaria's total external trade, the highest figure amongst all CEECs (Wallden, 1994: 385-389). The collapse of the USSR and the Comecon in the early '90s left Bulgaria with the titanic task of re-directing its foreign trade in an attempt to support employment and earn badly needed hard currency. Naturally during this process, access to the EC market became a top Bulgarian priority.
- *The very high share of agriculture for Bulgarian exports.* By 1991, agricultural exports accounted for almost a quarter of the total Bulgarian exports to the EC (European Commission, 1995). Fruit and vegetables in particular (for which the EC had 'toughened' its position for the second wave applicants), were of great importance to the Bulgarian agricultural sector since both product categories were export-oriented and consequently had been particularly hit by the loss of the Comecon markets (Commission of the EC, 1995a: 36-40). Finally, apart from its apparent importance for foreign trade, the role of agriculture in the overall Bulgarian economy was also crucial, accounting for 12% of the Bulgarian GDP and providing employment for 21.2% of the total workforce.
- *The very high share of textile and clothing for Bulgarian exports.* According to data provided by the European Commission (1994), these product categories in 1991 accounted for 14.9% of total Bulgarian exports to the EC with an annual growth rate of 74%, the highest amongst all CEECs. The Bulgarian insistence on more EC concessions for textiles and clothing products can therefore, be better understood against the background of a spectacular rise in its exports to the EC which was mainly a product of the growth in outward processing trade (OPT) from Bulgaria to the EC.

An overall assessment of the Bulgarian strategy

The strategy followed by the Bulgarian delegation during the seven rounds of its EA negotiations with the EC (May-December 1992) was marked by significant changes. Departing from an initial strategy which insisted on an early (almost 'unconditional') beginning and conclusion of the EA as a means of catching up with the first wave (Visegrads), the Bulgarian delegation gradually shifted towards a more aggressive strategy which 'evaluated' the agreement predominantly according to its consequences for the Bulgarian economy and to a lesser extent according to the political implications it may have had for the country's 'return to Europe'. This position is clearly reflected in the dismissive statements made by Bulgarian officials on the possible negative effects of a delayed conclusion, and also in the insistence of Bulgarian officials that their country should, at any cost, receive equal treatment to that granted to the Visegrads. In this respect, it can be argued that the Bulgarian delegation attributed far greater importance to the 'equal treatment' factor than to the 'catch up' factor during its Association negotiations with the EC.

It is beyond the scope of this book to evaluate the wisdom of the Bulgarian strategy and its long-term consequences for the country's relations with the EC or the economic effects that the EA had for the Bulgarian economy. What remains important for this chapter is how the Bulgarian strategy was affected by the EC's new 'corrected' offers to the second wave applicants and how the Bulgarian side understood and evaluated the balance between the 'equal treatment' and the 'catch up' factors.

The Romanian strategy: the predominance of the 'catch up' factor

The Romanian road to the Association negotiations was a troubled one. It was characterised by suspicion on behalf of the EC institutions concerning the government's commitment to free market reforms and to the protection of human rights. In fact, Theodore Stolojan, who succeeded Petre Roman as Prime Minister in October 1991, engaged in frantic efforts to restore his country's wounded credibility (a result of the miners' crisis in September 1991) in the EC and defended Romania's suitability to be included in the second wave of Association applicants (see chapter 5).

Romania's late entry into the Association game left little time and room for manoeuvre. When the Council finally authorised the Commission to begin exploratory talks with the Romanian government in December 1991, the country was just coming out of a major political crisis with a new government and was already lagging behind Bulgaria which had begun similar talks with the Commission in September. As a senior Romanian negotiator put it:

To be very frank, from a practical point of view, at the beginning we had not much time to develop a very complex scenario for the negotiations...The target of our delegation was to gain time (interview in the Romanian Mission to the EU, 21.3.97).

Having secured a very speedy conclusion - lasting just 20 days - of the exploratory talks with the Commission (*Agence Europe*, 6-7.1.92: 8), Romania was finally able to begin Association negotiations alongside Bulgaria in May 1992. Soon after the negotiations between the Commission and the Romanian delegation began, it became apparent that the Romanian delegation was prepared to follow a more 'flexible' line than that of their Bulgarian counterparts. As early as the second round, Association negotiations were reported to have made "substantial progress" (*Agence Europe*, 22-23.6.92: 10), while a senior Romanian negotiator admitted to being "surprised" by the number of issues in which agreement was reached from an early stage. By the end of the third round, only a few issues remained unresolved and the two sides were predicting that the agreement would be concluded "within a reasonably short space of time." (IP/92/717, 16.9.92).

The summer break therefore found the Romanian and the Bulgarian delegations in different positions. While the Bulgarians were already complaining to the British Presidency about the disappointing progress of their EA negotiations, the report by the Romanian Ministry of Trade and Tourism, which conducted the negotiations on behalf of the Romanian government, maintained that despite the two sides having:

...somewhat different views on steel and farm products...the Romanian side was willing to find solutions apt to speed up the conclusion of the Association accord with the EC (*BBC SWB*, 21.8.92: B/12).

Moreover, unlike the Bulgarian complaints for 'unequal treatment', the Romanian government made it clear that "the negotiations revealed that there were no significant differences between the treatment reserved to Romania in comparison to other countries" (*BBC SWB*, 21.8.92: B/12).

The resumption of negotiations after the summer was followed by agreement on two of the most difficult issues; the ECSC and the Textile protocols, while a complete draft text of the EA was also approved (IP/92/717, 16.9.92). The protocols on agricultural and processed agricultural products on the other hand, were left to be discussed alongside the protocol on the Rules of Origin in the fifth round of the negotiations scheduled for 12-13.10.92 in order to take account of the

Council's mandate on agriculture which was expected to be given on 6.10.92 (*BBC SWB*, 22.9.92: A1/3).

As in the case of the Bulgarian negotiations, the Council's offers on agriculture received a negative reception from the Romanian delegation. While the two sides agreed on the protocol for processed agricultural products and managed to resolve all other outstanding problems, the Romanian delegation insisted on the trilateral cumulation of the Rules of Origin. In addition, with respect to agriculture, it expressed "...the desire to obtain concessions comparable to those negotiated with the Visegrad countries" (IP/92/819, 14.10.92). As a result, a new (sixth) round was agreed despite earlier re-assurances that the October session would be the last one and that the agreement would be initialled at the end of the month.

While disappointed with the EC offers in the fifth round, the Romanian delegation was not distracted from its main objective of an early conclusion of the agreement. As a result, in the next round the Romanians were forced to accept the EC offers on the Rules of Origin and agriculture almost in their entirety,[16] thus clearing the way for the initialling of the agreement on 17.11.92 (*Agence Europe*, 18.11.92: 6 and Figure 6.3).

First Round (19-20.5.92)
EC delegation led by Mr. Gadieux (Deputy Director General in DG I). Romanian delegation led by Mr. Fota (Minister for Trade and Tourism). **Agenda**: Broad consensus on the principles and the main components of the agreement. Agreement that only limited issues will be discussed (Steel, Textile, Agriculture).
Second Round (18-19.6.92)
EC delegation led by Mr. Guggenbuhl (Head of Unit in DG I). Romanian delegation led by Mr. Pop (State secretary in the Ministry of Trade and Tourism). **Agenda**: Consensus on General Principles, Measures accompanying Trade Provisions, Financial co-operation, and Institutions. First exchange of views in Agriculture, Textiles, Transport and Rules of Origin.
Third Round (16-17.7.92)
EC delegation led by Mr. Guggenbuhl (Head of Unit in DG I). Romanian delegation led by Mr. Pop (State secretary in the Ministry of Trade and Tourism). **Agenda**: Agreement on Political Dialogue, General Principles, Common Provisions for Free Movement of Goods, Services, Establishment, Title V (Competition, Approximation of legislation, Payments etc.). Almost complete agreement on Economic, Cultural and Financial Co-operation. Progress on unilateral suspension clause. Further examination of Agriculture, Textiles, Industrial products, Rules of Origin and Customs Co-operation.
Fourth Round (14-15.9.92)
EC delegation led by Mr. Guggenbuhl (Head of Unit in DG I). Romanian delegation led by Mr. Pop (State secretary in the Ministry of Trade and Tourism). **Agenda:** Approval of the first draft agreement. Agreement (subject to confirmation) of the protocols on Customs Co-operation and Textiles. Decisive progress for the ECSC protocol.
Fifth Round (12-13.10.92)
EC delegation led by Mr. Guggenbuhl (Head of Unit in DG I). Romanian delegation led by Mr. Pop (State secretary in the Ministry of Trade and Tourism). **Agenda**: Final agreement on trade in industrial products. ECSC protocol agreed. Protocol on processed agricultural products and fisheries agreed. Further discussion on Agriculture and the Rules of Origin. Romania asked for concessions similar to those of the Visegrad.
Sixth Round (3-4.11.92)
EC delegation led by Mr. Guggenbuhl (Head of Unit in DG I). Romanian delegation led by Mr. Pop (State secretary in the Ministry of Trade and Tourism). **Agenda**: Final agreement on Agriculture, Interim Agreement, Rules of Origin.   **17.11.92**: The Romanian Europe agreement initialled. **1.2.93**: The Romanian Europe and Interim agreements signed **8.3.93**: The Romanian Interim agreement concluded **1.2.95**: The Romanian Europe agreement enters into force

Sources: *Agence Europe (various issues), BBC Summary World Broadcast (various issues), Personal interviews.*

Figure 6.3 Negotiating Rounds of the Romanian Europe Agreement

The 'capitulation' (as Bulgarian negotiators saw it) of the Romanian delegation in the sixth round was clearly detrimental to the efforts of their Bulgarian counterparts to secure a more generous Association deal. Nevertheless, such a 'capitulation' as well as the 'flexibility' shown by the Romanian delegation throughout the six rounds of the negotiations can be explained by a number of factors which relate to:

- *The political importance attached to the Association agreements by the Romanian government.* Unlike their Bulgarian counterparts, Romanian officials treated the agreement as a predominantly 'political' signal of their country's return to Europe. In this process economics, while still important, would inevitably have to come second. As the Romanian Prime Minister Nicolae Vocaroiou stressed in the signing ceremony of the Romanian Association agreement with the:

> The agreement is above all an important political act. It can have important consequences at a time when the process of transition to a market economy is encountering a number of difficulties which largely exceed initial expectations (*Agence Europe*, 1-2.2.93: 6).

Alongside the political importance it attached to Association, the Romanian government clearly favoured the conclusion of negotiations as soon as possible. The determination to 'catch up' with the Visegrads so that Romania could eventually negotiate entry to the EC from an equal footing was also driven by recent history. As a senior Romanian negotiator put it:

> Romania was traditionally very close to the EU. We were the first to be part of the GSP and the first to have an agreement with the EC. We thought it would be a mistake to be left third or fourth (interview in the Romanian Mission to the EC, 21.3.97).

- *The impact of iteration on the Romanian Association strategy.* The precedent set in the Visegrad agreements was accepted almost unquestionably by the Romanian delegation which entered the second wave of the Association game well aware of its inability to effectively challenge the precedent of the first wave or what the EC was currently offering. As a senior Romanian negotiator put it:

> I am inclined to say that there were not any difficulties during the negotiations, because we preferred to be very realistic. When we started the negotiations the first EAs were already signed. We realised that it would not be possible to go further than our colleagues from the three other countries have succeeded (interview in the Romanian Mission to the EC, 21.3.97).

The iterated nature of the EC's Association game in Eastern Europe also had a crucial impact in one more respect. The Visegrad case had already made it clear that non-compliance with the EC's offers would inevitably result in a long delay to the whole process. The Commission's request for a new revised negotiating mandate by the Council in order to break the deadlock in the first wave of EA negotiations 'cost' the Visegrads several months of delay without achieving a significantly improved deal. The 'punitive' effects of non-compliance, as demonstrated in the Visegrad case, played an important role in 'persuading' the Romanian delegation to accept the EC's agricultural offers during the fifth round of the negotiations. As a senior Romanian official explained: "We said it is better to be in, rather than waiting outside, particularly knowing the whole process of negotiations with the Visegrad three, where the Commission was obliged to ask for a new mandate which postponed very much the process." (interview in the Romanian Mission to the EU, 21.3.97).

- *The economic situation in the country at the time of the negotiation.* With regards to agriculture, the area which caused the greatest friction in all previous Association negotiations, the Romanian case was indeed a peculiar one. While agriculture accounted, in 1991, for 18.9% of the Romanian GDP and provided employment for 28.9% of the total labour force, its share of total Romanian exports to the EC was relatively small at just 6.1%. Moreover, in 1991 Romania was the only net importer of food in Eastern Europe and the CEEC with the largest agri-food trade deficit with the EC (Commission of the EC, 1995b and 1995c). As a country with a trade deficit in agriculture, but also with agriculture accounting for a small share of its exports to the EC, it is not surprising that the Romanian delegation was ready to accept a more 'restrained' regime in these products.

The inability of the Romanian agricultural sector to export during the first years of transition should not, however, conceal the Romanian readiness to 'exchange' a more restricted trade deal for an early conclusion of the agreement. In agriculture, for example, the Romanian delegation failed to include an EC commitment for future negotiations on an improved market access into the agreement,[17] while textiles were subjected to less favourable treatment than that granted to Bulgaria (interview in the Bulgarian Mission to the EC, 21.3.97), despite the fact that they were the biggest single product category in Romanian exports to the EC (see Table 6.3.). Moreover, in the Romanian agreement there is no Joint Declaration on the effect of the steel safeguard clause on future GATT-Romania trade arrangements.

Table 6.3 CEECs' Exports to the EC According to the EAs Product Categories[a], 1992

	Bul.	Rom	CSFR	Hun.	Pol.
Basic Products A (Annex IIa)	0.4	0.0	1.1	0.2	0.3
Basic Products B (Annex IIb)	0.6	0.4	0.0	0.2	0.7
Sensitive Products (Annex III)	8.7	29.9	26.3	20.1	23.4
Textiles (Protocol No. 1)	28.1	37.8	12.9	21.3	18.8
ECSC Coal (Protocol No. 2)	0.2	0.0	2.4	0.0	7.2
ECSC Steel (Protocol No. 2)	6.5	6.5	8.2	3.7	4.9
Other Industrial Products	55.5	25.4	49.1	54.5	44.7
Total	100	100	100	100	100

a.   Excluding agriculture
Source: European Commission, 1994

A final indication of the relatively worse trade deal (as compared with other Associated CEECs) granted to Romania can be seen in the share of Romanian exports which were finally included under 'sensitive' areas of the Association agreement (see Table 6.3). For example, 74.2% of Romanian exports to the EC came under product categories for which full liberalisation of the EC markets would take place within 5 years (as in the cases of Annex III and Protocol No. 2-steel) or more (as in the case of Protocol No. 1). For the rest of the Associated CEECs, however, the percentage (for the same product categories) varied between 43.3% (Bulgaria) and 47.4% (CSFR).

An overall assessment of the Romanian strategy

Assessing its negotiating strategy during the six rounds of its Association bargain with the EC it can be argued that the Romanian delegation chose a rather different path from that of their Bulgarian counterparts. Unlike the Bulgarians, for the Romanians the 'catch up' factor assumed far greater importance than the 'equal treatment' factor. The prioritisation of the fast conclusion of the Association negotiations with the EC was based on the great political significance attributed to the Association agreement by the Romanian delegation as well as on the conviction that the EC offers to the second wave applicants could not have been better than those of the Visegrads. The Romanian flexibility during the negotiations however, was also based on economic considerations. For example, unlike Bulgaria, the agricultural sector in Romania, although very large, was not in a position to export and as a result the Romanian delegation found it much easier to 'swallow' the EC's protectionism in this domain.

Nevertheless, the flexibility of the Romanian delegation was not without consequences. While the delegation achieved its goal of an early conclusion to its Association negotiations with the EC, the trade provisions included in the Romanian agreement were clearly less favourable than those included in the EAs of other CEECs. Moreover, Romania's flexibility throughout the course of the negotiations and particularly its 'capitulation' in the sixth round, not only undermined Bulgaria's tougher stance against the EC, but also jeopardised the second wave applicants' collective ability to secure a more generous Association deal.

While one may argue that the significance of Romania's capitulation was minor given the fact that the balance of power between the EC and the second wave applicants (even following a joint strategy) was already massively in favour of the EC, this chapter asserts that such a capitulation was particularly useful for the EC's position during the Association negotiations. Taking into consideration that from the outset the Association agreements were hailed by the EC as the vehicle which would assist the Associated partners' 'return to Europe', the preservation of the EC's reputation as a 'caring Hegemon' and an 'impartial judge' of the reform process in Eastern Europe was a crucial element of its involvement in the region. In this respect, the EC's offers could not be seen to be imposed upon the economically and politically weak CEECs as the result of old style power politics. Nor could the EC afford to appear to discriminate against the second wave applicants. In other words, the 'packaging' of the Europe agreements mattered. It is precisely on the crucial question of 'packaging' that divisions amongst the East European applicants proved so useful for the EC. There is no doubt that, having secured the agreement of the Romanian delegation, the EC was in a much better position to defend its offers and dismiss the Bulgarian decision to block the fifth round of negotiations as 'unreasonable'. Similarly, with the Romanian delegation ready to ratify any EC offer, Bulgarian claims of EC discrimination against the second wave applicants could also be easily discredited.

Conclusion: assessing the effects of iteration

Chapter 3 described the EC's Association game with the Visegrads as being 'nested' within the *Grand* game; that is a network of domestic and international games in which the EC was involved at the time of the negotiations. Viewing the EC as an actor simultaneously playing games in *multiple arenas* with *variable payoffs*, it was argued that the apparently sub-optimal choices made by the EC in its Association strategy made sense only within the wider context. It was thus concluded that certain elements of the EC's Association strategy (e.g. protectionism in agricultural products) could be better understood as the result of domestic or international pressures, rather than a direct response to the 'threat' emanating from the East European Association applicants themselves.

In addition to being 'nested' into a wider framework, however, the EC's Association game unveiled one more important characteristic, that of *iteration*. Rather than being negotiated simultaneously with all CEECs seeking Association, the Europe agreements were an iterated bargain spread over a long period of time and included only a small group of applicants at any one a time (see Figure 6.1). The iterated nature of the Association game had profound effects on the strategies of the participants in the second wave of negotiations. For the EC, the only actor able to participate in *all* different stages of this iterated process, the negotiations with Bulgaria and Romania provided a good opportunity to 'improve' its Association strategy. Such 'improvements' could take various forms; introducing further defence mechanisms for sensitive sectors (e.g. steel safeguard clause), restricting market access to certain products as a means of appeasing potentially disruptive domestic constituents (e.g. reduced quotas for fruit and vegetables) or tightening the conditionality clause in response to domestic and international changes (e.g. human rights and unilateral suspension clauses).

Similar to the *multiple arenas*-based analysis, *iteration* can also account for certain aspects of the EC's Association strategy in the second wave which otherwise would be difficult to comprehend. The EC's decision, for example, to introduce a specific safeguard clause in the steel sector for Bulgaria and Romania appears to be an unnecessarily punitive measure for the second wave applicants which, on their own merit, posed no real threat to the EC markets. Taking into consideration the problems experienced with Czechoslovak steel exports throughout 1992, and also the clear prospect of re-negotiating the EAs with the Czech and Slovak republics in the near future, the 'tightening' of the steel regime in the second wave could serve as a useful precedent. Thus, an apparently sub-optimal EC choice in relation to the second wave applicants becomes the best strategy if the full iterated nature of the EAs is taken into account (Tsebelis, 1990: 72-79).

The same can also be argued for agriculture. Why did the EC chose to be so harsh with the second wave applicants given their tiny share (0.5%) in the EC's agricultural imports? Why did the EC refuse a more general deal for the two countries as a means of helping their agriculture-based economies out of a depression? The answer to both questions lies to a large extent in the very nature of the EC's iterated involvement in the Association game. A more generous deal in agriculture for Bulgaria and Romania would almost certainly harm the EC's *reputation* (Axelrod, 1990) in Eastern Europe, sparking demands for similar treatment by the first wave of Association partners (whose combined agricultural exports to the EC were much higher that the those of the second wave), while also setting a dangerous precedent for future Association negotiations.

As far as the second wave applicants are concerned, it is clear that the iterated nature of the Association bargain had important implications for their negotiating strategies. In this respect it should again be noted that, unlike the EC, the Bulgarian and Romanian delegations did not participate in all phases of the iterated Association game and as a result were deprived of the important privilege of 'trial and error' enjoyed by the EC. While the precedent set by the Visegrad agreements, as well as the future extension of the EAs to other CEECs, were well-publicised and known to everybody, the two delegations had, nevertheless, 'one chance' to negotiate their Association agreements. What they got out of these negotiations would not be available for them to change in the future; no 'trial and error', no option for 'adjustments' or 'corrections' would be available to them.

The Bulgarian and Romanian one-shot Association game with the EC, however, was placed within a sequence of similar games which could not be ignored by the negotiating teams of the two countries. The EAs had a history and a future. Moreover, the signature of these agreements signalled the 'official' return of both countries into Europe and most importantly opened what was rightly or wrongly believed by the CEECs governments to be the way to eventual EC membership.

This chapter has argued that the iterated nature of the EC's Association game in Eastern Europe had a differential effect on the strategies followed by Bulgaria and Romania. For the Bulgarian delegation, the precedent set by the Visegrad agreements became something of a 'taboo'. Driven by the conviction that agreement was fundamental to the Bulgarian economy and also that a less generous treatment by the EC would manifest the country's *de facto* relegation to a second class partner, the Bulgarian strategy focused on the question of equal (and, if possible, better) treatment to that offered to the Visegrads. As the negotiations progressed and the EC's offers failed to satisfy Bulgarian demands, the Bulgarian delegation made it clear that it would defend the equal treatment taboo even at the expense of an early conclusion which could have important domestic implications as well as jeopardising the country's attempts to catch up with the Visegrads. The final outcome appeared to be something of a compromise. Whilst the EC's position remained unchanged on all major issues (human rights, steel safeguard clause, reduced agricultural quotas etc.) the Bulgarians were able to obtain minor concessions in the form of declarations at the end of the agreement or small improvements in the liberalisation timetable in some products (e.g. steel).

For the Romanian delegation on the other hand, the previous phases of the Association game had a different effect. Unlike their Bulgarian counterparts, they saw the precedent set by the Visegrad agreements as the maximum that their delegation could ever achieve over Association negotiations. Rather than using the Visegrad precedent as the bottom line of their negotiating strategy, they made it clear that they would be prepared to consider a less generous trade package in return for an early conclusion of their agreement. Such a strategy was clearly based on political considerations, primarily the conviction that the country's interests would be better served if Romania was to join the Association club as soon as possible, even at the expense of a less favourable trade deal. Indeed, the Association package secured by the Romanian delegation clearly reflected this strategy. While less generous compared to the ones signed with other CEECs, the Romanian agreement was initialled (17.11.92) one month in advance of the Bulgarian one (25.12.92). This month, however, proved to be crucial. The Romanian Europe agreement as well as the Interim agreement (dealing only with trade-related matters of the Europe agreement) were signed on 1.2.92. In just over a month, the Romanian Interim agreement received the Assent of the EP (12.2.93) and was officially concluded by the Council on 8.3.92. The Bulgarian Europe and Interim agreements, on the other hand, were signed on 8.3.93. However, its official conclusion was considerably delayed due to a largely unrelated quarrel within the Council and was not made possible until 6.12.93 (almost nine months later than the Romanian Interim agreement).

It is not the aim of this chapter to conclude which of the two strategies followed by the second wave applicants proved to be more successful. The extreme complexity of the agreements themselves and the large number of products and liberalisation timetables involved make comparisons between different EAs very difficult. But even when comparisons are possible, the final Association deal would have to be judged against each applicant's political and economic situation at the time of the negotiations and, most importantly, against its foreign policy priorities and objectives. What does remain clear however, is the fact that divisions amongst the East European applicants (caused, to a large extent, by the very nature of the Association bargain) did not help their collective bargaining position vis-à-vis the EC. Mayhew (1998: 42) has argued that internal disagreements within the Visegrad camp weakened the negotiating position of the first wave of Association applicants vis á vis the EC. A similar observation is also (and perhaps even more) applicable to the second wave applicants whose different understanding and expectations from their Association bargain with the EC prevented them from co-ordinating their strategies effectively, a move which would have clearly increased their chances of securing a more generous Association deal.

Notes

[1] The word 'peripheral' is used here to clarify the focus of the research and by no means implies that the Bulgarian and Romanian *Association arena* was 'superior' or more 'important' than other *arenas* in which the EC was involved at the time.

[2] See *Agence Europe*, 4.4.92: 6. See also interviews in the Bulgarian and Romanian Missions to the EU (21.3.97). In order to ease fears that the toughening of the conditionality principle constituted a discriminatory practice against Bulgaria and Romania, the Commission insisted that the absence of a similar clause from the Visegrad agreements was only due to the fact that these countries concluded their agreements before the signature of the Maastricht treaty and not because they were considered to be more 'reliable' partners than the second wave applicants. Furthermore, the Commission argued, Albania and the Baltic states were also subjected to a similar human rights clause for their co-operation agreements with the EC signed during the first months of 1992.

[3] Bulgaria was admitted as full member of the Council of Europe on 14.5.92 (*BBC SWB*, 14.5.92: A1/1) and the Bulgarian parliament ratified the European Convention of Human Rights on 5.8.92 (*BBC SWB*, 5.8.92: B/6). For the whole period of the Association negotiations, Romania continued to hold the status of an invited member of the Council of Europe which was granted to her on 3.2.91. The country became full member of the Council of Europe on 4.10.93. The Visegrads on the other hand were all members of the Council of Europe by February 1991. For more details on the participation in European multinational organisations see Clarke (1991).

[4] The two republics declared their independence on 25.6.91.

[5] The EC member states recognised the two republics on 15.1.92.

[6] See Commission Decision No. 92/433/EEC, OJ 1992, L238/24 and Commission Recommendation No. 92/434/ECSC, OJ 1992, L 238/26. Also, *Agence Europe*, 30.7.92: 9.

[7] The Council's statement on 12.5.92 amongst other things mentioned that "...Concerning the possible implementation of safeguard measures in application of the agreement, either because of violation of competition rules or for other reasons, appropriate quantitative solutions will be envisaged and, if needs be, adopted, in respect of the multilateral or international obligations of the parties. These measures will be taken in conformity with procedures planned for the implementation of the safeguard clause including immediate measures if necessary". See *Agence Europe*, 13.5.92: 7.

[8] Basic or Preferential Quantities are the average imports into the Community during the 'reference period' on which all trade concessions are calculated. The 'reference period' in the cases of CEECs were the three years prior to the negotiations (1991 or 1992) for which

complete data existed. In other words, if Bulgaria exported an average of 100 tonnes of fruit and vegetables during the 'reference period', the 'basic quantities' on which concessions would be calculated should have been 100 tonnes. Because of the 25% reduction agreed by the Council however, the 'basic quantities' would now have to be 75 tonnes.

[9] See the priorities set out by the Mr. Dimitrov for his government policy in 1992 (*BBC SWB*, 8.1.92. See also statement by Foreign Minister Ganev following his visit to Brussels in March 1992 (*BBC SWB*, 13.3.92).

[10] The new EC offer did not involve modification of the quantities qualifying for concessions, but relaxation of the rules relating to processing traffic. See *Agence Europe*, 3 and 7.10.92: 8.

[11] See *Agence Europe* 13.11.92: 8 and 7-8.12.92: 10. See also visit by Mr. Guggenbuhl to Bulgaria on 16.11.92 in order to resolve remaining technical problems with the Bulgarian delegation. *Together in Europe*, 15.11.92: 4.

[12] Rules of origin determine the economic nationality of goods and are usually attached in a separate protocol to all preferential agreements. They ensure that only products originating in an associated country benefit from preferential market access and define the conditions required for origin to be conferred on a product. As regards cumulation of the rules of origin, three main types can be distinguished: (i) *bilateral cumulation* operates between two associated partners (i.e. Bulgaria and the EU) and concerns materials only (i.e. excludes intermediate products- inputs); (ii) partial multilateral or *diagonal cumulation* allows cumulation for materials when several countries participate in an agreement (i.e. Association agreements with the Visegrads); (iii) *total multilateral cumulation* allows for the cumulation of all processing and transforming occurring within associated countries (i.e. EEA agreement). For more details on the Rules of Origin and their application in the Association agreements (Protocol 4), see European Commission (1994: 170-174).

[13] See Article 5, Protocol No. 2 in the Bulgarian agreement. Despite efforts by the Bulgarian delegation to avoid the inclusion of this clause into the final agreement, the EC position remained unchanged (interview in the Bulgarian Mission to the EC, 21.3.97).

[14] See Joint Declaration 18 at the end of the Bulgarian agreement. Also, two favourable EC Unilateral Declarations were included in the Bulgarian agreement in relation to Article 9 of the ECSC Protocol. See Unilateral Declarations No.s 4 and 5.

[15] See the EC's Unilateral declarations No. 3 at the end of the Bulgarian agreement.

[16] The only EC concession in the field of agriculture came in the form of some declarations at the end of the Romanian agreement in which the EC recognised the importance of 15 agricultural products for the Romanian agriculture. See interview in the Romanian Mission to the EC, 21.3.97.

[17] The compromise between the two parties provided for the attachment of a declaration at the end of the agreement in which the Romanian delegation expressed its wish for increased agricultural quotas in the future. However, no formal EC commitment was undertaken in this direction. See Declaration by Romania on Article 15 of the Interim Agreement (Art. 21 of the Europe Agreement) (Commission of the EC, 1992b).

PART III

THE EUROPE AGREEMENTS, EASTWARDS ENLARGEMENT AND THE EU's STRATEGY IN THE BALKANS

7 The Legacy of the Europe Agreements: Continuity and Change in the EU's Relations with Central and Eastern Europe and the Balkans

The pillars of the EC's Association strategy in Eastern Europe: conditionality, differentiation and compartmentalisation

Chapter 2 discussed how the principles of conditionality and differentiation formed the two basic pillars of the EC's Association strategy in Eastern Europe. In April 1990, the Commission fleshed out the conditionality principle by linking the calendar of the Association negotiations to the respect, on behalf of the Association applicants, of the rule of law; human rights; free multi-party elections and economic liberalisation with a view to introducing market economies. Conditionality was seen by the EC as a means of developing an effective 'carrot and stick' strategy aimed at ensuring the irreversibility of economic and political reforms in Eastern Europe. Its anticipated benefits would, therefore, be twofold. On the one hand, entry into the Association game would be the 'reward' for those CEECs committed to democratic values and the market economy. On the other, exclusion from the Association game would provide the worse performing CEECs with an incentive to engage in serious economic and political reforms.

In August 1990, the Commission fleshed out the differentiation principle. According to it the different political and economic profiles of the Association applicants illustrated the need to adapt each individual agreement to the circumstances of the country concerned. The specificity of the situation of each CEEC, in turn, implied "differentiation within and between the common elements comprising the future agreements". In fact, the differentiation principle enjoyed wide-spread support by the Association applicants which, following decades of irrational trade policies imposed upon them within the CMEA framework, were instinctively reluctant to negotiate 'collectively' with the EC and were naturally attracted to the idea of an Association deal specifically tailored to their own interests (interview in the Romanian Mission to the EU, 21.3.97.

The principles of conditionality and differentiation had indeed a crucial effect on the way in which the Association bargain was structured. The differentiation principle, for example, made it clear that the Association agreements would be negotiated bilaterally and not on a 'block to block' basis as, for example, had been the case of the Lomé Convention with the ACP countries. Moreover, a credible application of the conditionality principle meant that not all East European countries aspiring to Association could begin negotiating with the EC at the same time. Instead, they would have to be compartmentalised into different waves - depending on their performance in relation to the EC's prerequisites - and then invited to enter the Association game one at a time. As a result, following the Commission's recommendation in August 1990 and the Council's decision in September of the same year, Poland, Hungary and Czechoslovakia were selected to form the first wave of Association applicants, while Bulgaria and Romania (who had also expressed an interest in entering into the Association game) were left in the second wave.

Explaining the EC's position during the Association negotiations: beyond one-shot games

Chapter 2 examined the early development of the EC's Association strategy in Eastern Europe and looked at how the EC introduced different liberalisation timetables for different product categories according to the degree of their 'sensitivity' for the EC markets. Consequently, certain product categories (i.e. steel and textiles) were not subjected to the fast-track liberalisation applicable to most industrial products, while agriculture was altogether exempted from the establishment of the free trade area (FTA) between the EC and the Association applicants at the end of a ten-year transitional period. The special trade arrangements for the so-called sensitive sectors were presented by the EC as built-in feature of the Association agreements; non-negotiable and applicable to all CEECs aspiring to Association. Chapter 2 discussed how the EC resisted demands by the Association applicants for a more generous liberalisation timetable and stood firm to its commitment to protect its sensitive industries despite the fact that such a strategy often left the EC vulnerable to accusations of excessive trade protectionism.

The EC's caution during the first wave of Association negotiations is, at one level, puzzling. The EC's refusal to agree on more generous trade concessions for the CEECs was not only incompatible with the EC leaders' early promises for full support of the process of economic and political transformation in Eastern Europe, but it also constituted a disproportionately harsh reaction to the small trade threat posed by the Visegrad applicants whose combined share of the EC's total external trade in 1990 did not exceed 2.4% (The European Commission, 1994: 545). What is seemingly even more puzzling is the fact that the EC's protectionism intensified further during the Association negotiations with the second wave applicants, despite the fact that Bulgaria and Romania posed an even smaller trade threat (in 1990 their combined share of the EC's total external trade was 0.58%) than the Visegrad applicants.

This book argued that the EC's inability to 'translate' positive rhetoric into generous trade concessions for the CEECs cannot be fully understood if the Association negotiations with the first and second wave applicants are studied 'independently' as one-shot games played in a vacuum. In order to account for the contextual factors that affected the EC's strategy during the Association negotiations, chapters 3 and 6 utilised the concepts of games in *multiple arenas* with *variable payoffs* (Tsebelis, 1990) and *iterated games* (Tsebelis, 1990, Axelrod, 1990). The two concepts were used outside the theoretical rigidity of 'full blown' game theory. Instead, this book followed the example of a wide range of analysts (e.g. Putnam, 1988; Bates *et al.*, 1998; Radaelli, 1998; Friis, 1998), who used formal models as frameworks for contexualising and enhancing our understanding of empirical evidence. In this respect, the analysis provided in this book builds on Scharpf's observation that "a game-theoretic representation can often provide useful and precise abstractions of extremely complicated real life constellations" (1997: 45).

Games in multiple arenas with variable payoffs

The concept of games in *multiple arenas with variable payoffs* (Tsebelis, 1990: 60) was used in chapter 3 in order to illustrate how the Association game was 'nested' within a broader network of intertwined and interdependent games played at both the *Domestic* and *International arenas* (what was described in Figure 3.2 as the *Grand game*). Applying

Tsebelis' argument to the EC's Association game with the first and second wave applicants, chapter 3 argued that the EC's inability to accept a more generous Association package was in most cases related, not to the direct threat posed to its interests by the Association applicants themselves, but instead to the EC's attempts to maximise its payoffs in the entire network of games in which it was involved at the time (i.e. the *Grand game*). Hence, EC preferences that may seem profoundly sub-optimal within the context of an one-shot game, can be seen in a rather different perspective when studied within the context of games in *multiple arenas* (with *variable payoffs*) and vice versa.

Against this background, chapter 3 argued that generous agricultural concessions to the Association applicants (though perhaps feasible within the context of an one-shot game) were likely to undermine the EC's bargaining position within the GATT negotiations and particularly vis à vis the US which had long been arguing for the relaxation of EC's protectionist practices in international agricultural trade. Domestically, more concessions to Eastern Europe would almost certainly infuriate the agricultural lobby, the patience of which had already been seriously tested by the proposed CAP reform and the EC's compromises in the GATT negotiations. A similar situation was described for the cases of textiles and steel where the EC also discovered that concessions to the CEECs were either likely to undermine its position at an international level and/or put at risk important domestic reform agendas.

The *multiple arenas*-based analysis should not only be restricted to the EC's inability to deliver generous concessions in trade-related issues. Chapter 3 also discussed how a more concrete promise to the CEECs in relation to future EU membership would almost certainly undermine the EC's efforts to delay (beyond the conclusion of the Maastricht negotiations) the opening of enlargement negotiations with the EFTA countries. On the other hand it was argued that a *multiple arenas*-based analysis is less useful in explaining the EC's outright rejection of the CEECs' demands for the relaxation of restrictions on free movement of workers. In this case, the CEECs as the largest 'pool' of illegal immigration presented the main (not a secondary) threat to the EC's interests. Nevertheless, reference to other peripheral games such as the EC's economic recession (and its implications on unemployment and social security bills) can offer additional resources for the understanding of the EC's position on this matter.

So why did the Association game fail, in most cases, to attract 'priority treatment' over other peripheral games of the EC's *International* and *Domestic arenas*? In other words, why did the EC prefer to 'sacrifice' a generous Association package for the CEECs in order to strengthen (or, rather, not to undermine) its position in other domestic and international bargains? References to the EC's small economic stakes in Eastern Europe during the early 1990s may be valuable in answering these questions. Whilst investment and trade between the two sides grew massively in comparison to their pre-1989 levels, in real terms the amount of EC's trade and investment directed to Eastern Europe remained rather insignificant. In this respect, the size of the EC's anticipated payoffs from the Association game was clearly smaller than the size of its anticipated payoffs from other, economically more important, peripheral games such as GATT or the CAP reform.

The EC's small economic stakes in Eastern Europe can, therefore, account for the CEECs' inability to 'seduce' the EC into a more generous Association deal. Neither could the CEECs 'bully' their way into a more favourable result. Unlike the EC's strong agricultural lobby or the powerful American and Japanese opposition within the GATT bargain, the Association applicants had no effective means of resisting the EC's offers. Chapters 2 and 6 discussed the poor co-ordination of the CEECs' strategies during the Association negotiations and their fragmented opposition to the EC's protectionism (caused, to an extent, by their compartmentalisation into different waves). Moreover, for all Eastern European countries the 'cost of exclusion' (Moravcsik, 1994: 59) from the Association agreements remained prohibitively high. In turn, their profound inability to bear the consequences of 'no agreement' (Putnam, 1988: 442) rendered the threat of defective behaviour, as a means of 'bullying' the opposition into more concessions, obsolete.

For the EC on the other hand, the economic implications of defective behaviour in the Association game were always much smaller than those facing the CEECs. Only when combined with overall security considerations did the cost of 'no agreement' increased and became a sufficient reason for the relaxation of the EC's caution vis à vis the first and second waves of Association applicants. To this end, chapter 3 discussed how the deterioration of the situation in Yugoslavia and the wider security concerns caused by the Moscow coup in August 1991, assisted the unlocking (as a result of more generous EC offers) of the stagnated negotiations with the Visegrads as well as the advancement of the Bulgarian and Romanian requests for the opening of Association negotiations.

Iterated games

One of the main implications of the Association applicants' compartmentalisation into different waves was the fact that the EC's Association game in Eastern Europe would be spread over a long period of time and be repeated for a number of times. The effects of iteration on the EC's negotiating strategy vis à vis the second wave applicants was examined in chapter 6. Similarly to the *multiple arenas*-based analysis offered in chapter 3, chapter 6 argued that the EC's negotiating position vis à vis the second wave applicants should not be studied in isolation, but in relation to the Association game's 'past' and anticipated 'future'. In this respect, the selection of sub-optimal preferences at a particular phase of an *iterated game*, may be necessary for the maximisation of a player's payoffs during the entire period of the game (Tsebelis, 1990: 73) or for the preservation of its *reputation* vis à vis previous or future negotiating partners (Axelrod, 1990: 151, Tsebelis, 1990: 156).

The EC's need to preserve its *reputation* vis à vis existing and potential Association partners as well as to maximise its payoffs during the entire period of the Association game had been central themes in the analysis of the second wave of Association negotiations provided in chapter 6. Hence, the reasons which led the EC's insistence on 'improved conditionality' (Guggenbuhl, 1995: 240) for the second wave applicants should not be solely confined to the poor human rights records and the rather sluggish pace of political reform in Bulgaria and (particularly) Romania. In addition to taking into account the 'peculiarities' of the two Balkan countries, such a change of strategy was in keeping with the new constitutional arrangements agreed in Maastricht and, in particular, with the incorporation of Article F into the new treaty which made a clear reference to the European Convention for the Protection of Human Rights and Fundamental Freedoms of 1950.

Most importantly, the insertion of the human rights and automatic suspension clauses into the second *wave* of EAs gave the EC an opportunity to address a far wider audience. It was not only an indication that the EC had learnt its lesson from the unfolding crisis in the former Yugoslavia, but also a vehicle for the reinforcement of the EC's *reputation* as an uncompromising supporter of human rights. The reinforcement of such a reputation was significant, particularly as the EC was soon to engage in Association negotiations with the constituent republics of the disintegrating Czechoslovakia as well as with the Baltic states where the treatment of the Russian speaking minorities had been a matter of concern.

A similar analysis was also used in order to account for the deterioration of the EC's trade-related offers (i.e. steel and agriculture) to the second wave applicants despite the latter posing an insignificant trade threat to the EC. Chapter 6 argued that the reduction of the quantities of fruits and vegetables qualifying for trade concessions under the EAs, reinforced the EC's protectionist *reputation* (which had already been established for meat and dairy products since the Visegrad agreements) and extended it to cover Mediterranean products. Moreover, the insertion of a specific safeguard clause for steel not only made clear that the EC had got the message from the row over Czechoslovakian steel imports in summer 1992, but also created a precedent which would allow the EC to deal more effectively with similar incidents in the future.

References to the iterated nature of the Association game can, therefore, provide additional resources for the understanding of the EC's position during the second *wave* of Association negotiations. Without such references, the insertion of an 'improved conditionality' clause and, in particular, the tightening of the EC's agricultural and steel offers to Bulgaria and Romania would seem a disproportionately punitive measure for the two Balkan countries and as such a profoundly sub-optimal preference. Nevertheless, when the preservation of the EC's *reputation* and the maximisation of its payoffs during the entire period of an *iterated game* are taken into consideration, the changes of the EC's strategy during the second wave of Association negotiations can be put into a clearer perspective.

The Bulgarian and Romanian exclusion from the first wave of Association negotiations

The reasons behind the Bulgarian and Romanian exclusion from the first wave of Association applicants were explored in chapters 4 and 5. Chapter 4 looked at the response of the EC's member states to the two Balkan countries' requests for entry into the Association game. It was argued that whilst the Bulgarian and Romanian governments were successful in persuading the EC-12 that their countries were fit to enter the Association game, the economic and political appeal of the two Balkan applicants was clearly much smaller than that of the Visegrad group. Sluggish economic reforms and political uncertainty in the two countries deterred foreign investment and consequently reduced incentives for faster integration into the EC's economy. In terms of trade, Bulgaria's and Romania's combined share of the EC's total external trade was four times smaller than that of the Visegrad group in 1990. As far as individual EC member states were concerned, by 1990 the combined volume of Bulgarian and Romanian trade was just above 10% of the Visegrad equivalent in Germany, around 20% in Italy and Britain and less than 30% in France (Table 4.1).

Bulgaria's and Romania's political appeal to the EC member states was also limited. Chapter 4 argued that neither Bulgaria nor Romania managed to secure effective and consistent patronage for the strengthening of their relations with the EC, similar to that enjoyed by their Visegrad counterparts through their special relationship with Germany. In the case of Romania, the potential of its special relationship with France could not be fully exploited given Paris' scepticism about the process of EC widening. Italy, on the other hand, whilst keen to assume the role of patron for the two Balkan countries (in particular Romania), lacked the necessary credibility mainly due to its governmental instability and the large size of its economy's sensitive sectors. The same can also be argued for Greece whose patron credentials were seriously undermined by the bad shape of its economy, its inflexible foreign policy over the 'Macedonian issue' (a source of constant disagreement in Greek-Bulgarian relations) as well as by its small influence within the EC.

Chapter 5 looked at the response of the Commission and the European Parliament to the Bulgarian and Romanian Association requests. Once again it was argued that Bulgaria's and Romania's delayed entry into the Association game was due to their inability to persuade the two EC institutions that their progress down the path of political and economic reform was comparable to that of the Visegrad group. In Romania, the reform record of the NSF government was poor, whilst its conduct of the first multi-party elections was severely criticised by the European Parliament. Moreover, the bloody suppression of the students' demonstration in June 1990, not only eliminated the country's chances of inclusion in the first wave of Association applicants, but eventually led the Commission (following sustained pressure by the EP) to freeze the EC's relations with the NSF government for the second half of 1990. In Bulgaria, on the other hand, whilst the situation remained comparatively better than in Romania, political and economic reforms lagged behind those of the Visegrad group. The victory of the former communist party (BSP) in the first multi-party elections raised doubts over the continuation of the reform process in the country, whilst prolonged political instability during the summer of 1990 (at a time when the EC selected the composition of the first wave of Association applicants) did little to assist the country's bid for speedy integration into the EC.

The compartmentalisation of Bulgaria and Romania into the second wave of Association applicants had important implications for the way in which the two countries negotiated their Association to the EC. In chapter 6 it was argued that the iterated nature of the Association bargain (which was itself a by-product of the compartmentalisation of the Association applicants into different waves) provided the EC with an opportunity to adjust its Association strategy in order to take into account important internal and international developments as well as the experience gained by the negotiation of the Visegrad agreements (see above). The iterated nature of the Association bargain also had important implications for the negotiating strategies of the second wave applicants. Chapter 6 argued that for the Bulgarians, the precedent set by the Visegrad agreements became something of a 'taboo'. The preservation of their country's 'equal treatment' with that offered to the Visegrads was, therefore, elevated to the highest priority of the Bulgarian delegation, one that was worth following even at the expense of delaying the conclusion of the negotiations with the EC. For the Romanians on the other hand, their Association with the EC was perceived as the beginning of a process which would eventually lead to full EC membership and as such it was given a much more 'political' meaning. Their delegation firmly believed that the actual content of the agreement was of secondary importance. What mattered most was its early conclusion, even with less favourable terms than those offered to the first wave applicants, so that Romania could 'catch up' with the Visegrads in the 'race' for EC membership.

Under such fundamentally different perceptions of the iterated nature of the Association bargain the two delegations found it increasingly difficult to co-ordinate their positions vis à vis the EC's offers. The Bulgarian delegation often accused the Romanian strategy of being submissive and damaging for both applicants' bargaining positions (interview in Bulgarian Mission to the EC, 21.3.97), while the Romanian delegation dismissed the Bulgarian strategy as being unrealistic and irrelevant (interview in Romanian Mission to the EC, 21.3.97). The different negotiating strategies followed by the Bulgarian and Romanian delegations, nevertheless, should not only be attributed to their different perceptions of the Association bargain's iterated nature. Differences in foreign policy priorities and objectives, in composition of trade with the EC and in economic and political situations in each of the two Balkan applicant countries are factors that also need to be taken into consideration if their different negotiating strategies during the Association bargain are to be fully understood.

The legacy of the Association agreements and the process of EU enlargement

Chapter 2 discussed the EC's immediate reaction to the revolutions in Eastern Europe during the last months of 1989. It was argued that the EC's strategy for economic and political reconstruction in the region was elaborated against a background of high uncertainty and rapid change. The unique nature of the events in Eastern Europe meant that no pre-existing blueprint for action could be selected by the EC in its attempt to stabilise the situation in the region. Against this background, all available policy options carried significant risks, whilst none of them escaped criticism and doubt. The idea for a radically restructured CMEA, for example, favoured by President Delors (Speech/90/1, 17.1.90) and Commissioner Andriessen[1] in early 1990, received a hostile reception by most East European governments which saw it as a threat to their hard-earned economic and political independence from the Soviet Union (CEPR, 1992: 4). Moreover, such an idea was dismissed by many commentators as an attempt to artificially prolong intra-regional trade which, for many decades, had been based on irrational and politically motivated economic policies (Baldwin et al., 1992: 74-75; Inotai, 1994: 36-40; Mayhew, 1998: 86-89).

The idea of creating a body similar to the Organisation for European Economic Co-operation (OEEC) which was responsible for the management of the Marshal Plan in post-War Europe, was also problematic. Whilst an OEEC-type of organisation could serve as a useful platform for the distribution of the G-24 aid and the promotion of regional co-operation in Eastern Europe, its credibility was jeopardised both by the very small volume (as compared to the Marshal Plan) of the G-24 assistance (Van Ham, 1993: 177-179; Inotai, 1994: 29-32) and by the lack of the necessary mechanisms and expertise in the CEECs needed for the absorption of a Marshal Plan-type of assistance programme. (Cadieux, 1991: 253; Zecchini, 1991: 256-260, Rood, 1991: 26).

Finally, the suggestion for the creation of a Europe-wide trade agreement in which both the EC and all the CEECs would be full members was also rejected. Despite the fact that such an arrangement was favoured by the President of the EBRD Jaques Attali[2] and, later, by other prominent economists (Balwin, 1994), the plan resembled President Mitterrand's idea of a 'European Confederation' too much to attract the sympathy of Eastern European governments and those EC member states which remained committed to the EC's closer relations with the region.

Therefore, from a variety of risky options the conclusion of a series of bilateral Association agreements with the CEECs based on the principles of conditionality and differentiation was selected by the EC as the best strategy for assisting economic and political transformation in Eastern Europe. In fact, such a strategy carried with it many advantages. It was both cheaper than the Marshall Plan and free from the prejudices associated with the CMEA. Moreover, at a time of radical change within the EC, it promised a cautious and controlled pace of rapprochement with Eastern Europe, while at the same tome it was thought to provide the necessary mechanisms for ensuring the irreversibility of reforms in the region.

The selected strategy, nevertheless, was not free of risks. The bilateral linking of the CEECs to the EC was bound to increase their dependency on the EC and weakened the prospects of regional co-operation in Eastern Europe.[3] Contrary to the EC's early expectations,[4] most East European governments did not perceive regional co-operation as supplementary to their 'return to Europe', but rather as an unwanted deflection from their ultimate goal of EU and NATO membership. In this respect it can be argued that whilst the Association agreements managed to respond to the calls for the strengthening of the EC's relations with the CEECs during the early stages of transition, in the longer run they failed to create an alternative framework of co-operation (outside the immediate EU structures) which could ease the pressure exerted by the CEECs' for a speedy and full EU membership. Against this background, the East European record of regional co-operation remained poor. Several regional schemes such the Quadrangorale,[5] the initiative for Black Sea Economic Co-operation[6] and the Greek-inspired Balkan Initiative[7] have either fallen into obscurity or are still struggling to get off the ground. Even the relatively more successful formations such as the CEFTA[8] and the Baltic Free Trade Area[9] are lacking permanent structures for policing trade liberalisation and competition rules, while at a political level they both remain at an embryonic stage (Mayhew, 1998: 89; Dangerfield and Goryunov, 2001).

With most of the regional formations either discredited or low on the CEECs' list of priorities, the EC's later attempts to revitalise regional co-operation in Eastern Europe had limited success. Both Copenhagen (1993) and Essen (1994) European Councils paid considerable lip service to regional co-operation, but the money allocated by the Phare programme in this direction was far too modest to make a real impact.[10] Clearly, the most successful EC initiative for the promotion of better relations amongst the CEECs was the French-inspired Pact on Stability in Europe (1995) which assisted the settling of some regional disputes (e.g. the Romanian-Hungarian Treaty of Understanding, Co-operation and Good Neighbourliness of September 1996). Nevertheless, as Sedelmeier and Wallace (1996: 377) argued, this scheme was more an attempt on behalf of the EC to develop preventive diplomacy in the region (in the shadow of the Bosnian war and the failures of the CFSP), rather than an initiative aimed at providing 'positive incentives' for the strengthening of regional co-operation in Eastern Europe.

The principle of compartmentalisation found perhaps its most clear manifestation in the publication of the Commission's *avis* (part of the Agenda 2000 document) on the membership applications of the 10 East European candidates (The Commission of the EC, 1997). The Commission's *avis* essentially confirmed the existence of a multi-tier Eastern Europe and called upon only five East European membership applicants (the Czech Republic, Estonia, Hungary, Poland and Slovenia) to begin fast-track accession negotiations with the EU. For the remaining five applicants (Bulgaria, Latvia, Lithuania, Slovakia, Romania), accession negotiations were to proceed at a much slower pace and their prospect of EU membership was effectively moved to the distant future.

Following the new realities created by the war in Kosovo, however, the EU's policy of compartmentalisation became increasingly unsustainable. Soon after his appointment as Commissioner for Enlargement, Guenter Verheugen (Gerhard Schroeder's former Minister for Europe) argued strongly for a more inclusive enlargement process where all East European applicants would be allowed to begin fast-track accession negotiations with the EU.[11] This change of policy was seen by many as an attempt by Prodi's Commission to defend itself against accusations of discriminatory practices against the second wave of accession applicants as well as a means of rewarding Bulgaria's and Romania's crucial support (against a very sceptical domestic audience) for NATO's campaign in Yugoslavia.

Hence, the Commission's Progress Reports on enlargement published on 13.10.99[12] argued for the inclusion of Bulgaria, Latvia, Lithuania, Romania and Slovakia into the fast lane of accession negotiations. The Commission's proposals were agreed by the Helsinki European Council in December 1999 (Doc 99/16, 10/11.12.99) and the formal opening of fast-track accession negotiations with the former second wave applicants took place on 28.3.00. Whilst important at a symbolic level, in practical terms the EU's move did little to reduce the pre-existing gap between the first and the second group of membership applicants which, since then, has continued to widen, thus confirming the existence of a *de facto* compartmentalised Eastern Europe.

In retrospect, the principles of bilateralism and compartmentalisation that underpinned the EU's Ostpolitik for most of the last decade have not only undermined regional co-operation in Eastern Europe but have also ultimately failed to control the pace of the EU's rapprochement with the CEECs. Back in 1991, for example, the EC made it clear that the Association agreements should be separated from the question of membership and rather be treated as arrangements which had value 'on their own'. Nevertheless less than eighteen months after the conclusion of the first wave of EAs, the EU's position was to change at the Copenhagen European Council (June 1993). Full membership had now became a mutual objective, while the Association agreements were soon to be incorporated within the broader framework of a pre-accession strategy (agreed by the Essen European Council in December 1994). A year later, the Madrid European Council (December 1995) committed the EU to opening accession negotiations with the CEECs within the six months following the conclusion of the IGC that led to the Treaty of Amsterdam. Indeed, following the publication of the Agenda 2000 in July 1997, the formal opening of the first wave of accession negotiations took place in London on 12.3.98, whilst within the next two years the EU was engaged in fast-track accession negotiations with all ten of the East European applicants.

In fact, the EU's inability to control the pace of its rapprochement with the CEECs over the last decade raises questions about the preparation of its forthcoming enlargement. The failure of the Amsterdam IGC to tackle the enlargement-related agenda revealed the magnitude of the problem. Later, the bitter disagreements over the reform of the EU's internal policies (on the basis of the Commission's Agenda 2000 proposals) in view of enlargement was yet another indication of the members states' reluctance to bear the financial burden of an enlarged EU. The compromise reached in the Berlin European Council (March 1999) over the next financial framework (2000-2006) did settle some of the financial uncertainties of enlargement, but still the details of the reform of the CAP and the Structural Funds remain unresolved. More recently, the Nice Treaty addressed the problems of institutional reform, but here too the final arrangement is not free from confusion and uncertainty.

Today, even the frontrunners of the process of EU enlargement are facing an uphill struggle in their efforts to secure early entry into the club. Amongst Eastern Europe's best performers a lot of political capital has been invested on the assumption that the first wave of the EU's eastwards enlargement will take place by 2004. Economic planning too is crucially dependent upon early entry into the EU. Yet the 2004 horizon for full EU membership is by no means certain. The rejection of the Nice treaty in the Irish referendum in summer 2001 posed the first major challenge in this direction. Greece's threat that unless Cyprus is included amongst the first wave of countries to join the EU, it will block the entire enlargement process may also frustrate the membership aspirations of the East European applicants. Moreover, with the most difficult chapters (i.e. agriculture) of the accession negotiations still open, nobody can predict with certainty whether the 2004 deadline can be met or which of the five frontrunners will be ready to join by that time.

Against this rather uncertain background, the absence of a credible multilateral framework in Eastern Europe, caused to a large extent by the EU's legacy of bilateralism in the region, may prove very costly indeed. Such a multilateral framework could be useful in absorbing (at least temporarily) the shock of a possible delay in the process of EU enlargement and could provide an acceptable 'waiting room' before full EU membership. So far, the European Conference – the only forum that brings together all EU membership applicants – has manifestly failed to provide such an alternative. From the outset, its establishment by the Luxembourg European Council (December 1997) was regarded more as an attempt to entertain the EU's refusal to grant Turkey candidate status,[13] rather than to provide a true multilateral framework aimed at fostering closer co-operation amongst the EU membership applicants.

The challenge of accommodating Eastern Europe's 'losers': the European Union and the Balkans

Irrespective of the short-term progress of the enlargement negotiations, however, strong regional formations will almost certainly be needed in order to accommodate Eastern Europe's 'losers' both politically and economically. The promotion of such schemes in the Balkans may be one of the greatest challenges for the EU's Ostpolitik in the coming years. For the best part of the last decade the EU's Balkan strategy was overshadowed by its disastrous handling of the early stages of the Yugoslav crisis in 1991-92 and the subsequent catastrophic wars in Croatia and Bosnia. With its confidence and credibility severely wounded as a result of the Yugoslav fiasco, the EU's strategy in the region was to remain hesitant and, many would argue, incoherent and seemingly ignorant of the inter-related nature of the region's economic and political problems. Instead, the EU's relations with the Balkan countries were based on a series of bilateral agreements the depth of which was determined by the local regimes' degree of compliance with the conditionality principle.

Hence, those considered to have progressed sufficiently down the path of political and economic reform were eventually allowed to negotiate Europe agreements with the EU. This category included Bulgaria and Romania and, since 1995, Slovenia. Further down the ladder of contractual relations with the EU stood countries not directly involved in the Yugoslav wars where the pace of reform remained slower. For the countries of this category (i.e. Albania and later FYROM) the EU provided assistance through the Phare programme and trade concessions in the form of a Trade and Co-operation agreement. In a third category stood the countries directly involved in the Bosnian conflict with which the EU did not establish bilateral relations and which benefited only from the EU's humanitarian operations in the region.

The end of the Bosnian war in 1995 opened up new opportunities for the EU's strategy in the Balkans. On 26-27.2.96 the EU's General Affairs Council launched the Regional Approach for the Balkans (Pres96/33, 27.2.96). The EU's initiative was meant to supplement the Dayton agreement and the OSCE efforts in the former Yugoslavia as well as to provide a framework for promoting stability, good-neighbourliness and economic recovery in South-East Europe. Specially tailored clauses of economic and political conditionality – emphasising the respect of minority rights and the improvement of bilateral relations in the region – formed the cornerstones of the Regional Approach.[14] For the five eligible countries (Albania, Bosnia, Croatia, FRY, FYROM), compliance with these new conditionality clauses became the passport to improved access to the EU markets through autonomous EU trade concessions, financial and economic assistance through the OBNOVA (aid for the republics of former Yugoslavia) and Phare programmes and eventual establishment of 'normal' contractual relations with the EU in the form of Trade and Co-operation agreements.[15]

However, from the outset, the success of the Regional Approach was fatally undermined by the lack of sufficient financial resources to cope with the devastation caused by the Yugoslav wars on the region's economy and infrastructure. Moreover, the EU's initiative was far less 'regional' than its title indicated. Bulgaria, Romania and Slovenia, already linked to the EU by Association agreements, did not have any meaningful relation with it. Neither did Greece or Turkey. In addition, the strengthening of the conditionality principle meant that very few Balkan countries could benefit from the full advantages of the Regional Approach. Thus, by the end of 1998 the EU's relations with the with the wider Balkans presented an astonishing variety and included:

- a full member of the EU (Greece)
- a member of the first wave of enlargement applicants (Slovenia)
- two members of the second wave of enlargement applicants (Bulgaria and Romania)
- a membership applicant, whose current eligibility for negotiating entry was denied by the EU (Turkey)
- two members of the Regional Approach with Phare eligibility and a Trade and Co-operation agreement with the EU (Albania and FYROM)
- a member of the Regional Approach eligible for Phare funding and autonomous EU trade concessions, but without a Trade and Co-operation agreement with the EU (Bosnia)
- a member of the Regional Approach included into the scheme of autonomous EU trade concessions, but with neither Phare eligibility nor a Trade and Co-operation agreement with the EU (Croatia)
- a country without any official contacts with the EC (FRY).[16]

The escalation of the crisis in Kosovo during the first months of 1999 and the subsequent NATO's bombing of Yugoslavia in June 1999 marked yet another watershed for the EU's strategy in the region. The Vienna European Council in December 1998 had already recognised the difficulties of the existing EU policies in the region and had called for a broader and more integrated approach based on a 'common strategy' for the Western Balkans (Doc/98/12, 11/12.12.98). The Kosovo war clearly accelerated this process and affected the EU's relations with the countries of the region. The launch of the Stability Pact on 10.6.99 was the first example of the EU's changing strategy.[17] Bringing together a very large number of countries and organisations (including the EU, the US, Russia, the IMF, the UN the OSCE and others) the Stability Pact sought to create a framework for the co-ordination of military and economic efforts to stabilise the region and to contribute to the consolidation of lasting peace, democracy and economic prosperity. For this purpose, Bodo Hombach (a former Chief of Staff in Gerhard Schroeder's Chancellery) was appointed special co-ordinator of the Stability Pact and chair of its governing body: the 'South Eastern Europe Round Table'.

Within the wider context of the Stability Pact, in June 1999 the EU launched a new type of relationship with the countries of the region:

the Stabilisation and Association process (SAP). The Stabilisation and Association agreements (SAAs) were made available to five countries - Albania, Bosnia, Croatia, Macedonia and FRY - provided they comply with the EU's enhanced conditionality principle as this was elaborated within the context of the Regional Approach. In terms of their structure and content, the SAAs borrowed heavily from the EAs. Both types of agreements included provisions for asymmetrical trade liberalisation, financial assistance, co-operation in a wide range of policies (including JHA) as well as the strengthening of Political Dialogue between the two parties (The Commission of the EC, 1999). The SAAs, however, placed greater emphasis upon regional co-operation, democratisation, the development of civil society and institution building in South-east Europe. In strong contrast to the EAs, the SAAs made explicit reference to future membership into the EU. To this end the Feira European Council in June 2000 made it clear that all South-east European countries could potentially be considered as candidates for EU membership provided they fulfilled the 1993 Copenhagen criteria.

Today almost two years since the launch of the Stability Pact the Balkan countries remain amongst Eastern Europe's 'losers'. Slovenia as the only Balkan representative in the first wave of membership applicants is perhaps the only exception to this rule. Bulgaria and Romania although presently involved in accession negotiations with the EU are unlikely to join in the foreseeable future. Recent electoral results in both countries[18] are unlikely to contribute to their faster integration into the EU. In Croatia and FRY the arrival of Stepan Mesic and Vojislav Kostunica have marked a rapid drive towards democratisation. Responding to these positive developments in May 2001 the EU initialled a SAA with Croatia whilst FRY (particularly since Milocevic's extradition to the Hague) is likely to follow in the near future. The reform process in both countries, however, remains fragile and the future of the domestic coalitions that support it uncertain. In Bosnia and Albania progress has been slower. The political systems of both countries have been extremely volatile and their governments have not yet managed to assume full control over their territory and curb the power of criminal gangs and war lords. Despite these uncertainties, however, the EU has signalled its intention to open SAA negotiations with both countries in the early months of 2002. Finally, in FYROM, the first country to sign a SAA with the EU in April 2001 and until recently a model of moderation in the Balkans, the situation is precarious. The recent outbreak of violence between the government forces and Albanian extremists has left the country in limbo, with the prospect of an all-out civil war still remaining a distinct possibility.

Against this background the EU's efforts to accommodate Eastern Europe's 'losers', particularly those in the Balkans, is likely to be a task as crucial and challenging as enlargement itself for it is clear that the success of the EU's internal development is inextricably linked to the stability and welfare of its neighbours. The breaking of the vicious circle of political and economic underdevelopment in the Balkans, however, will require far more than tutoring local politicians about the benefits of economic and political reform. It will, first of all, require a realisation by all concerned (including the EU) that the region will either recover collectively or it will not recover at all. Within this context the pursuit of inclusiveness must be paramount. Economic recovery in the region will also require a far greater commitment on behalf of the EU (and other Western benefactors) to provide the necessary financial resources needed for such an undertaking as well as a new pan-European trade arrangement which will alleviate the 'hub and spoke' effects (Baldwin, 1994, Sapir, 2000) to those countries that are likely to remain excluded from the full benefits of the Single Market for the foreseeable future. To this end, proposals for an Association of Association Agreement (AAA); a Pan European Free Trade Area (PEFTA) or a Pan European Custom's Union (PECU) need to be urgently pursued. In the longer run, however, the European Union's attempts to assist Europe's more fragile democracies can only be successful if the inclusive character of the European integration process is preserved. A meaningful prospect of full entry into the European Union will also be the best weapon for defeating the 'underdog culture' (Diamantouros 1994) that has so dogged the Balkans in the past and the only guarantee that the region will finally progress towards a new era of stability and economic development.

Notes

---

[1] See Andriessen's Communication on the changes in Eastern Europe (Commission of the EC, 1990b: 3). The idea of a restructured CMEA was also supported by a number of economists in Eastern Europe, particularly from countries which were not yet fully committed to economic liberalisation (e.g. Bulgaria and Romania). For more details see Zaman (1990, 1991); Pogonaru (1990); Arojo (1990); Vachkova and Todorova (1990). All sources cited in Wallden (1994: 240).

[2] Attali proposed the idea of such a Europe-wide trade agreement convinced that "a succession of bilateral trade agreements [between the EC and the CEECs] could only lead to frustration". For more details see *Agence Europe*, 18.6.92.

[3] For an early warning on the need for promoting multilateralism and regional co-operation in Eastern Europe see Bonvicini et al. (1991: Chapter 7).

[4] See, for example, Delors' speech before Strasbourg European Council, *Speech/89/87*, 7.12.89.

[5] The scheme was created by Italy in 1989 and involved (alongside Italy) Austria, Hungary and Yugoslavia. It was later renamed Hexagonale following the inclusion of Czechoslovakia in 1990 and Poland in 1991.

[6] The Black Sea Economic Co-operation Declaration was signed on 25.6.92 by Albania, Armenia, Azerbaijan, Bulgaria, Georgia, Greece, Moldova, Romania, Russia, Turkey and Ukraine.

[7] The inaugural meeting of the Balkan Initiative was held in Crete on 3.11.97 including top-level representatives from Greece, Turkey, Bulgaria, Romania, Albania and Yugoslavia.

[8] CEFTA was first created by Poland Hungary and the Czech and Slovak republics on 21.12.92. The scheme was later enlarged with Slovenia (1996) and Romania (1997).

[9] The Baltic Free Trade Area was created by Estonia, Latvia and Lithuania soon after the three republics declared their independence from the Soviet Union in 1991.

[10] Over the period 1992-1996 the money allocate by the Phare programme for the promotion of regional co-operation amounted to 160.8 million ECUs. This figure is less than 3% of the total Phare assistance in Eastern Europe over the same period. See Mayhew (1998: 141).

[11] See for example, Verheugen's speech during his hearing at the European Parliament, 1.9.99.

[12] For an overview of the Progress Reports, see IP/99/751, 13.10.99.

[13] Turkey was finally granted candidate status by the Helsinki European Council (December 1999).

[14] In April 1997 the General Affairs Council set specific preconditions for each country before being allowed to deepen their relations with the EU. In addition more general preconditions were also included under the titles of 'human rights, rule of law', 'respect for and protection of minorities' and 'market economy reforms'. See PRES/97/129, 29/30.4.97.

[15] Albania signed a Trade and Co-operation agreement with the EU in 1992. Albania and FYROM joined the Phare programme in 1991 and 1993 respectively.

[16] FRY did initially benefit from autonomous EU trade concessions within the context of the Regional Approach, but in 1998 the country's relations with the EU were effectively frozen following the escalation of the Kosovo crisis.

[17] The establishment of the Stability Pact was originally envisaged by the General Affairs Councils on 8 & 26.4.99 (see PRES/99/94 of the Special Council Meeting - General Affairs - Luxembourg, 8.4.99 and 2173 and PRES/99/118 of the Council Meeting - General Affairs - Luxembourg, 26.4.99). The plan was then approved by the Council on 17.5.99 (see PRES/99/146 of the 2177th Council Meeting - General Affairs - Brussels, 17.5.99) and was officially launched by the Cologne special international meeting on 10.6.99.

[18] In the Romanian presidential election in December 2000, the reformist governing coalition Democratic Convention (DC) suffered a crushing defeat and former President Ion Iliescu returned triumphant to power. In Bulgaria, the party of the former King Simeon won the parliamentary election June 2001 after defeating the reformist UDF of former PM Ivan Kostov.

Bibliography

Adamiec J. (1993), *East-Central Europe and the European Community, A Polish Perspective*, RIIA Discussion Papers, No. 47, Royal Institute of International Affairs, London.

Agence Europe, various issues.

Allison T.G. (1971), *The Essence of Decision: Explaining the Cuban Missile Crisis*, Little Brown, Boston.

Arojo Z. (1990), "SIV: Varianti na Preustrojstvoto [CMEA: Alternative Solutions for Perestroika]", *Mezhdunarodni Otnosheniya*, No. 6.

Arts M. J. and Lee N. (1994) (eds), *The Economics of the European Union: Policy and Analysis*, Oxford University Press, New York.

Assemblee Nationale (1991a), [Discussion on the crisis in the textile sector], Sceance du 29 Mai 1991.

Assemblee Nationale (1991b), [Discussion on the international negotiations in the textile sector], Sceance du 14 Juin 1991.

Assemblee Nationale (1991c), [Discussion on aid policy in Eastern Europe], Seance du 11 Octobre 1991.

Assemblee Nationale (1992a), [Discussion on GATT negotiations], Sceance du 16 Avril 1992.

Assemblee Nationale (1992b), [Ratification of the Friendship and Co-operation treaty with Romania], Sceance du 15 Mai 1992.

Assemblee Nationale (1992c), [Discussion on CAP reform], Sceance du 27 Mai 1992.Avramov R. (1993), "Opening of the Bulgarian Economy?", in Nikolov K. (ed), *Bulgaria and the European Community*, Working Papers No. 3b/93, Centre of European Studies, Sofia, December.

Axelrod R. (1981), "The Emergence of Co-operation Among Egoists", *American Political Science Review*, Vol. 75, pp. 306-18.

Axelrod R. (1990), *The Evolution of Co-operation*, Penguin Books, London.

Balazs P. (1992), "How Can the Community Be Expanded?", *The New Hungarian Quarterly*, No. 125, Vol. 33, Spring.

Baldwin R (1994), *Towards an Integrated Europe*, Centre for Economic Policy Research, London.

Baldwin R. *et al.*(1992), *Monitoring European Integration, iii: Is Bigger Better? The Economics of EC Enlargement*, CEPR, London.

Barnes I. and Barnes P. (1995), *The Enlarged European Union*, Longman, New York.

Bates R.H *et al.* (1998), *Analytic Narratives*, Princeton University Press, Princeton.

Baun M. (2000), *A Wider Europe: the process and politics of European Union enlargement*, Rowman & Littlefield Publishers Ltd, Lanham.

BBC Summary World Broadcast, various issues.

Bensainou D. (1995), "Les Fonds Structurels: Quelle Application Aux PECO?", *Economie Internationale*, CEPII, No. 62, 2e Trimester, 1995.

Bideleux R. and Taylor R. (1996) (eds), *European Integration and Disintegration. East and West*, Routledge, London.

Biedenkopf K. (1994), Problems of German and European Policy Towards the East, *Perspectives*, No. 3.

Black M. (1962), *Models and Metaphors*, Cornell University Press, New York.

Black S. (1997), *Europe's Economy Looks East*, Cambridge University Press, Cambridge.

Bonvichini G. (1991) (ed), *The Community and the Emerging European Democracies*, Royal Institute of International Affairs, London.

Brabant Van J. (1999), *Remaking Europe: the European Union and the transition economies*, Rowan & Littlefield Publishers inc, Lanham.

Brown J.F. (1992), "Crisis and Conflict in Eastern Europe", *RRF/RL Research Report*, Vol. 1, No. 22, 29 May.

Buckwell A., Haynes J., Danidova S., Kwiecinski A. (1994), *Feasibility of an Agricultural Strategy to Prepare the Countries of Central and Eastern Europe for EU Accession*, Study prepared for the Commission's DG IA, December.

Bulmer S. (1994a), "Institutions and Policy Change in the European Community: The Case of Merger Control", *Public Administration*, Vol. 72, No. 3.

Bulmer S. (1994b), "The Governance of the European Union: A New Institutionalist Approach", *Journal of Public Policy*, Vol. 13, No. 4.

Bulmer S, Paterson W. (1996), "Germany in the European Union: Gentle Giant or Emergent Leader", *International Affairs*, Vol. 72, No. 1.

Burgess A (1997), *The New Domination of the East*, Pluto Press, London.

Buzelay A. (1989), "Convergences et Redistributions dans la Perspectives 1992", *Revue Francaise d' Economie*, Vol. IV, No. 3.

Cadieux J-L. (1991), "The Commission of the European Communities", in OECD, *The Transition to a Market Economy*, Vol. 1, Paris.

Caporaso J. (1996), "The European Union and Forms of State: Westphalian, regulatory or post-modern?", *Journal of Common Market Studies*, Vol. 34, No. 1, March, pp. 29-52.

CEPR (1992), *The Association Process: Making Work*, Occasional Paper No. 11, Centre for Economic Policy Research, London.

Clarke D.L. (1991), "European Multinational Organisations: A Primer" in *Report on Eastern Europe*, 9.

Cloos et al (1994), *La Traité de Maastricht: Genèse, Analyse, Commentaires*, Bruylant, Brussels.

Coffey J.I. and Solms F. (1995), *Germany, the EU and the Future of Europe*, Centre of International Studies, Monograph Series, No. 7, Princeton University.

Coffey P. (1976), *The External Economic Relations of the EEC*, The Macmillan Press Ltd, London.

Cofos E. (1992), "I Elada ke ta Valkania pros to 2000 [Greece and the Balkans towards 2000]", in Elliniko Idrima Amyntikis ke Eksoterikis Politikis, *Epetirida Amintikis ke Exoterikis Politikis* 1990-1991, Athens.

Cohen M., March J. and Olsen J. (1972), "A Garbage Can Model of Organizational Choice", *Administrative Science Quarterly*, 17, March.

Coleman C. J. (1973), *The Mathematics of Collective Action*, Aldine, Chicago.

Collinson S, Miall H. and Michalski A (1993), *A Wider European Union? Integration and Co-operation in the New Europe*, RIIA Discussion Papers, No. 48, The Royal Institute of International Affairs, London.

Couloumbis T. (1992), "Greece and the European Challenge in the Balkans", in Hellenic Foundation for European and Foreign Policy, *The South-East European Yearbook 1991*, Athens.

Couloumbis T. (1993), "The Security Dimension: Bulgaria's Integration in Europe", in Nikolov K. (ed), *Bulgaria and the European Community*, Working Papers No. 3b/93, Centre of European Studies, Sofia, December.

Couloumbis T. and Yannas P. (1993), "Greek Security in a Post Cold War Setting" in Hellenic Foundation for European and Foreign Policy, *The South-East European Yearbook 1992*, Athens.

Cram L. (1994), "The European Commission as a Multi-Organisation: Social Policy and IT Policy in the EU", *Journal of European Public Policy*, Vol. 1, No 2, Autumn.

Cremona M. (1997), "Movement of Persons, Establishment and Services", in Maresceau M.(ed.), *Enlarging the European Union*, Longman, London.

Croft S., Redmond J., Rees G.W., and Webber M. (1999), *The Enlargement of Europe*, Manchester University Press, Manchester.

Curzon Prize V., Landau A., and Whitman R. (1999) (eds), *The Enlargement of the European Union: issues and strategies*, Routledge, London.

Cviic C. (1991), *Remaking the Balkans*, Pinter Publishers, London.

Dangerfield M. and Goryunov V. (2001) (eds), *Subregional Dimensions of European Union Enlargement*, University of Wolverhampton, May.

Dawisha K. (1990), *Eastern Europe, Gorbachev and Reform. The Great Challenge*, Second Edition, Cambridge University Press, Cambridge.

De Gust K.L. (1989), "European Security in the of Glasnost", *European Affairs*, Vol. 4, Winter.

Devuyst Y. (1995), "The European Community and the Conclusion of the Uruguay Round" in Rhodes C. and Mazey S. (eds), *The State of the European Community*, Third Edition, Lynne Riener, Boulder.

Diamantouros N. (1994), "Cultural Dualism and Political Change in Post-Authoritarian Greece", *Centro de Estudios Avanzados en Ciencias Sociales: Estudios Working Papers,* Madrid.

Donnelly M. (1993), "The Structure of the European Commission and the Policy Formation Process", in Mazey S. and Richardson J., (eds), *Lobbying in the European Community*, Oxford University Press, Oxford.

Donnelly M. and Richie E. (1994), "The College of Commissioners and their Cabinets", in Edwards G. and Spence D. (eds), *The European Commission*, Longman, London.

Drabek Z. (1993), "A Call for Re-negotiation of the Europe Agreements", *Bulgaria and the European Community*, Centre for European Studies, Sofia.

Drabek Z. (1993), "Call for Re-negotiation of the Europe Agreement", in Nikolov K. (ed), *Bulgaria and the European Community*, Working Papers No. 3b/93, Centre of European Studies, Sofia, December.

Dyson K., Featherstone K. (1997), "Jacques Delors and the Re-Launch of Economic and Monetary Union: A Study of Strategic calculation, Brokerage and Cognitive Leadership", Paper Delivered to the fifth biennial international conference of the *European Community Studies Association (USA)*, Seattle, Washington, May/June.

Dyson K., Featherstone K., Michalopoulos G. (1994), *"The Politics of EMU: The Maastricht Treaty and the Relevance of Bargaining Models"*, Prepared for delivery at the 1994 Annual Meeting of the *American Political Science Association*, The New York Hilton, September.

East European Reporter, various issues.

EC Mission to Bulgaria (1990), [Benavides report on political situation in Bulgaria), 21 March (unpublished and confidential document).

EC Mission to Romania (1990), [De Lange report on political situation in Romania), 2 January (unpublished and confidential document).

Edwards G. and Spence D. (1994) (eds), *The European Commission*, Longman, London.

EKEM (1993), *Triminiea Ekthesi gia ta Valkania* [Quarterly Report for the Balkans], No 2, Athens, December 1993.

Eleftherotypia, [Greek daily], various issues.

Elster J. (1989), *Solomonic Judgements: Studies in the Limitations of Rationality*, Cambridge University Press, New York.

Eskenazi I. (1993), "Bulgarian Association with the EC", in Nikolov K. (ed), *Bulgaria and the European Community*, Working Papers No. 3b/93, Centre of European Studies, Sofia, December.

Etzioni A. (1961), *A Comparative Analysis of Complex Organisations*, Free Press, New York.

Etzioni A. (1967), "'Mixed Scanning': A 'Third' Approach to Decision Making", *Public Administration Review*, Vol. 27.

Eurobarometer (1990), *Public Opinion in the EC*, No. 34, The Commission of the EC, December.

Eurobarometer (1991), *Public Opinion in the EC*, No. 36, The Commission of the EC, December.

European Access, various issues.

European Communities (1978), *Collection of Agreements Concluded by the European Communities*, Volume 3, Brussels.

European Communities (1978), *Treaties Establishing the European Communities,* Brussels.

European Trade Union Institute (1992), *Social Aspects of the Assistance Programmes to Central and Eastern Europe and the Commonwealth of Independent States*, ETUI, Brussels.

European Trade Union Institute (1992), *The Association Agreements between the European Community and Poland, Hungary and Czechoslovakia: A trade Union View*, ETUI, Brussels.

Eurostat (1990), *Basic Statistics of the Community*, 27th Edition, Luxembourg.

Eurostat (1991), *Basic Statistics of the Community*, 28th Edition, Luxembourg.

Eurostat (1992a), *Foreign Statistical Yearbook 1991*, Luxembourg.

Eurostat (1992b), *Basic Statistics of the Community*, 29th Edition, Luxembourg.

Eurostat (1993), *Basic Statistics of the Community*, 30th Edition, Luxembourg.

Eurostat (1994a), *Basic Statistics of the Community*, 31st Edition, Luxembourg.

Eurostat (1994b), *Country Profile: Romania 1992*, Luxembourg.

Eurostat (1996), *Country Profile: Central and Eastern European Countries 1994*, Luxembourg.

Evans P., Jacobson H, Putnam R. (1993) (eds), *Double-Edged Diplomacy: International Bargaining and Domestic Politics*, University of California Press, California.

Forster A. and Wallace W. (1996), "Common Foreign and Security Policy: A New Policy or Just a New Name" in Wallace H. and Wallace W. (eds), *Policy-Making in the European Union*, Third Edition, Oxford University Press, Oxford.

Friedman J. (1971), "A Non-co-operative Equilibrium for Super-games", Review of Economic Studies, Vol. 38, 1971.

Friis L. (1997), *When Europe Negotiates: From Europe Agreements to Eastern Enlargement?*, Institute of Political Science, University of Copenhagen, Copenhagen.

Friis L. (1998), "Approaching the 'Third Half' of the EU Grand Bargaining- The Post-Negotiation Phase of the 'Europe Agreement Game", *Journal of European Public Policy*, 5, 2: June.

Fulop M. and Poti L. (1990), "An East European Party Census", Policy Paper Series, *The Hungarian Institute of International Affairs*, Budapest, March.

Galtung J. (1971), "A Structural Theory of Imperialism", *Journal of Peace Research*, No 2.

Galtung J. (1973), *The European Community: A Superpower in the Making*, George Allen and Unwin Ltd, London.

Galtung J. (1991), "A Structural Theory of Imperialism", in Little R. and Smith M., *Perspectives on World Politics*, Second Edition, Routledge, London.

Glenny M. (1996), *The Fall of Yugoslavia: the third Balkan war*, 3rd edition, Penguin Books, New York.

Gorbachev M. (1988), *Perestroika. New Thinking for our Country and the World*, Updated edition, Fontana, London.

Gourevitch P. (1978), "The Second Image Reversed: the International Sources of Domestic Politics", *International Organisation*, 32, 4, Autumn.

Govaere I. (1997), "Trade-Related Aspects of Intellectual Property Rights in the Europe Agreements: Stimulus or Limitation to Parallel Imports?", in Maresceau M.(ed.), *Enlarging the European Union*, Longman, London.

Grabbe H. and Hughes K. (1997), *Eastward Enlargement of the European Union*, The Royal Institute of International Affairs, European Programme, London.

Grant C. (1994), *Delors: Inside the House that Jacques Built*, Nicolas Brealey Publishing, London.

Greco E. (1994), "Italy's Policy towards the Yugoslav Crisis", in Hellenic Foundation for European and Foreign Policy, *The South-East European Yearbook 1993*, Athens.

Green D. and Shapiro I. (1994), *Pathologies of Rational Choice Theory*, Yale University Press, New Haven.

Green D. and Shapiro I. (1995), "Pathologies Revisited: Reflection on our Critics", *Critical Review*, Vol. 9.

Gregory R. (1989), "Political Rationality or Incrementalism? Charles E. Lindblom's Enduring Contribution to Public Policy Making", *Policy and Politics*, No. 17, Vol. 2.

Grunert T., "Decision Making Processes in the Steel Crisis Policy of the EEC: Neocorporatist or Integrationist Tendencies?" in Meny Y. and Wright V. (eds), *The Politics of Steel: Western Europe and the Steel Industry in the Crisis Years (1974-84)*, De Gruyter, Berlin.

Guggenbuhl A. (1995), "The Political Economy of Association with Eastern Europe", in Laursen F. (ed.), *The Political Economy of European Integration*, The European Institute of Public Administration, Netherlands.

Haas E. B. (1958), *The Uniting of Europe: Political, Social and Economic Forces 1950-1957*, Stanford University Press, California.

Haas E. B. (1975), "Is There A Hole in the Whole? Knowledge, Technology, Interdependence and the Construction of International Regimes", *International Organisation*, Vol. 29, Summer.

Hamilton C.B. and Winters L.A. (1992), "Opening Up International Trade with Eastern Europe", *Economic Policy*, No. 14.

Handl V. (1993), "Germany and Central Europe: Mitteleuropa Restored?", *Perspectives*, No 1.

Handl V. (1993), "Developments in Germany and Czech-German Relations", *Perspectives,* No. 2.

Harris, G. (1996), "Re-inventing the Union: The European Parliament in a Wider Europe". Paper presented to the Conference of the *International Studies Association* held in San Diego on 16-20 April.

Harsanyi J. (1977), *Rational Behavior and Bargaining Equilibrium in Games and Social Situations*, Cambridge University Press, Cambridge.

Hauner M. (1994), Germany? But Where Is It Situated?, *Perspectives*, No. 3.

Hellenic Foundation for Defence and Foreign Policy (ELIAMEP) (1993), *The South Eastern European Yearbook 1992*, Athens.

Hill C. (1993), "The Capability-Expectations Gap, or Conceptualising Europe's International Role", *Journal of Common Market Studies*, Vol. 31, No. 3, September.

Ibanescu M. (1994), "Romania", in Tracy M. (ed.), *East West European Agricultural Trade: The Impact of Association Agreements*, APS-Agricultural Policy Studies, Prague.

Ida K. (1993), "When and How Do Domestic Constraints Matter? Two-level Games With Uncertainty", *Journal of Conflict Resolution*, 37, September.

Inotai A. (1994), "Transforming the East: Western Illusions and Strategies", *The New Hungarian Quarterly*, No. 133, Vol. 35, Spring.

Ioakimidis P. (1992), "Greece, the EC and the Eastern European Countries: An Overview", in Hellenic Foundation for European and Foreign Policy, *The South-East European Yearbook 1991*, Athens.

Ioakimidis P. (1993), Evropaiki Politiki Enosi [European Political Union], Themelio, Athens.

Kathimerini, [Greek daily], various issues.

Katzenstein P.J. (1976), "International Relations and Domestic Structures: Foreign Economic Policies of Advanced Industrial States", *International Organisation*, Vol. 30, No 1, Autumn.

Kazakos P. (1994), "Transformation in South-eastern Europe and the Role of the West" in Hellenic Foundation for European and Foreign Policy, *The South-East European Yearbook 1993*, Athens.

Keesing's Record of World Events, various issues.

Keohane R. (1984), *After Hegemony. Cooperation and Discord in the World Political Economy*, Princeton University Press, Princeton.

Keohane R. (1986), "Realism, Neorealism and the Study of World Politics", in Keohane Robert (ed), *Neorealism and its Critics*, Columbia University Press, New York.

Keohane R. (1991), "Co-operation and International regimes" in R. Little and M. Smith (ed), *Perspectives on World Politics*, Second Edition, Routledge, London.

Keohane R. and Hoffmann S. (1991). *The New European Community: Decision Making and Institutional Change*. Westview Press, Boulder/Oxford.

Keohane R. and Nye J. (1972) (eds), *Transational Relations and World Politics*, Harvard University Press, Cambridge.

Keohane R. and Nye J. (1977), *Power and Interdependence*, Little Brown, Boston.

Kingdon J. (1984), *Agendas, Alternatives and Public Policy*, Harper Collins Publishers, Michigan.

Kissinger H. (1966), "Domestic Structures and Foreign Policy", *Daedalus*, Spring.

Kolankiewicz G. (1994), "Consensus and Competition in the Eastern Enlargement of the EU", *International Affairs*, Vol. 70, No. 3.

Kramer H. (1993), "The European Community's Response to the 'New Eastern Europe'", *Journal of Common Market Studies*, Vol. 32, No. 2.

Krasner S. (1983) (ed), *International Regimes*, Cornel University Press, Ithaca.

Lakatos L.A. and Schaffer H.W. (1996), *Coming to Terms with Accession,* Forum Report of the Economic Policy Initiative No. 2, Institute for East West Studies, London.

Lange de H. (1988), "Taking Stock of the EC-EFTA Dialogue" in Jamar H. and Wallace H. (eds), *EEC-EFTA: More than Just Good Friends?* College of Europe, Bruges.

Langer A. (1993), "What Sort of Cooperation in Security Policy Between Bulgaria and the EC?", in Nikolov K. (ed), *Bulgaria and the European Community*, Working Papers No. 3b/93, Centre of European Studies, Sofia, December.

Langewiesche R. (1997b), "Phare Social Dialogue Programmes: Some Lessons from 18 Months of Experience: A Structural Reflection", *Transfer: European Review of Labour and Research*, Vol. 3, No. 2.

Langewiesche R. (1997a), "The Social Dimension in the Eastward Enlargement of the European Union", paper presented in the *International Industrial Relation Association*, European Regional Congress, Dublin, August.

Le Monde, various issues.

Light D. and Phinnemore D. (2001) (eds), *Post-Communist Romania: coming to terms with transition*, Palgrave, Basingstoke.

Lindblom E.C. (1959), "The Science of 'Muddling Through", *Public Administration Review*, No. 19.

Lindblom E.C. (1964), "Context for Change and Strategy: A Reply", *Public Administration Review*, No. 24.

Lindblom E.C. (1965), The Intelligence of Democracy, The Free Press, New York.

Lindblom E.C. (1977), Politics and Markets, Basic Books, New York.

Lindblom E.C. (1979), "Still Muddling, Not Yet Through", *Public Administration Review*, No. 39.

Lord C. (2000) (ed), *Central Europe: core or periphery?*, Copenhagen Business School Press, Handelshøjskolens Forlag.

Luce R.D. and Raiffa H. (1957), *Games and Decision,* John Wiley and Sons, New York.

Mannin M. (1999) (ed), *Pushing Back the Boundaries: the European Union and Central and Eastern Europe*, Manchester University Press, Manchester.

March J. and Olsen J. (1989), *Rediscovering Institutions: The Organisational Basis of Politics*, The Free Press, New York.

Maresceau M. (1993), "Europe Agreements: A New Form of Cooperation between the European Community and Central and Eastern Europe", in Muller Graff P.C. (ed.). *East European States and the European Communities: Legal Adaptation to the Market Economies*, ESCA-Series, Vol. 2, Nomos Verlagsgesellschaft, Baden-Baden.

Maresceau M. (1997) (ed), *Enlarging the European Union*, Longman, London.

Marshall B. (1992), "Migration into Germany: Asylum Seekers and Ethnic Germans", *German Politics*, Vol. 1, April.

Martonyi J. (1992), "The EC and Central Europe", *The New Hungarian Quarterly*, No. 128, Vol. 33, Winter.

Mayhew A. (1998), *Recreating Europe: The European Union's Policy towards Central and Eastern Europe*, Cambridge University Press, Cambridge.

Mazey S. and Richardson J. (1993) (eds), *Lobbying in the European Community*, Oxford University Press, Oxford.

Mazey S. and Richardson J. (1994), "The Commission and the Lobby" in Edwards G. and Spence D. (eds), *The European Commiss*ion, Longman, London.

Messerlin P. (1993), "The EC and Central Europe: The Missed Rendez-Vous of 1992?", *Economics of Transition*, Vol. 1, No.1.

Montaguti E. (1997), "The Europe Agreements' Anti Dumping Provisions in the EC-CEECs Relations", in Maresceau M.(ed.), *Enlarging the European Union*, Longman, London.

Moravcsik A. (1991), "Negotiating the Single European Act: Natioanl Interests and Conventional Statecraft in the European Community" in Keohane R. and Hoffmann S., *The New European Community: Decision Making and Institutional Change.* Westview Press, Boulder/Oxford.

Moravcsik A. (1993), "Preferences and Power in the European Community: A Liberal Intergovernmentalist Approach", *Journal of Common Market Studies*, Vol. 31.

Moravcsik A. (1994), "Preferences and Power in the European Community. A Liberal Intergovernmentalist Approach", in Blumer S. and Scott A. (eds), *Economic and Political Integration in Europe. Internal Dynamics and Global Context*, Blackwell Publishers.

Morgenthau H. (1978), *Politics Among Nations: The Struggle For Power and Peace.* Fifth Edition Revised, Alfred A. Knopf, New York.

Morse E. (1976), *Modernisation and the Transformation of International Relations*, Free Press, New York.

Muller-Graff P.C. (1993) (ed), *East European States and the European Communities: Legal Adaptation to the Market Economies*, ESCA-Series, Vol. 2, Nomos Verlagsgesellschaft, Baden-Baden.

Muller-Graff P.C. (1997), "Legal Framework for Relations between the European Union and Central and Eastern Europe: General Aspects", in Maresceau M. (ed), *Enlarging the European Union*, Longman, London.

Nastase A. (1991), "La Roumanie et son Destin Europeen", *Revue des Deux Mondes*, September.

Nello S. and Smith K. (1998), *The European Union and Central and Eastern Europe: the implications of enlargement in stages*, Ashgate, Aldershot.

Nikolov K. (1993) (ed), *Bulgaria and the European Community*, Working Papers No. 3b/93, Centre of European Studies, Sofia, December.

Nikolov K. (1998) (ed), *Bulgaria in An Integrated Europe*, Edition 1996-97, CES Working Papers, Centre of European Studies, Sofia, April.

Nugent N. (1995b), "The leadership Capacity of the European Commission", *Journal of European Public Policy*, Vol. 2, No. 4, December.

Opt K.D. (1999), "Contending Conceptions of the Theory of Rational Action", *Journal of Theoretical Studies*, Vol. 11, No. 2.

Padoan P.C. (1993), "Opening of the Bulgarian Economy: Problems and Prospects", in Nikolov K. (ed), *Bulgaria and the European Community*, Working Papers No. 3b/93, Centre of European Studies, Sofia, December.

Pagonaru F. (1990), "Uniunea Est-europeana de Plati, o Posibila Solutie Pentru Asiguranea Convertibilitati? [East European Payments Union: A Possible Solution for the Problem of Convertibility]", *Tribuna Economica*, No. 22, 1 June.

Paparizov A. (1993), "European Integration Beyond Maastricht", in Nikolov K. (ed), *Bulgaria and the European Community*, Working Papers No. 3b/93, Centre of European Studies, Sofia, December.

Perry D.M. (1992), "Bulgaria: A New Constitution and Free Elections", *RFE/RL Research Report*, 3 January.

Peters G. (1996), "Agenda Setting in the European Union", in Richardson J. (ed), *European Union: Power and Policy Making*, Routledge, London.

Peters R. (1967) (ed), *Hobbes*, Peregrine Books, Middlesex.

Pettifer J. (1994), "Greece, Albania and the Greek Minority Question" in Hellenic Foundation for European and Foreign Policy, *The South-East European Yearbook 1993*, Athens.

Phinnemore D. (1999), *Association: stepping-stone or alternative to membership?*, Sheffield Academic Press, Sheffield.

Pinder J. (1991), *The European Community and Eastern Europe*, Pinter Publishers, London.

Pollack M.A. (1997), "Delegation, Agency and Agenda Setting in the European Community", *International Organisation*, Vol. 51, No. 1, Winter.

Preston C. (1995), "Obstacles to EU Enlargement: The Classical Community Method and the Prospects for a Wider Europe", *Journal of Common Market Studies*, Vol. 33, No. 3, September.

Princen S. (2001), "A Tale of Traps, Trade and Two-Level Games: negotiating trapping standards in the transatlantic relation", paper presented in the *ECPR Joint Sessions*, Grenoble, 6-11 April 2001.

Putnam R. (1988), "Diplomacy and Domestic Politics. The Logic of Two Level Games", *International Organization*, 42, 3, Summer.

Radaelli C. (1998), "Game Theory and Institutional Entrepreneurship: Transfer Pricing and the Search for Co-ordination in International Tax Policy", *Policy Studies Journal*, Vol. 26, No, 4.

Rasmussen E. (1990), *Games and Information*, Basil Blackwell, Oxford.

Reinicke H.W. (1992), *Building a New Europe: The Challenge of System Transformation and Systemic Reform*, Brookings Occasional Papers, The Brokings Institutions, Washington, D.C.

Richardson J. (1996) (ed), *European Union: Power and Policy Making*, Routledge, London.

Rieger E. (1996), "The Common Agricultural Policy: External and Internal Dimensions", in Wallace H. and Wallace W.(eds), *Policy Making in the European*.

Risse-Kappen T. (1996), "Exploring the Nature of the Beast: international relations and comparative analysis meet the European Union", *Journal of Common Market Studies*, Vol. 34, No. 1.

Rollo J. and Smith A. (1993), "The Political Economy of Eastern European Trade with the European Community: Why So Sensitive?", *Economic Policy*, No. 16.

Rollo J. and Wallace H. (1991), "New Patterns of Partnership" in Bonvichini *et al.*, *The Community and the Emerging European Democracies*, Royal Institute of International Affairs, London.

Rood Jan. Q. Th. (1989), "The Functioning of Regimes in an Interdependent World", in Rosenau J. and Tromp H. (eds), *Interdependence and Conflict in World Politics*, Avebury, Sydney.

Rood Jan. Q. Th. (1991), "The EC and Eastern Europe over the Longer Term" in Bonvichini *et al.*, *The Community and the Emerging European Democracies*, Royal Institute of International Affairs, London.

Rosenau J. (1967) (ed), *Domestic Sources of Foreign Policy*, Free Press, New York.

Rosenau J. (1969) (ed), *Linkage Politics: Essays on the Convergence of National and International Systems*, Free Press, New York.

Ross G. (1994), "Inside Delors Cabinet", *Journal of Common Market Studies*, Vol. 32, No. 4, December.

Ruggie J. (1975), "International Responses to Technology: Concepts and Trends", *International Organisation*, 29, 3, Summer.

Ruhl L. (1995), "Germany and the Extended Europe", *German Comments*, No. 37, Bonn, January.

Sapir A. (1999), "Trade Regionalism in Europe: towards and integrated approach", *Journal of Common Market Studies*, Vol. 38, No. 1, March, pp. 151-162.

Scharpf F.W. (1977), "The Joint-Decision Trap: Lessons from German Federalism and European Integration", *Public Administration*, Vol. 66, 1988.

Scharpf F.W. (1997), *Games Real Actors Can Play*, Westview, Boulder.

Schneider G. and Decerman L.E. (1994), "The Change of Tide in Political Co-operation: a Limited Information Model of European Integration", *International Organisation*, Vol. 48, No. 4, Autumn.

Schneider G. and Seybold C. (1997), "Twelve Tongues, One Voice: An Evaluation of European Political Co-operation", *European Journal of Political Research*, Vol. 31, No. 3.

Schneider G., Weitsman P. and Bernauer T. (1995) (eds), *Towards a New Europe: Stops and Starts in Regional Integration*, Praeger, Westort/London.

Scott A. (1977), "The Logic of International Interaction", *International Studies Quarterly*, Vol. 21, September.

Sedelmeier U. (1994), "The European Union's Association Policy towards Central and Eastern Europe: Political and Economic Rationales of Conflict", *SEI Working Paper*, No. 7, Sussex European Institute, Falmer.

Sedelmeier U. (1995), "Competing Policy Recommendations for Europe Association and the Limits of a Trade Liberalisation Approach to Integration: Some Illustrations from the Case of Steel", paper presented at the UACES Research Conference *Integration within Wider Europe*, Birmingham, 18-19 September.

Sedelmeier U. and Wallace H. (1996), "Policies towards Central and Eastern Europe", in Wallace H. and Wallace W. (eds), *Policy-Making in the European Union*, Third Edition, Oxford University Press, Oxford.

Shaffer M. (1995), "The Applicability of Three-Game Analysis to the EC-Visegrad Negotiations for the Europe Agreements", paper presented at the UACES Research Conference *Integration in a Wider Europe*, 18-19 September.

Shafir M. (1992), "Romania's Tortuous Road to Reform", *RFE/RL Research Report*, 3 January.

Shikova I. (1996), "The European Union in the Mirror of Public Opinion", in Nikolov K. (ed), *Bulgaria in an Integrated Europe*, Centre for European Studies, CES Working Papers, No. 1/96, Sofia, June.

Shlaim A. and Yannopoulos G.N. (1978) (eds), *The EEC and Eastern Europe*, Cambridge University Press, London.

Simon H. (1976), *Administrative Behaviour*, Third Edition, The Free Press, New York.

Simon H. (1982), *Models of Bounded Rationality* (2 vols.), MIT Press, Cambridge.

Skak M. (1993), "Bulgaria's Policy Towards the EC", in Nikolov K. (ed), *Bulgaria and the European Community*, Working Papers No. 3b/93, Centre of European Studies, Sofia, December.

Slatinski N. (1993), "Bulgaria's Place in European Security", in Nikolov K. (ed), *Bulgaria and the European Community*, Working Papers No. 3b/93, Centre of European Studies, Sofia, December.

Smith A. (2000), *The Return to Europe*, Macmillan Press, Basingstoke.

Smith K.E. (1998), *The Making of the EU Foreign Policy: The Case of Eastern Europe 1988-1995*, Macmillan, London.

Smith M. (1994), "The Commission and External Relations" in Edwards G. and Spence D. (eds), *The European Commission*, Longman, London.

Smith M. (2000), "Negotiating New Europes: the roles of the European Union", *Journal of European Public Policy*, Vol. 7, No. 5, pp. 806-822.

Spulber N. (1963), "Changes in the Economic Structures of the Balkans: 1860-1960", in Jelavich C. and Jelavich B. (eds.), *The Balkans in Transition*, University of California Press, Berkley, 1963.

Stawarska R. (1992), "Poland's Association with the EEC", *Polish Western Affairs*, Vol. XXXIII, No. 1.

Steinbruner J. (1974). *The Cybernetic Theory of Decision: New Dimensions of Political Analysis*, Princeton University Press, Princeton.

Steinmo S., Thelen K. and Longstreth F. (1992) (eds), *Structuring Politics: Historical Institutionalism in Comparative Analysis*, Cambridge University Press, Cambridge.

Stevens C. (1992), "The EC and the Third World", in Dyker D. (ed), *The European Economy*, Longman, London.

Stevens C. (1996), "EU Policy for the Banana Market" in Wallace H. and Wallace W. (eds), *Policy-Making in the European Union*, Third Edition, Oxford University Press, Oxford.

Stuart P. (1997), "Germany, the Visegrad States and the Dual Enlargement of the European Union and Nato", paper presented in the *BISA Conference*, Leeds, 1997.

Sukova-Tosheva A. (1994), "Bulgaria", in Tracy M. (ed.), *East West European Agricultural Trade: The Impact of Association Agreements*, APS-Agricultural Policy Studies, Prague.

Swain G. and Swain N. (1993), *Eastern Europe Since 1945*, Macmillan, London.

Tang H. (2000) (ed), *Winners and Losers of EU Integration: policy issues for Central and Eastern Europe*, World Bank, Washington D.C.

Tangerman S., Josling T.E., Munch W. (1994), *Pre Accession Agricultural Policies for Central Europe and the European Union*, Study prepared for the Commission's DG IA, December.

Tarditi S., Senior-Nello S., Marsh J., Blaas G., Kelly L., Nucifora A., Thiele H. and Bastiani A. (1994), Agricultural Strategies for the Enlargement of the European Union to Central and Eastern European Countries, Study prepared for the Commission's DG IA, December.

The Commission of the EC (1989), [Action Plan for Poland and Hungary], COM (89) 470, 26 September.

The Commission of the EC (1990a), [Report on Relations Between the Community and the Countries of East Europe], SEC (90) 4 January, (unpublished and confidential document).

The Commission of the EC (1990b), [Implications of Recent Changes in Central and Eastern Europe for the Community's Relations with the Countries Concerned], SEC (90) 111/2, 17 January, (unpublished and confidential document).

The Commission of the EC (1990c), [Commission's proposals for the Visegrad EAs], SEC (90) 717 final, 18 April.

The Commission of the EC (1990d), [Commission's proposals for the extension of the Phare programme], SEC (90) 843, 2 May.

The Commission of the EC (1990e), [Commission's proposals for the extension of the Phare programme], COM (90) 318 final, 6 July.

The Commission of the EC (1990f), [Commission's proposals for the general outline of the Association agreements], COM (90) 398 final, 27 August.

The Commission of the EC (1991), [Commission's proposal for granting medium-term financial assistance to Bulgaria] COM (91) 88, 19 March.

The Commission of the EC (1992a), *Scoreboard of G-24 Assistance, Summary ECU Tables and Graphics*, Brussels, 8 April.

The Commission of the EC (1992b), [Romanian Interim agreement], COM (92) 510 final, 21 December.

The Commission of the EC (1993a), [Bulgarian Europe Agreement], COM (93) 45 final, 18 February.

The Commission of the EC (1993b), *The Agricultural Situation in the Community:1992*, Brussels.

The Commission of the EC (1993c), [Commission's Communication on the Competitiveness of the European Textile and Clothing Industry], COM (93) 525 final, 27 October.

The Commission of the EC (1994), "The Economic Inter-Penetration between the European Union and Eastern Europe", Directorate General for Economic and Financial Affairs, *European Economy: Reports and Studies*, No. 6.

The Commission of the EC (1995a), *Agricultural Situation and Prospects in the Central and Eastern European Countries: Bulgaria*, Working Document produced by Directorate- General for Agriculture (VI).

The Commission of the EC (1995b), *Agricultural Situation and Prospects in the Central and Eastern European Countries: Romania*, Working Document produced by Directorate- General for Agriculture (VI).

The Commission of the EC (1995c), *Agricultural Situation and Prospects in the Central and Eastern European Countries: Summary Report*, Working Document.

The Commission of the EC (1997), [Agenda 2000], COM (97) 2000 final, 15 July.

The Commission of the EC (1999a), [Stabilisation and Association Agreements], COM (99) 235, 26 May.

The Commission of the EC (1999b), *European Economy: Supplement C. Economic Reform Monitor*, No. 3, October.

The European Parliament (1988), Directorate General for Committees and Delegations, Secretariat of the Political Affairs Committee, *"General Summary of the Human Rights Situation in the Countries of Eastern Europe for the Information of Members of the Inter-Parliamentary Delegations to those Countries"*, Luxembourg/Brussels, 30 August, unpublished.

The European Parliament (1995), Directorate General for Research, *Agricultural Strategies for the Enlargement of the EU to Include CEECs*, Research and Documentation Papers.

The European Parliament (1996), Task Force on the Intergovernmental Conference, *Briefing on the 1996 Intergovernmental Conference and the Enlargement of the EU*, No. 36, Luxembourg, May.

The European Parliament, *Debates of the European Parliament*, various issues.

The Financial Times, various issues.

The Guardian, various.

The House of Commons, *Parliamentary Debates*, various issues.

Tiersky R. (1992), "France in the New Europe", *Foreign Affairs*, Vol. 72, No. 2.

To Vima, [Greek weekly], various issues.

Todorova M. (1993), "Bulgaria in the European Context", in Nikolov K. (ed), *Bulgaria and the European Community*, Working Papers No. 3b/93, Centre of European Studies, Sofia, December.

Tracy M. (1994) (ed), *East West European Agricultural Trade: The Impact of Association Agreements*, APS-Agricultural Policy Studies, Prague.

Troxel L. (1992), "Bulgaria's Gypsies: Numerically Strong, Politically Weak", *RFE/RL Research Report*, 6 March.

Tsebelis G. (1988), "Nested Games: The Cohesion of French Politics", *British Journal of Political Science*, No. 18.

Tsebelis G. (1990), *Nested Games: Rational Choice in Comparative Politics*, University of California Press, Berkeley.

Tsebelis G. (1994), "The Power of the European Power as a Conditional Agenda Setter", *American Political Science Review*, Vol. 88.

Tsoukalis L. (1993), *The New European Economy: The Politics and Economics of Integration*, Second Revised Edition, Oxford University Press, New York, 1993.

Ullman R. H. (1991), *Securiting Europe*, Princeton University Press, Princeton.

Vachkova-Todorova K. (1990), "Imat li Budeshche Otnosheniyata SIV-EIO" [There is a Future for Relations Between the EC and the CMEA], *Mezhdunarodni Otnosheniya*, No. 7.

Van Den Bempt P. and Theelen G. (1996), *From Europe Agreements to Accession,* European University Press, Brussels.

Van Den Bossche A.M. (1997), "The Competition Provisions in the Europe Agreements: A Comparative and Critical Analysis", in Maresceau M.(ed.), *Enlarging the European Union*, Longman, London.

Van Den Hende L. (1997), "EU Safeguard Measures under the Europe Agreements: The Settlement of Trade Disputes" in Maresceau M.(ed.), *Enlarging the European Union*, Longman, London.

Van Ham P. (1993), *The EC, Eastern Europe and European Unity. Discord, Collaboration and Integration Since 1947*, Pinter Publishers, London.

Veremis T. (1992), "Greek-Turkish Relations and the Balkans", in Hellenic Foundation for European and Foreign Policy, *The South-East European Yearbook 1991*, Athens.

Veremis T. (1993), "A Redefinition of Security Considerations in the South-eastern Europe", in Hellenic Foundation for European and Foreign Policy, *The South-East European Yearbook 1992*, Athens.

Wallace H (1991b), "The Europe that Came in from the Cold", *International Affairs*, Vol. 67, No. 4.

Wallace H. (1991) (ed), *The Wider Western Europe: Reshaping the EC/EFTA Relationship*, The Royal Institute of International Affairs, London.

Wallace H. and Wallace W. (1996) (eds), *Policy-Making in the European Union*, Third Edition, Oxford University Press, Oxford.

Wallace H. and Wallace W. (2000) (eds), *Policy-Making in the European Union*, Fourth Edition, Oxford University Press, Oxford.

Wallace H. and Wessels W. (1989), *Towards a New Partnership: The EC and EFTA in the Wider Western Europe*, EFTA Occasional Paper, No. 28, EFTA Secretariat, Geneva.

Wallden S. (1993), *I Simfonies Sindesis tis Evropaikis Kinotitas me tin Roumania ke tin Voulgaria* [The Association Agreements between the EC and Romania and Bulgaria], Idiki Meleti No. 1, Balkan Unit, EKEM, Athens.

Wallden S. (1993b), "Bulgaria's Association with the EC: Beyond Disillusionment", in Nikolov K. (ed), *Bulgaria and the European Community*, Working Papers No. 3b/93, Centre of European Studies, Sofia, December.

Wallden S. (1994), *Valkaniki Sinergasia ke Evropaiki Oloklirosi* [Balkan Co-operation and European Integration], Papazisis, Athens.

Wallden S. (1994b), "Voulgaria ke Evropaiki Kinotita [Bulgaria and the European Community]", in Hellenic Foundation for European and Foreign Policy, *Epetirida Amintikis ke Exoterikis Politikis 1993-1994*, Athens 1994.

Waltz K. (1959), *Man, the State and War: A Theoretical Analysis*, Columbia University Press, New York.

Waltz K. (1970), "The Myth of National Interdependence", in Kindelberger C. (ed), *The International Corporation: A Symposium*, MIT Press, Cambridge.

Waltz K. (1979), *Theory of International Politics*, Addison-Wesley, Massachussets.

Weidenfeld W. (1997) (ed), *A New Ostpolitik: Strategies for a United Europe*, Bertelsmann Foundation Publishers, Gutersloh.

Wightman G. (1993), "The Czech and Slovak Republics" in White S., Batt J. and Lewis P. G. (eds), *Developments in East European Politics*, Macmillan, London.

Wijkman P (1991), "The EEA Agreement - At Long Last", in *EFTA Trade 1990*, EFTA Secretariat, Economic Affairs Department, November.

Winters A. (1992), "The Europe Agreements: With a Little Help from our Friends", in CEPR, *The Association Process: Make it Work*, CEPR Occasional Paper, No. 11.

Wolfers A. (1962), *Discord and Collaboration*, Johns Hopkins University Press, Baltimore.

Woolock S. and Hodges M. (1996), "EC Policy in the Uruguay Round" in Wallace H. and Wallace W., *Policy Making in the European Union*, Third Edition, Oxford University Press, Oxford.

Wright M. (1946), *Power Politics*, Holmes and Meier, New York.

Wright V. (1993), "France: Recent History and Politics" in Regional Surveys of the World, *Western Europe 1993*, Europa Publication limited, London, 1993.

Young A. (2001), "Extending European Co-operation: the European Union and the 'new' international trade agenda", paper presented in the *ECPR Joint Sessions*, Grenoble, 6-11 April 2001.

Zaman G. (1990), "CAER-Spre o Reformare Radicala [CMEA: Towards a Radical Reform]", *Tribuna Economica*, No. 36 (7 September) and No. 37 (14 September).

Zanga L. (1994), "Albanian Statistics: Filling the Information Void", *RFE/RL Research Report*, Vol. 3, No 10, 11 March.

Zartman W. (1971), *The Politics of Trade Negotiations between Africa and the European Community: The Weak Confront the Strong*, Princeton University Press, New Jersey.

Zecchini S. (1991), "Economic Reform and Western Assistance", in OECD, *The Transition to a Market Economy*, Vol. 1, Paris.

Note on EC Documents:

Many of the EC documents quoted in this book have been accessed in the Internet. Sources beginning with *IP* (e.g. *IP/98/274*) refer to press releases by the Commission. Sources beginning with *Speech* (e.g. *Speech/90/20*) refer to speeches made by the Commission's officials. Sources beginning with *Pres* (e.g. *Pres/98/86*) refer to press releases by the Council. Sources beginning with *Doc* (e.g. *Doc/89/2*) refer to press releases by the European Council. All these documents are available in the EC's *Rapid* Database.

Index